WHEN THE YEAR ENDS IN ONE

HOW TOTTENHAM HOTSPUR'S 1991 FA CUP WIN SAVED THE CLUB AND TRANSFORMED ENGLISH FOOTBALL

EWAN FLYNN

pitch

First published by Pitch Publishing, 2025

1

pitch

Pitch Publishing
9 Donnington Park,
85 Birdham Road,
Chichester, West Sussex,
PO20 7AJ
www.pitchpublishing.co.uk
info@pitchpublishing.co.uk

A CIP catalogue record is available for this book
from the British Library.

ISBN 978 1 83680 138 2

Typesetting and origination by Pitch Publishing

MIX
Paper | Supporting
responsible forestry
FSC
www.fsc.org   FSC® C010615

Printed and bound on FSC® certified paper in line with
our continuing commitment to ethical business practices,
sustainability and the environment.

Printed and bound in India by Thomson Press

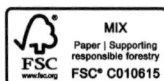

Contents

Prologue

DRESSED IN his dark suit and the formal club tie he never particularly relishes wearing, Terry Venables strides purposefully on to the lush Wembley turf, determined to rally his players who have gathered in a daze near the centre circle. His face, usually so demonstrative, offers no tell of the panic he must be fighting to suppress. Barely 15 minutes of the 1991 FA Cup Final have elapsed, and Venables's Tottenham have just fallen behind. Far more damagingly, however, Paul Gascoigne, the team's totemic midfielder, whose preternatural performances have – against a backdrop of existential crisis for the club – somehow enabled Spurs to navigate a path to this, English football's most revered occasion, is being loaded on to a stretcher. Gascoigne's tearful departure, with a career-threatening injury, appears to snuff out hope of an unparalleled eighth FA Cup triumph. Worse still, it obliterates the deal for the player – scheduled to complete immediately after the final – promising emaciated Tottenham a world-record transfer fee from Lazio. Without this injection of funds to tackle the club's mountainous debt, the Midland Bank's receiver can no longer be expected to stay his hand. The team will be broken up, Venables will leave, and what will happen to Tottenham Hotspur Football Club from there is anybody's guess.

Whoever said, 'It's lucky for Spurs when the year ends in one'?

Chapter One

Gazzamania

SUPERFICIALLY, THE summer of 1990 seemed ripe with promise for Tottenham Hotspur. The club had finished the 1989/90 campaign third in the First Division. After two full seasons in charge, the declaration Terry Venables had made when first arriving as manager about bringing the league title to White Hart Lane appeared far less outlandish than it had. Not least because Spurs always seemed to prosper in seasons where the year ended in one. They'd won the FA Cup as a non-league side in 1901, then repeated the feat in 1921; 1951 had been marked with the club's first First Division title, while 1961 saw Spurs complete a historic 'double'. A League Cup followed in 1971, while the FA Cup had been captured again in 1981.

Moreover, England's thrilling run to the 1990 World Cup semi-finals gave succour to the entire domestic game. At last, a chance appeared to be presenting itself to English football whereby its desperate image of death, disaster and male violence, played out in the stands of decaying Victorian-built stadiums, could be decisively shed.

The poster boy for this optimistic new dawn was Spurs' Paul Gascoigne. His potent blend of on-pitch panache allied with raw, unrefined charisma and vulnerability had taken an audience of over 25 million people on a life-affirming journey that ended with his tears in Turin as England lost to West Germany on penalties. It's a remarkable figure given that only five years earlier, in the wake of the revulsion caused by the Heysel disaster and the horror of the Bradford City stadium fire, both the BBC and ITV had contemplated whether to let club football slip quietly from their schedules. As Neil Harman wrote in his 90/91 season preview for the *Daily Mail*, 'Football needs a groundswell of good feeling, not the bitterness that has followed its leap from one terrible tragedy to another. Perhaps Gazza can cleanse us ... Reach for the sky, lads – lead them there, Gazza.'

In the monolithic media landscape of the early 1990s, the chronicling of Gascoigne's meteoric rise to white-hot fame was unavoidable. Only Princess Diana could rival the celebrity he suddenly 'enjoyed'. The term 'Gazzamania' was quickly coined to describe the phenomenon. As Brian Glanville, writing in *The Times*, sagely observed ahead of the new season, 'Gazza is public property now, with all the attendant risks.' Icelandic defender Gudni Bergsson, who arrived at Spurs soon after Gascoigne had signed in 1988 and was billeted in the same Waltham Abbey hotel while they adjusted to London life, explains the new reality after the World Cup. 'After Italia 90, we went on a pre-season tour of Ireland. The attention and pressure on Gazza, wow, it was mayhem. Gary Lineker was more used to that side of things than the rest of the squad. Those two were John Lennon and Paul McCartney, whereas the rest of us combined weren't even George Harrison and Ringo. We didn't matter at all.' The team's goalkeeper, Erik Thorstvedt, laughs at the memory. 'Suddenly, Gazza was the most popular person in Britain, and he's having to be smuggled in and out of the training ground in the trunk of cars and stuff like that. It was absolutely crazy.'

The thirst for a glimpse of Gascoigne reached far beyond the British Isles. Tottenham's opening league game of the season versus Manchester City – at a sold-out White Hart Lane – reportedly attracted a 300 million worldwide television audience. Obligingly, he supplemented two fine Lineker goals with a late solo effort of his own in a 3-1 win. Commentator Jonathan Pearce recalls travelling to Sunderland with the official Tottenham party to cover their next fixture. 'The chairman, Irving Scholar, let us go up there with the team. I think we flew into Newcastle. After the game, we got on the coach from Roker Park to the airport, and Gazza only had his shorts on. He'd given everything else – kit, tracksuit, the lot – away. He said, "Don't worry, lads. My mum's picking me up 'cos I'm staying up here tonight." But we were flying back down from a different airport, so the last thing we saw before entering the terminal was Gazza, stripped down to his shorts, stranded at the wrong airport. He'd become a global superstar during that summer. I don't think it changed him at all. There are so many great stories about him from then. Looking back now, though, they have a tinge of "Whoops, where is this all leading to?"'

Within ten days of the season's opening, the rapacious demand for a pound of Gascoigne's flesh saw him go directly from training on Monday morning to a photo shoot for one of his many new sponsors, on to Madame Tussauds to pose for his impending waxwork before heading across to the BBC in Shepherd's Bush for a sit-down chat with Terry Wogan. Having witnessed the hysteria of the crowd of thousands who had gathered outside the studio to greet their new idol, the avuncular host warned Gascoigne of 'tall poppy syndrome'. 'We have a tradition in this country, certainly among the press, where as soon as you become enormously successful, there reaches a point where they decide "we're going to knock him off the parapet now".'

Gascoigne's reply showed how steep the learning curve ahead would be, 'I'm working so hard to behave myself … I just want to be one of the lads. I want to stay one of the lads. They're trying to make me something I'm not.' Recognising the naive inadequacy of his guest's answer, Wogan could only sign off by saying, 'I just hope the tabloids will be kind and you'll be able to have a happy and enjoyable life.'

Not bloody likely, given the ferocious circulation war between the Rupert Murdoch-owned *Sun* and Robert Maxwell's *Daily Mirror*. Both were desperate to be Gascoigne's official patrons and continue to pump him up before revelling in the inevitable fall from grace. *The Sun* got his signature and rushed the *Paul Gascoigne Story* cartoon strip into print. Having missed out, *The Mirror* expedited knocking him down. In a press interview at the time, Gascoigne wrestled with his transformed life. 'Sometimes I feel like doing a runner for a few days to just hide … The publicity I've had has been great, but I'm worried I'm being built up so high. They're just waiting for anything that goes wrong. I feel better on the pitch. I'm safe there with my boots and strip on. When I'm in the centre of the pitch, no one can get to me.'

Paul Stewart, who shared a house with Gascoigne that season, reflects, 'Gazza loved the fame, and I think that's where things started to get difficult for him. He didn't fully realise the press wasn't always going to write glowingly about him. And when they were nasty, he wanted to have a go back. You can't win at that. The papers down in London were much harsher than in the north, where we'd both come from. They were always looking to cause trouble, planting girls in hotels and setting up confrontations. What they went on to do to him was disgusting.'

To ward off the potential for burnout amid this frenzy, Venables imposed a moratorium on Gascoigne undertaking commercial activities for the 72 hours before games. Not that those outside the Tottenham coaching staff could see any sign of impaired performance. Quite the opposite. In his next match after the Wogan interview, Gascoigne underlined why, in his case, it was time to absolutely believe the hype. Derby County were thrashed 3-0. Gascoigne's hat-trick past his England World Cup team-mate, goalkeeper Peter Shilton, included two outrageous bending free kicks, steered into opposite top corners of the net. He'd get four in a League

Cup match later in the same month, and on and on it went from there.

Gascoigne's dubious reward was to be rendered as a latex puppet on *Spitting Image*, which perhaps prompted Margaret Thatcher – badly in need of his rub during the dog days of her administration – to invite him to Downing Street. In the view of the broadcaster and encyclopaedia of all things Tottenham Hotspur, Danny Kelly, 'Gazza went on to be beyond special that year. His 90/91 was as good a season as any Spurs player has had. I'd hold it up against virtually anything I can think of in English football. Liam Brady, Cristiano Ronaldo, Gareth Bale, maybe they were on a par, but certainly no better.'

Chapter Two

Tottenham Hotspur PLC

PAUL GASCOIGNE'S brilliant hat-trick against Derby on Saturday, 8 September was swiftly put in the shade by the less-welcome news emanating from White Hart Lane the next day. City editor Jeff Randall's *Sunday Times* column revealed, 'Robert Maxwell, the media magnate and owner of the *Daily Mirror*, has entered into secret talks that could give him effective control of Tottenham Hotspur, one of Britain's most famous football clubs.' Alarmingly, Randall revealed the context behind this potential takeover. The club was sinking beneath debts exceeding '£10 million'.

'The fact that Spurs – once assumed to be one of the wealthiest football clubs in Britain – is in deep financial trouble will come as a shock to many of its fans … Even the playing staff and Spurs' manager, Terry Venables, have been told nothing,' explained Randall, before setting out the undesirable choice now faced by the Tottenham board. Find a 'white knight' investor like Maxwell, or sell the team's star names.

It would transpire that £10 million severely underestimated the gargantuan scale of Tottenham's liabilities. How was this even possible? The club's debt was almost incomprehensible in the ecosystem of the 1990 First Division. But therein lay Spurs' problem. They were not comparable to any of the other clubs in the Football League. Since 1983, Tottenham Hotspur Football Club had been a mere subsidiary of Tottenham Hotspur PLC.

* * *

Irving Scholar and Paul Bobroff were the men who had charted this unique path for the football club. They had taken over by stealth in 1982 when the escalating cost of building White Hart Lane's West Stand had run the previous regime into financial difficulties. Scholar had been a Spurs fanatic since childhood. Having passed through St Marylebone Grammar School, he'd done sufficiently well in the property game to make it financially expedient for him to relocate to Monaco. At first, the debonair Scholar offered his expertise to help the club out of the West Stand mess. Rebuffed by the board, he began targeting Tottenham shares registered in the name of women. His calculation that these had likely been passed on by late husbands proved shrewd. He offered them cash. They gladly accepted. In partnership with Bobroff – another property man sharing a fondness for Spurs – this strategy gave them sufficient clout to force the Emergency General Meeting required to bring about regime change.

The pair quickly hatched plans to refinance the club. As Scholar explains in his autobiography *Behind Closed Doors*, 'The answer, when it came, was blindingly simple. Why not float Tottenham Hotspur on the stock exchange ... At that time, in the early Eighties, the financial markets were quite buoyant. The stock market was in the middle of its bull phase, and there seemed to be a lot of new money in the City.'

Garth Crooks, Ossie Ardiles and Danny Thomas – the first two in bowler hats – dutifully posed clutching a copy of the *Financial Times* to signify Tottenham Hotspur becoming the first sporting club in the world to float on the stock exchange. Scholar and Bobroff sought to raise £3.8 million. While the erstwhile duo were entitled to declare the issue a triumph given it was four times oversubscribed, inauspiciously, on the first day of trading, shares bought at £1 a pop fell to 90p. They would remain stubbornly below the £1 mark for over three years.

A week on from the flotation, Bobroff – newly installed as chairman of Tottenham Hotspur PLC (Scholar became chairman of Tottenham Hotspur Football Club soon thereafter) – staked out his vision of the company's future. 'We have said, from the start, we would like to found a broadly based leisure company – and that means we are ready to look at acquisitions ourselves.' Spurs were no longer just in the market for centre-halves and centre-forwards. Buying up companies to boost the share price – or to use the business pages' lingo, 'diversifying' – was now a fundamental part of Tottenham Hotspur's *raison d'etre*. To quote the fabled line often attributed to Keith Burkinshaw – who resigned as manager within seven months of Spurs entering this brave new world – 'There used to be a football club over there.'

In the spring of 1985, Spurs unveiled an 'innovative' deal with Danish kit supplier Hummel, who were keen to break into the British sportswear market. Rather than simply wearing shirts featuring the manufacturer's chevrons and receiving a commission for each replica sold, Tottenham would become the UK distributor for Hummel International. It was now up to Spurs to get Hummel gear on sale alongside Adidas's and Nike's wares in sports shops and to chase up any revenue generated. An entire range called 'Hoddle in Hummel', marketed with photos of Glenn Hoddle lolling around in preppy polo shirts and yacht club shorts, was designed. Besides a few loyal Spurs fans compelled into making purchases out of loyalty, few beyond north London were interested. Spurs were also responsible for supplying kit to other teams signed up by Hummel over the next five years.

It did not go well. Wimbledon's 1989 centenary shirt wasn't delivered until 1990, while that same year, Southampton resorted to dedicating a whole page in their matchday programme entitled 'This problem has been caused by Tottenham Hotspur PLC'. It sought to explain to disappointed young Saints and their parents why replicas hadn't been available in the club shop in the run-up to

Christmas. As unsold Hummel stock began piling up in the Ferry Lane warehouse, Tottenham's newly appointed chief executive, Bob Holt, recommended closing down the Hummel UK operation – which had never turned a profit – and 'throwing away the key'. Eventually, in March of 1990, that's what happened. Tottenham Hotspur PLC was left to cover Hummel UK's £1 million losses and write off the nearly £3.5 million it had spent setting up the failed enterprise.

Hummel wasn't the only diversification mis-step. In April 1987, the celebrated City man Tony Berry had been brought on to the PLC's board. Berry, like Scholar, a long-standing fan who'd trained with the club as a schoolboy, had invested £410,000 in Tottenham and was promising plenty more where that came from. The Blue Arrow recruitment company he'd built up was in the process of acquiring Manpower, the world's largest temporary employment agency, for $1.3 billion. Berry had bedazzled the financial world, who admiringly wondered how a firm with humble beginnings in St Albans was in a position to take over an American behemoth. If Berry's business brilliance could rub off on Spurs, the PLC would be quids in. His mere presence saw the share price shoot up to £2.50 during the summer of 1987. Before the year was out, guided by Berry, Tottenham Hotspur became the owners of two small textile companies, as £2.5 million was stumped up for Stumps (cricket clothing) and Martex, who did a garish line in women's knitwear. Both companies underwent a rapid reversal of fortune under Tottenham's leaky umbrella. By the summer of 1989, profit was turned into loss. Subsequently, Martex and Stumps ceased trading, with Spurs owing a further £1 million to a former Martex director.

A deal to produce merchandise for the England team ahead of Euro 88 was another Spurs swing-and-miss. England's participation in the tournament lasted all of six days. They lost their three group-stage matches to Ireland, the Netherlands and the USSR. As if that wasn't enough to put off potential buyers of England tat, rampant hooliganism accompanied the team's appalling results.

Perhaps the £120,000 Tottenham spent just before the European Championship on a 75 per cent stake in Synchro Systems – whose software ran the membership and ticketing arrangements for several football clubs, including Spurs – was an attempt to hedge their bets. The England fans' misbehaviour led Margaret Thatcher's government to press ahead with a long-mooted and highly contentious identity card bill for football that would force all fans to buy computer-readable ID cards to enter matches. Sports minister Colin Moynihan talked up the prospect of legislation being in place for the 1989/90 season. While Irving Scholar publicly spoke out against the proposals, the PLC – of which he was the major shareholder – stood to benefit from its implementation. Synchro would suddenly have a captive market and a glut of new football customers. However, in the wake of the Taylor Report into the 1989 Hillsborough disaster, plans for a compulsory football ID card scheme were scrapped. Spurs ended up giving Synchro Systems – which had maxed out a £1.5 million overdraft while providing little tangible benefit to the PLC – away for £1.

Tony Berry's star was on the wane by then. The financing of Blue Arrow's takeover of Manpower, which had furnished his burgeoning reputation, had come under intense scrutiny. It transpired that half the shares in the rights issue to fund the buyout had gone unsold. Blue Arrow's brokers tried to flog them around the City with limited success. That they then chose to suppress the fact that shares worth around £200 million remained in their hands led to ultimately aborted criminal proceedings being launched against them. In May 1989, Berry fell under personal investigation by the Department of Trade and Industry (DTI) for a £25 million loan of Blue Arrow's money – allegedly without the formal blessing of the company's board – to a colourful developer transforming part of Canvey Island. Proceedings against

Berry were eventually dropped, but the damage had been done. He was a pariah in the City, and as a result, the hope surrounding his elevation to the Tottenham board had given way to recrimination among his fellow Spurs directors.

Tottenham weren't alone in being buffeted by the financial tremors that characterised the final years of the Eighties following 1987's 'Black Monday' stock market crash. Nor were their directors unique in believing know-how and success in one sector preordained profit in another. Fatally for Scholar and Bobroff – and the prospects of their PLC – they'd made a botch job of what should have been their bread and butter.

The fire that had taken 56 lives at Valley Parade led to stringent demands on clubs to conduct safety work on their stadiums. Tottenham's East Stand – home to the beloved 'Shelf', which offered 11,000 fans the best elevated standing view in the country – had insufficient emergency exits and was threatened with having its capacity reduced by half. The Tottenham board had three options: downsize the stand to comply, rebuild it completely at an estimated cost of £12 million or retrofit the East Stand within its existing perimeters for £4.8 million. Scholar and Bobroff settled on the latter. Under the plan, those fans on the Shelf would be shunted to the Paxton Road end and replaced in the East Stand by 36 executive boxes courting the more moneyed and compliant calibre of supporter. What followed, according to Simon Inglis in his seminal book *Football Grounds of Britain*, 'turned out to be one of the most retrogressive, badly managed and overpriced stand refurbishments ever carried out in British football'.

Scholar – who took every opportunity to remind anyone who would listen that he was a Spurs fan first and foremost, football club chairman and PLC major shareholder second – exhibited the heavy-handed paternalism that came so naturally to so many of those in the boardrooms of the Football League's clubs. As a Tottenham supporter, it is inconceivable he was unaware of the sentimental attachment those who stood on the Shelf had for the terrace – a bond akin to Liverpool supporters' connection to the Kop. Nevertheless, he opted to crack on with no consultation.

Spurs fan-turned-activist Annelise Jespersen takes up the story. 'We found out the club had already applied for planning permission for the work when they were saying they hadn't. I still have the reply to a letter I sent the club asking for clarification about the rumoured work. It essentially said, "Nothing to see here, guv." They'd put a planning application in to Haringey just before the 1988 FA Cup tie with Port Vale. No mention of that had been made to fans. They'd even brought a game forward to start the work without explaining why. The club's official line was that "no definite agreement had been reached, and Spurs fans will be the first to know". I got the reply to my letter in March. They'd already submitted the planning application in January.'

Despite having had ample time to reflect on the saga, Scholar showed no contrition. In his 1992 autobiography, he wrote, 'I must say I was unaware of any other club ever consulting its supporters prior to putting in a planning application to improve facilities.'

Jespersen explains what happened next. 'When the planning application was about to be heard, 20 or 30 of us turned up at the council's building, and I think the councillors were shocked to find Spurs fans opposing the plans. The planning meeting was put back to May, which gave us more home games to organise other fans. That's how Left on the Shelf was formed.'

At the end of the final game of the 87/88 season, the fan group staged a sit-in to bring attention to their cause. An unsatisfactory compromise was reached. A 3,000-capacity 'Shelf' was retained in front of the all-important executive boxes.[1] Ironically, the Tottenham board could have side-

---

1   The reprieve proved only fleeting. The 1990 Taylor Report recommended all major stadiums be converted to all-seater.

stepped the two-month delay inflicted by the postponement of the planning decision. As the scheduled work was being carried out within the stand's existing structure and didn't materially change its appearance, Spurs need not have submitted a planning application in the first place.

Contractor Wimpey was now up against it to ready the stand for the opening game of the 88/89 season against Coventry. Six hours before the kick-off of what should have marked the much-anticipated Spurs debut of Gascoigne, the game was postponed on safety grounds. Spurs were docked two points by the Football League and then had to employ a barrister to argue the points deduction down to a £15,000 fine. Wimpey was dismissed but later won a High Court ruling that ordered Spurs to pay it the £900,000 they had tried to withhold. Once finally completed, the East Stand refit came in at a reported £8.6 million, approaching double its original estimate. The finished stand was an eyesore – with restricted-view seats caused by the vast pillars required to hold up its new roof.

Rounding off this fiasco, the roof was almost inadvertently responsible for a human tragedy. The old East Stand roof – which contained an abandoned ramshackle press box – had been due to come down during the 1988 close season. The slipping schedule, however, saw the order of works re-jigged, and it remained in place for a further year. Paul Gascoigne, fast garnering a reputation for mischief in the early days of his Tottenham career, scaled his way up to the dilapidated structure. While he scoped pigeons through the sight of his air rifle, the rotten floorboards gave way beneath him. Gascoigne plunged in the region of 20 feet, his fall being broken by the seats below. Miraculously, he walked away with only minor injuries.

Significantly for the financial imbroglio enveloping the club, it was Gascoigne's signing – for a then British record fee – that had necessitated Tottenham switching their banking facilities from Barclays to the Midland Bank.

Taking on a faltering prospect like Tottenham Hotspur PLC was symptomatic of a number of poor judgements by the Midland. Despite being one of the UK's biggest banks, bad debts resulting from a downturn in the UK property market at the end of the 1980s, an unsuccessful acquisition of a US subsidiary earlier in the decade and a number of shaky loans made to countries in the developing world provoked panic of there being a run on the Midland.

Attempting to shore itself up, the bank looked to claw back money where it could. Tottenham's sizeable overdraft came into sharp focus. As chairman of the PLC and only too aware of his fiduciary duties, Bobroff saw the sale of star players as the solution. As far as Scholar – chairman of the football club and the largest single shareholder in the PLC – was concerned, this was anathema. Flotation and diversification were supposed to be the means by which the football club could afford top players. Now, the football club was being asked to cover the losses of a string of failed businesses.

In the summer of 1989, Scholar was still determined 'to dare' and 'do'. Venables told Scholar that Gary Lineker could be tempted back to England from Barcelona for a very reasonable fee. The prospect of Lineker, Gascoigne and Chris Waddle combining in a Tottenham team was as exciting as anything witnessed since the club's 1960s 'glory, glory' days. Venables promised to raise the £1.5 million needed for the Lineker deal – which included the capture of young midfielder Nayim – through player sales. The transfer was structured so that Spurs would pay one instalment up front and the balance by the start of August 1990.

However, on the day of Lineker's White Hart Lane unveiling, Scholar took a call from Marseille's maverick president Bernard Tapie. The French club wanted Waddle and, following a bout of haggling, agreed to pay £4.5 million for the winger – which at the time was the third-highest transfer fee in football history. The front cover of *The Spur* fanzine wryly captioned a picture of a smiling Lineker beside

Venables with the striker saying, 'I can't wait to play up front ahead of Chris Waddle', to which his new manager responds, 'Er, Gary? There's something I've been meaning to tell you ...'

Both Venables and Scholar insisted that Waddle's departure was a decision founded in footballing rather than financial imperatives. Scholar promised Venables he could reinvest all the money over and above the £1.5 million needed to cover the purchases of Lineker and Nayim in the team. Venables quickly pursued the purchases of Steve Sedgley from Coventry and Pat Van Den Hauwe from Everton. But above his head, a boardroom storm was brewing. Bobroff wanted to apply the brakes and divert the Waddle money to prop up the ailing PLC. Scholar, contrastingly, was determined to honour his commitment to Venables, and pushed both transfers through.

Nevertheless, the fact that the rest of the Waddle inheritance went unseen by Venables led to a souring of the relationship between him and Scholar. Scholar had wooed Venables to White Hart Lane with a commitment to bankrolling an assault on the title. But a new reality had kicked in. As the disillusioned manager explained, 'At the moment, I couldn't lay out a fiver on a World Cup star.' Henceforth, when their paths crossed on matchdays, Venables went out of his way to avoid speaking to Scholar.

The Waddle episode proved even more damaging to Scholar's entente with Bobroff. The one-time partners now began to conspire against each other. (The irony of one of their fellow directors, Douglas Alexiou, being a specialist in divorce law was lost on no one.) Bobroff struck first, in September of 1989. He argued that both the PLC and the football club needed to be led by the same person to ensure a unity of purpose. He requested that Scholar keep his shares but resign as a director. The response? In as many words, Scholar told him to do one. Bobroff was now in an exposed position without the telling support of the other heavyweight directors. Seizing the moment, Scholar rounded on him. Against his will, Bobroff was forced to resign as chairman. He bitterly signed an agreement to go, but demanded that the other board members buy out his shareholding. A mealy-mouthed public statement was released saying he'd left Tottenham to 'pursue other business interests'.

However, Scholar's 'victory' was reversed within a week. Bobroff had taken legal advice during that time and had been told that the agreement he'd been railroaded into signing wouldn't hold if tested in court. And Scholar couldn't buy Bobroff out because to do so would take him above the 30 per cent threshold, requiring him to bid for the entire company, which he was unwilling to do. Therefore, the only recourse available was to scrap the agreement. Bobroff was quietly reinstated as PLC chairman. At the December 1989 Annual General Meeting, he tried putting a brave face on this shambles. Addressing one fan-shareholder's concerns about 'boardroom shenanigans', he acknowledged the 'unsettling' effect they'd had on supporters. But he then insisted the board was 'united and happy with the direction the club was taking'. Cue much rolling of eyes from the AGM floor.

This stalemate held throughout the rest of the 1989/90 season. The team's surge to third place, followed by the star turns of Gascoigne and Lineker at the World Cup, meant the boardroom strife receded from the consciousness of most Spurs fans.

However, the troubles were only lying dormant for a while, as the city editor of the *Sunday Times* well understood. The huge and looming presence of Robert Maxwell, waiting in the wings, was soon to bring them spewing back to the surface.

Chapter Three

Bob's Your Uncle

IRVING SCHOLAR had always been a slick salesman. But attempting to champion Robert Maxwell's credentials as the person to safeguard Spurs' future, he floundered. 'Mr Maxwell's record in football is exemplary. You have to remember that he's taken control of two clubs, which were both in the Third Division and secured promotion to the First Division for both of them ... There are mixed feelings about Mr Maxwell becoming involved, but unfortunately those people who criticise him don't know the man.'

Scholar had become close to Maxwell during their time together on the Football League's television committee. So close, in fact, that he came to refer to Maxwell as 'Uncle Bob'. Both men found common cause in their belief that the Football League, and its fusty management of the game, urgently required reform or revolution.[2] Throughout the 1980s, Maxwell had tested the League's rule book to its limits.

As with so many elements of his life, when it came to his interest in football, untangling fact from fiction proved difficult. Maxwell had entered the world as Ján Ludvik Hoch, born into a Jewish family facing terrible poverty in rural Czechoslovakia. The direction of his life changed when

---

2 Scholar had most recently been perturbed by the Football League's decision in August 1990 to expand the First Division to 22 teams from the 1991/92 season. In his view this would dilute the quality of the top tier and make it a less attractive product.

Hitler invaded his homeland in 1939. Aged 16, he took up arms against the Nazis. His mother, father, grandfather and three of his siblings all perished in Auschwitz. Hoch fought in a division of the French army created for Czech exiles, then following France's surrender, he made it to England and rejoined the fight, serving with the 6th North Staffordshire regiment. He later received the Military Cross for bravery and settled on his new Anglicised name.

After the war, Maxwell's charm, resourcefulness and intelligence – which included a remarkable ability for languages – saw him set up a highly successful publishing house, Pergamon Press. The company identified an untapped niche, printing scientific research that grateful academics would virtually hand over for free. It therefore made sense to relocate Pergamon to Oxford, where it could be close to the university.

Maxwell quickly recognised football's uniquely held place in British society. And keen to fit in, he declared allegiance to Arsenal. It would, however, have been unseemly to come to the Gunners so late in life. Accordingly, Maxwell manufactured an elaborate backstory. As a child – without the money to pay for a ticket – he'd snuck through a gap in a fence to witness an exhibition game played by Arsenal in Czechoslovakia. It's a great tale. The problem with it is that the only record the Arsenal Historical Society has of the club visiting Czechoslovakia before World War Two is a friendly against Slavia Prague in May of 1926. Maxwell would have been a two-year-old at the time.

Maxwell's mendacious tendencies led him to severe difficulties in 1971. Following an investigation into his sale of Pergamon, he'd been caught cooking the company's books. Maxwell's racket was placing orders with Pergamon from within the stable of his other shrouded companies to maximise its profitability and bump up the sale price. There was no way of spinning the Department of Trade and Industry's judgement. 'Notwithstanding Mr Maxwell's acknowledged abilities and energy, he is not, in our opinion, a person who can be relied on to exercise proper stewardship of a publicly quoted company.'

For most careers in business, such a shameful verdict would have proved fatal. Maxwell, whose brass neck was copper-bottomed, wasn't one to accept defeat. He found a loophole that allowed him to repurchase Pergamon at a fraction of his artificially inflated sale price and began casting around for ways to launder his reputation. Oxford United's run-down Manor Ground was on Maxwell's doorstep, and by 1981, the U's – like so many of English football's financially struggling clubs – were on the brink.[3] Maxwell figured out he could get his name in the press as the city's footballing saviour for next to nothing.[4] Some reports say his rescue of Oxford cost him £128,000. Others say he effectively got the club for free by guaranteeing to underwrite its debts.

Wherever the truth lies, Maxwell's 'investment' offered a handsome return in the publicity it generated. Whether it was heroically wading into the terraces to restore calm when crowd trouble broke out between Oxford and Portsmouth fans or causing a storm by proposing to merge Oxford with Reading – who he announced he'd agreed to buy – to create Thames Valley Royals, Maxwell lapped it up. Although a wave of fierce fan protest thwarted the 'Royals project', Maxwell was unperturbed. In February 1984, the *Daily Mirror* broke the news that he had struck a 'staggering £10 million' deal with Martin Edwards to take control at Manchester United. Negotiations – if they ever seriously took place – went nowhere, but Maxwell was fast becoming a celebrity.

A month later, he was linked to a rescue of Derby County, which faced an Inland Revenue winding-up order. Despite

---

3 Maxwell began renting the vast Headington Hill Hall site in 1959. In 1960, Headington United changed their name to Oxford United. Two years later the club was elected to the Football League, where they replaced the financially indebted Accrington Stanley.

4 That Maxwell would subsequently use the Manor Ground's pitch as his own personal helipad and urinal sat incongruously with his 'saviour' status.

Football League rules prohibiting individuals from being involved in the running of multiple clubs, Maxwell did follow through this time. He circumvented the authorities by installing his son Ian as chairman. Maxwell could now declare himself a two-time saviour while stressing Derby and Oxford would operate autonomously. Such claims were somewhat undermined – as was his supposed passion for football – by his suggestion to Oxford manager Jim Smith that he coach both teams simultaneously.

But with Maxwell's patronage, both clubs scaled two divisions to reach English football's top flight. Oxford arrived in 1985, not merely surviving but winning the League Cup at Wembley; while Derby joined them in 1987. The Rams being the bigger club, Maxwell reshuffled the pack. Another of his children, Kevin, took the chairman's seat at the Manor Ground. And – to the surprise of absolutely no one – Maxwell inserted himself into that position at Derby. By then, he'd bought the *Daily Mirror*, fulfilling his long-held ambition of being a newspaper proprietor and sticking it to Rupert Murdoch, who had gazumped him for *The Sun* and *News of the World* in 1969. Reportedly, Maxwell's edict to his sports editor was, 'Make sure my name appears on the sports pages every day.' To aid this task, Maxwell went to war with the Football League. An agreement with Elton John to buy Watford was eventually stymied in the High Court.

By the end of the decade, Maxwell was unquestionably one of the most influential people in Britain. His speed dial was a who's who of world leaders. While his renamed Maxwell Communications Corporation's £2.6 billion leveraged buyout of US publishing giant Macmillan appeared to confound economists and financiers alike, it gave him further chance to lord it over his great rival Murdoch.

The timing of Jeff Randall's explosive *Sunday Times* revelation about Maxwell's desire to buy into Spurs was all the more fascinating because the man himself had been noisily signalling his intention to get out of football. A week before the story broke, he'd announced Derby were up for sale while lamenting, with little justification given the afterglow radiating from the 1990 World Cup, that 'football in Britain could not be in a sorrier state'.

Randall kept digging. Seven days after his initial article, his column – fast becoming a must-read for Spurs fans – disclosed that overtures to Maxwell had been made by Irving Scholar well before the start of the 90/91 season. Even more worryingly for those tracking the club's flatlining fiscal health, Randall exposed that Scholar had been forced to go cap-in-hand to borrow £1.1 million from Maxwell because the club was about to default on the second instalment due to Barcelona for Lineker and Nayim. Had that happened, Barça, by rights, could have repossessed the players. So urgent was Scholar's need that he'd agreed to guarantee the loan Maxwell provided against assets of his private company, Holborn Property. Fatefully, Scholar had kept his solicitations to Maxwell a secret from his fellow directors and shareholders in the PLC who, under City regulations, were entitled to know. Scholar's flimsy defence was to claim that Maxwell had insisted on absolute confidentiality.

No sooner had Maxwell's cover been blown than he began making regular – not to mention bombastic – statements on the state of play at the club. In an interview with ITV's *News at Ten*, he explained, 'Irving Scholar is a good friend of mine, and he approached me in July to help Spurs raise some money by a new rights issue, and I said "yes" subject to contractual conditions.' Maxwell stressed he was not looking to take over custodianship of the club. His would be a supporting role. 'I'm an old-age pensioner who doesn't have the time.' The sentiment was crudely underlined in a subsequent radio interview: 'I'm just a boy who can't say no. If I was a woman, I'd be pregnant the whole time.'

He also used the spotlight to fire a thinly veiled shot across Bobroff's bows: 'I'm flashing the yellow card at those involved in squabbles. It is inconceivable that I or anybody else would entertain having discussions about rights issues or becoming involved in any way with a club where some of the board are behaving like grown-up children.' Seasoned observers of Maxwell's modus operandi wondered whether – having scooped the publicity of being associated with Spurs – he was now seeking an off-ramp from Tottenham High Road before it became time to pony up for the £13 million stake in the club.

Emboldened by Maxwell's pronouncement, Scholar went after Paul Bobroff again. Three board meetings in four days, described as 'highly charged' by Harry Harris in *The Mirror*, finally got the job done. Bobroff – against his will – was voted out as PLC chairman. Douglas Alexiou was stuffed into the breach that Scholar – with Maxwell's help – had pried open. But the coup only went so far. Bobroff refused to resign as a director, bringing to mind the old cliche about deckchair rearrangement on the *Titanic*.

Having hinted immediately after Bobroff's dismissal that his rights issue could go ahead, Maxwell showed no urgency to proceed. The Tottenham board was left hopelessly entrenched, stewing on the splenetic divisions that had brought the club to this sorry point. As one insider put it in contemporary newspaper reports, 'There's blood on the Spurs walls.' The Midland Bank – whose worsening financial position soon resulted in its own chairman being deposed – was becoming very agitated indeed. Not least because Tottenham Hotspur PLC's financial advisors decided to sever ties with the company, while the Stock Exchange intimated its desire to investigate the Maxwell affair.

Insolvency practitioner David Buchler – a passionate Spurs fan and ex-schoolmate of Bobroff's – recounts how he was drafted in to navigate a way forward. 'I think during the latter part of autumn 1990, the board realised they needed some help, so they came to me.' It's a measure of how dicey the situation had become that Buchler remembers being introduced to Stephen Adamson from Ernst and

Young in stark terms. 'This is Stephen, the receiver for the Midland Bank.'

'From my perspective, going in to help,' says Buchler, 'it was clear there were two clans. It really boiled down to a disagreement over the future of one player, Paul Gascoigne. Irving Scholar wanted the best for the team – that was his focus, rather than what was involved in running a publicly listed company. Paul [Bobroff] perhaps could have been a bit gentler with Irving. The breakdown in their relationship is what prolonged the situation for so long.'

Like any good counsellor in an acrimonious divorce, Buchler set out to moderate and lower the temperature within White Hart Lane. It was no small challenge. 'I remember one board meeting where I said, "We really need to stop all these leaks to the press. They aren't helping the situation." Everyone agreed. The next morning, I picked up the newspaper, and there was a blow-by-blow account from the perspective of each faction, faithfully reproduced by the journalists they were friendly with.'

It was open season on Tottenham in the press. Even the news of a £4 million kit deal with Umbro to start the next season, which included an upfront payment of £1.1 million – the exact amount needed to settle the Maxwell loan – was quickly countered by a *News of the World* spoiler. This claimed that double-winning captain Danny Blanchflower, reportedly living on £20 per week while thought to be suffering from Alzheimer's, was yet to receive money from Spurs due to him from a benefit match played six months ago.

Scholar's position as a director looked increasingly wobbly as, for nearly four weeks, Tottenham failed to issue a circular to shareholders explaining goings-on at the company, as was required by the Stock Exchange. When Tottenham's solicitors Ashurst Morris Crisp finally submitted a report to the Exchange, it made grim reading for the company's major shareholder. It had not been necessary for Scholar to keep his fellow directors in the dark about Maxwell. The agreement between the two permitted Scholar to divulge their dealings to the Tottenham board, provided they were also bound to confidentiality. In the law firm's view, the fact that Scholar had amended his undertaking to comply with his own, more restrictive, interpretation of the clause, and backdated it, 'had the effect of misleading the board' and was 'improper'.

On 19 October, the Stock Exchange suspended shares in Tottenham Hotspur PLC. Having flouted the Companies Act and Tottenham's articles of association, Irving Scholar's position as a director was untenable. He stepped down from the company's board within ten days of the share suspension but retained his status as football club chairman and major shareholder in the PLC.

Following the issuing of a brutal censure of Tottenham by the Stock Exchange, *The Guardian*'s dismayed financial editor, Alex Brummer, urged the Department of Trade and Industry to investigate. 'The Stock Exchange should never need to tell the board of a publicly quoted company that it should have "adequate procedures to enable a business to be conducted in a satisfactory manner". That it feels obliged to lecture Tottenham on how to conduct itself speaks volumes for the way corners were cut. Bad blood among board members is nothing new, nor is the desire for a quick fix to a financial problem. However, the nature of Irving Scholar's dealings should send shivers down the spines of investors and fans.'

Watching on aghast as this internecine carnage had begun playing out, a small group of Spurs fans felt unable to sit idly by on the sidelines. Lawyer, long-time White Hart Lane season ticket holder and veteran of the Left on the Shelf campaign, Steve Davies was among the first to start organising Tottenham supporters. 'I was horrified by the idea of Maxwell. It was a sign of desperation. It was well known he was a crook. People had been intimidated from criticising him because he would immediately sue. He wasn't a gem. What you want is someone who cares about the club and intends to take it forward – and hopefully has some money as well. There was no evidence he fitted that bill. It was another sign of Irving Scholar's poor judgement that he got involved with someone like that. I think Scholar felt he could hang on with Maxwell's backing, but Maxwell was an epic bullshitter … full of bluster. But was he ever going to actually produce the money? Did he even have it? I walked past him once at *The Mirror* building. He stared at me. I wish I'd had the confidence to say something to him because I'm normally quite good at that, but I didn't. My overriding sense was Spurs will be nowhere if we get this buffoon in charge, so we've got to do something about it.

'There was a bit of a moment in the late Eighties and early Nineties that came along with the football fanzine movement where you felt something in the air, that supporters were entitled to have a voice. It was an interesting exercise for those of us who wanted to do something in taking collective action, pre-internet. How do you reach people? We used to put posters up around Tottenham, but by the next day, they'd be fly-posted over. So we weren't massively effective at first. The Football Supporters' Association helped us convene the first meeting in late September 1990 at the University of London Union.'

Annelise Jespersen explains her motivation for attending along with around 50 others that night. 'I was involved in social justice, so getting stuck in first over the Shelf and then again after the news about Maxwell seemed a natural extension of that. Not that I was a professional activist or anything. But if there was something to be done, I wanted to help. The club was in trouble. We owed all this money to the Midland Bank, and what would happen if they called it in? In hindsight, it's easy to think they'd never have been willing to do that, but football didn't hold the place it does now in the national picture. I doubt anyone was asking questions about Spurs in Parliament.

'We were perhaps a bit optimistic in asking Scholar and Maxwell to come to the ULU meeting, but Steve, Bernie

Kingsley, James Loxley and I took things forward from there. I was working full-time. But I was young, and had a lot of energy. I spent untold hours handing out leaflets and writing letters to the Midland, the club and press. I don't think we ever had designated roles. You just gravitate to what you're good at. We agreed to hold meetings on the first Saturday home game of each month at the Railway Tavern. The first time we did, it wasn't clear whether it was just the regular pre-game drinkers or people who'd actually seen our leaflet. So I got up on a table and said this is what we're here for. I never got any pushback. I think having an unusual name and a loud voice made me stand out. From then on, people would ask, "Are you Annelise?" and take a leaflet.'

'Why did we settle on the name TISA [Tottenham Independent Supporters' Association]?' says Davies. 'We had to make it clear we were independent. I was in the supporters' club – and I'm sure they felt slightly antagonistic to us at the start because they'd been around a long time – but their affiliation with the club made it difficult for them to take a view on anything. While I don't think supporters' associations should be commenting constantly on things like transfers, when it comes to issues concerning the club's entire future, it's time to step in.'

Jespersen agrees that staking out their independence was critical. 'After Left on the Shelf, there'd been an attempt to co-opt the opposition. A group called the Tottenham Community Liaison Committee had been set up, which had a couple of fan representatives on it. When I wrote to Scholar to introduce TISA, he replied, telling me to speak to them.'

So, with TISA's independence established, what were the group's aims? 'The immediate one,' says Jespersen, 'was that we reckoned individual Spurs fans held about 20 per cent of the shares in the company. Loads of people had that nominal share to hang on the wall to say they owned a stake in the club. We wanted to mobilise those fans to express concerns legitimately to the board. [There was even some initial heady talk of a rights issue by fans to raise the money to clear the debt.] Tactically, we wanted to have a credible voice at the AGM that they had to hold before the end of 1990 and be able to say "we represent X number of shareholders, and you have to listen". Looking at the original TISA leaflets, we called for: "Fans to be consulted on changes; regular meetings between supporters and the club; the company to be run in a professional way; the success of the football team to be the main aim of the company [*plus ça change*] and greater accountability of the board." That doesn't sound too unreasonable now, does it?'

Chapter Four

The Manager – Can You Take the Pressure?

UNABLE TO spend any money at Spurs as the 1990/91 season began unfolding, Terry Venables committed to printing his own. The Monopoly-style banknotes for *The Manager* board game he was busily developing in one of his more successful side hustles were stamped with his signature on behalf of the Banco De Venables.[5] The Tottenham manager's frustrations at his real-life plight poured out in the game's back-of-the-box blurb. 'The measure of success in football can be a dilemma. Are you considered a successful manager if your club makes £5 million profit but your team gets relegated? Or if you lose £5 million but come top of the league, are you more or less of a success? The object of *The Manager* is not only to win the championship but stay handsomely in profit, too. Football is a game. But it is also a business and a big one at that. *The Manager* is all about the business game of football. And in our game, at the end of the day, the one with the most money will win. If you don't, there's always next year, isn't there? – if you're still around.'

---

5 Venables had long possessed a keen entrepreneurial eye beyond football. As an 18-year-old player at Chelsea, on the advice of an accountant, he'd formed his own limited company. He'd then invested in a Soho tailoring business, Thingummywigs (a cap for women with fake hair sewn in, designed to cover their hair rollers) and later collaborated on the more lucrative *Hazell* detective novels that were adapted for television.

As will be of great significance later on in this story, it was during Venables's attempts to secure funding to take his board game to market that he first came into the orbit of financial fixer Eddie Ashby.

The Manager's release in shops coincided with the news of Robert Maxwell's intention to buy into the drowning club. By then, Venables, who'd lost his mother to cancer that August, had entered the final year of his Tottenham contract. He began briefing, in no uncertain terms, that he'd had his fill of being subservient to directors. 'If we get Maxwell as well as Scholar, then we all move one step down towards the boot room, myself included. I'm past worrying about who is supposed to own the club ... Ever since we got paid directors and the City became involved with football clubs, we have been heading rapidly for the day when the English manager is reduced to the continental coach. I'm supposed to be the whizz-kid boss with the business acumen as well as the football brain. But I have no alternative at the moment but to concentrate all my energies solely on the team.'

The eclectic cast of characters in the squad he'd assembled responded with a string of winning results that saw Spurs undefeated in their first ten games and roused talk of a title bid. 'Terry protected us from the financial situation,' recalls midfielder David Howells. 'We only saw what we read in the press. There weren't any meetings among the players because we never felt that was necessary. Terry was honest with us.

'His training was always vibrant. You understood the purpose of his sessions, which isn't always the case in football. He'd do things in training we'd never seen before. He was so confident in his ability and trusting that he let Malcolm Allison and John Lyall come in and take training when they were out of work a couple of times. It was tremendous for us. No other manager I played under was confident enough to do something like that. All credit to Terry. Handing over your team to someone else in that way is a precious thing. He was a genuinely funny bloke, too. Sometimes with managers, you'd feel you had to laugh if they cracked a joke, but Terry had a brilliant sense of humour.'

One way and another, comedy was a constant feature of life at Tottenham's training ground. Indeed, the facilities were a running joke among the Spurs players and staff. One of Irving Scholar's early moves in his partnership with Paul Bobroff had been to sell off the training ground Tottenham owned at Cheshunt, to Tesco. After a brief stay at a rented site in Enfield, where players had been required to share a canteen alongside the gawking employees of consumer electrics firm Thorn EMI, Spurs took up residence at a sports ground at Chase Lodge in Mill Hill. The English Heritage-listed house on the site offered a splendid fit with the image of Spurs as one of English football's great aristocrats fallen upon hard times.

Physio John Sheridan recalls life at Mill Hill with an incredulous smile: 'The old building was Grade II-listed. I'd planned to put my treatment room in there, but they said we couldn't change any of the colours – the walls were dark grey – and we weren't allowed to move the electrical sockets. It wasn't fit for purpose. I found two old Portakabins and the cross-section to attach them on *Exchange & Mart*. They came from one of the North Sea oil rigs. We couldn't connect them to the mains electricity. Not ideal for a treatment room! We had to install this big old diesel generator, which was a nightmare. Whenever I ordered the physio supplies, I'd have to buy the fuel for it, too. The first one we had was really unpredictable. Come winter, there were times when I'd have to jump-start the battery using my car so that I could start treating these players worth millions. Luckily, I'd worked on the production line for Vauxhall Motors before training as a physio, which came in handy.'

Power wasn't the only thing in short supply. 'There were toilets in the cabin but no running water. If we wanted that, we had to collect it from the house. Inevitably, one of the players – I'll leave you to guess who – decided to take a dump in the lav. We had to go and get a load of buckets of water from the main building to try and flush it. Us physios were a different breed back then.'

Gudni Bergsson – whose arrival at Spurs from the amateur ranks of Icelandic football owed much to the 1988 Miss World competition being held in London, where the agent for Miss Iceland (who took the crown) put in a good word for Bergsson to his counterpart for Miss Ireland, who happened to be a good friend of Venables – was amazed by the privations of Mill Hill. 'It was a bit grim. The showers were absolutely minging. The hot water ran out after two minutes, and then it would be ice cold. I was a bit taken aback because we had some pretty good facilities at home and a lot of warm water with our hot springs!

'I remember when it started to get a bit nippy in November and December, saying to Roy Reyland, our kit man, "Come on Roy, when are you going to get the proper warm training kit out?" He'd always reply, "No, no, no, Gudni. We need to keep that back until it's absolutely freezing so that you appreciate it." I think he was having to be a bit tight with the kit because he didn't have that much of it and maybe worried the players would nick it. We were only wearing a thin top and shorts, shivering our arses off.'

By contrast, Bergsson's Nordic team-mate, Erik Thorstvedt, received multiple sets of training kit for each session. Roy Reyland explains: 'The foreign lads weren't the best dressers, and Gazza used to burn Erik's clothes. To guard against this, I started to give Erik three sets of kit. One to wear to drive to training, one to wear during the session and one to go home in.' Tottenham's commercial manager, Mike Rollo, who spent plenty of time at Mill Hill recording interviews for the premium rate Spurs Line he'd developed to generate revenue for the club, recalls a scene he witnessed when arriving early one morning. 'Gazza was one of the first in – I could see he was fussing around with something and giggling like a schoolboy. The next thing I hear there's this big hullabaloo. Gazza comes racing out of the changing rooms at full pelt. Erik is in hot pursuit behind. It turned out when Erik had gone to put his goalie gloves on, he'd found something unwelcome inside.'

Thorstvedt is philosophical about behaviour that, in today's game, would be considered beyond the pale. 'When the players are warming up nowadays, they do all that stuff like touching hands to release good chemicals in the body. Whereas, it's fair to say, in our era at Tottenham, we had a piss-taking culture. Some of it wasn't all that funny, but some of what went on was hilarious.'

Thorstvedt's reply is instantaneous when asked for his favourite training ground tale. 'Ahhh, Gazza and the ostrich.' The goalkeeper is referencing an incident destined to live forever in club folklore. As the Tottenham squad – minus the AWOL Gascoigne – gathered on the practice pitch wondering what innovative drill Venables had in store and where their star man was, the midfielder arrived dragging a burlap sack. Upon closer inspection, it was clear to the players that whatever its contents were, they were moving. Gascoigne could hold on no longer, and out of the bag came a disorientated ostrich – wearing a Spurs shirt bearing Steve Sedgley's number. The impressive length of Sedgley's neck was a recurring source of material for Gascoigne's unique form of banter. 'He got it from Paradise Park in Hoddesdon, which was a funny little zoo,' smiles Thorstvedt, 'I used to take my kids there.'[6]

Paul Walsh is somewhat of an outlier among the Spurs players who played under Venables, as he isn't wholly positive

---

6   Others have their own favourite Gazza stories. Roy Reyland recalls the time a fully clothed Gascoigne jumped into a lake while the team were taking a stroll around the grounds of their hotel before an important away match. 'When he came back up to the surface he said, "I nearly caught it." He thought he'd seen a fish. Ludicrous but harmless fun.'
    Nayim remembers his team-mate driving his car on to the Mill Hill training pitches and churning them up by doing 'rallies'.
    For John Sheridan it's the time Gascoigne hopped over a fence in the middle of a training session in search of a stray ball. 'We didn't see him again until the next morning when he turned up with the ball under his arm and said, "It took me a while to find it!"'

about the experience or glowing about Gascoigne. 'You laugh at things like the ostrich. Everyone laughed. Who else could be bothered to get a fucking ostrich and bring it into training? It's more aggravation than it's worth. And then you've got to scuttle around the place trying to catch it. It was a funny moment. But how do you then get the players to refocus? There were too many distractions like that at Spurs.

'A couple of times, Gazza pissed me off, and we had a bit of a wrestling match which I eventually got the better of. Terry tried to break it up, saying, "Come on, Paul." I told him, "Well, sort golden bollocks out then. He thinks he can do what he likes all the time." Every day, someone would dig for something to give someone else a load of stick over. Mabbsy [captain Gary Mabbutt] was the only one who set a good example to the younger lads, and Lineker tended to stay out of it, too. But there were quite a few of us who were taking the piss and behaving unprofessionally. Don't get me wrong, I was a big part of that. Underneath all that bullshit on the surface, I realise looking back there was a lot of stuff going on with people. But it was always fronted out with bravado.

'Terry's approach was ... I can clearly remember him saying, "You're adults, and I'm going to treat you as adults." I shook my head and thought, "Fucking hell, if only you knew what we were getting up to." We weren't adults. We were like a bunch of kids, acting like a bunch of kids. As a professional, you know the code of conduct and what's allowed. But I'd come from Liverpool, where there were enough strong characters in the dressing room to ensure nothing got out of hand. At Spurs, it felt like people were crossing the line every day. But looking back at my part in what went on – I've thought a lot about this – if I could speak to Terry now, I'd apologise. He gave me a chance at a big club when I left Liverpool, and really I fucked it up.'

It's worth pointing out that for all their championship pedigree, Liverpool's players weren't above reproach for a lack of professionalism. During the 1990/91 season, Steve McMahon made headlines for a prank that went dangerously sideways. Following a night out, McMahon reportedly leaned through team-mate Glenn Hysén's taxi window and pulled his tie so tightly the Swedish defender lost consciousness. With his wife unable to free him, the driver was forced to make an emergency stop to prevent Hysén from dying of asphyxiation. Later in the year, across Stanley Park at Everton – twice title winners in the 1980s – Peter Beagrie was involved in an infamous incident where, following a night on the sauce, he was unable to enter what he thought was the team hotel, and so decided to drive a motorcycle through its glass front. The winger required 50 stitches.

The prevalent drinking culture in English football still had several years left to run. Nayim, whose football education was conducted at Barcelona's salubrious La Masia complex, remembers his shock when, returning from one of his first away matches with Spurs, the team bus made an unscheduled pit stop. 'It was to go to an off-licence and buy lots of beer. I couldn't believe it. I asked Terry Venables, who'd managed me at Barça, "What's going on here?" He told me, "That's the culture in England, so you'll have to get used to it."

'It was the same in the players' lounge. It was different for me because I was born in Ceuta [the Spanish territory in north Africa] and don't drink because I'm Muslim. But even in Barcelona, the players would only have one glass of wine with a meal, and that was it. The Spurs players came to love a night out with me as I could always drive them back home safely to their houses afterwards!'

'The discipline was very slack,' reflects Thorstvedt. 'Maybe it took some foreign influence for English football to change. I think the English game really needed to go through that. Terry had a great football brain and was a sensible guy who was clearly respected among the players – a players' manager. But, I think he felt you can't change people and must adapt to how they are. I'd played in Germany for a couple of seasons before I came to Spurs. I was so impressed by how football was run there. You got weighed constantly. If you trained poorly, you might not get picked at the weekend. It was all so professional. Then, when I came to England, it was all about what happened at 3pm on Saturday. There was no support whatsoever to help me settle in.

'I stayed three months in the Swallow Hotel with Gazza – he'd been kicked out of his first one – and every week, there'd be 20 bottles of champagne on his tab because all his mates from Newcastle would be staying with him. My impression was that Spurs were picking up the bill. I felt the players had a power over the club that they didn't have in other countries. You're shocked when you come to a new place and see how different things are. But after a few months, you get used to it. The training culture might not have been as good as in Germany, but there was this immense will to win. Before a match, there would be laughing and joking in the dressing room, but once the players came in from the warm-up, it was like turning on a switch. I've literally seen guys headbang the wall, getting up for it.

'Just as astounding was how much they could drink at night and then still be able to go out and perform. There were many good players in that Tottenham team, but their attitude on the pitch and how they went for it was incredible to me. I must say that's a British thing. You get blitzed during World War Two, and you just clear the rubble and get on with it. It was the same with the IRA bombings when I was there. Lots of Norwegian tourists were frightened, but Londoners were straight back on the tube to work.'

Perhaps stoicism in the face of the club's crumbling financial edifice – allied with Gascoigne's sparkling form – accounted for Tottenham's potent start to the season. The final match in the sequence of results unblemished by defeat was a 2-1 away win at Nottingham Forest, secured with a David Howells winner at the death. The versatile youth-team graduate had bagged Tottenham's opener, too, in addition to clearing one off the line. It's a game that he ranks among his best in a Spurs shirt.

However, rather than Howells's heroics, *The Mirror* was more interested in the captivating testimony of Forest's callow new signing from the League of Ireland, Roy Keane. It concerned Gascoigne's behaviour during the match. 'I couldn't believe it. He kept telling me I was rubbish. And that was one of the compliments. Some of the things he was saying to me were unbelievable. Most are unrepeatable.'

Interactions between Keane and his Tottenham counterparts would become a feature of the tussles between the clubs that season. (If you know, you know. And if you don't, rest assured we'll get there later.) The paper also excoriated Gascoigne for a 'four-letter flare-up' with an associate of Forest manager Brian Clough. And for swearing in front of children – some of whom were blind – which, supposedly, somehow made his offence even more egregious.

Liverpool undoubtedly considered the Gascoigne-inspired Spurs a threat to their grip on the First Division. The defending champions arrived at White Hart Lane in early November in ominous form, having won nine and drawn one of their opening ten league fixtures. Kenny Dalglish strung five across the back while Steve McMahon attempted to subdue Gascoigne by fair means or foul. Having been robbed by Gascoigne in his own half, McMahon checked his progress with what professional wrestling commentators would describe as a stiff clothesline across the throat. He gladly accepted the yellow card that came his way.

Deep in the second half, after Liverpool had established an unassailable 3-1 lead, he inexplicably escaped further sanction when smashing an elbow into Gascoigne's face. The midfielder's wink to the camera, having solemnly pleaded his innocence to the official, only added to the sense of injustice. Gascoigne, understandably, had little time for the referee's words of condolence as he tried to stem the blood flowing from his nose but imprudently pushed him away. Gary

Mabbutt quickly intervened to calm things down. But with the match being shown live to a vast television audience on ITV, Gascoigne's combustible temperament – particularly in the face of provocation – would, from then on, face inspection every time he set foot on the field.

The defiance Venables had coaxed from his side in adversity could not be sustained after the Liverpool defeat. Incidents that in more serene times could have been dismissed with a laugh were instead interpreted as emblematic of the club's dire straits. Having finished their pre-match meal in a west London hotel ahead of December's league game at Stamford Bridge, the Spurs players found the team bus had been towed away for a parking infraction. A fleet of taxis was hailed, but Spurs received a £20,000 fine for their belated arrival and then succumbed 3-2 to the Blues, with Gary Lineker missing a penalty. A disappointing home draw with Sunderland, which had required Paul Walsh's two-goal intervention from the bench and a last-minute Lineker leveller to rescue a point, was followed by defeat at Maine Road.

The subsequent 2-1 home win over lowly Luton came at a heavy price. Nayim and Pat Van Den Hauwe were both dismissed before half-time. Nayim for 'foul and abusive language', while Van Den Hauwe further enhanced his 'psycho' reputation with a tackle *The Guardian*'s David Lacey described as 'designed to separate Iain Dowie from his legs'. In Lacey's match report, he praised the players for taking their medicine from referee David Elleray without protest. Elleray, however, revealed years later in his memoir that he had been 'completely broken' by the players' conduct and had only spared Gascoigne from a red card for a string of invective at the interval because 'he could not find the courage to dismiss him'. Elleray also disclosed that following that exchange, he'd seriously contemplated handing his whistle to his linesman and walking out on the match.

The suspensions stemming from the Luton game, coming at the busiest time of the season, exacerbated the strain on a squad being hollowed out by the sale of fringe players like Guy Butters and Bobby Mimms. Such moves by the football club's hierarchy to recoup money wherever possible were designed to forestall unwelcome conversations between the PLC board and the Midland about the need to cash in more bankable assets.

Although Spurs would subsequently achieve only a solitary further home league win in the season, the Luton game was transformative for one of the team's more maligned players. Paul Stewart had arrived at White Hart Lane the day before Paul Gascoigne in 1988 for a similarly lavish fee. Venables had long admired Stewart's combative centre-forward play and beat off competition from Everton for his signature. Stewart recalls Venables's powers of persuasion. 'I was a northern lad who didn't intend to come south. But I went down to meet Terry, and he had a glass of champagne waiting for me, which was a touch of class. I ended up signing there and then. I wanted to keep the news out of the press as I was getting married that summer, and I didn't want to ruin my wife's wedding day. She was a twin, so it was always going to be a wrench moving to London.

'People talk about the north–south divide – believe me, it's real. The way people live up north is very different to London. The first time I set eyes on the team bus at Spurs was a real eye-opener for me in terms of that. I came from Man City, where we had a bog standard coach to take us to away games. Then, at Tottenham, I remember seeing that black double-decker Holsten bus for the first time. There are chefs on it, and you're handed a menu. You can order steak cooked how you like it and a choice of white or red. Other teams used to hate us for it – it wound them up no end. They thought we were flash southern softies. But that was alright by us 'cos once we got on to the pitch, we could hold our own. Mostly because we had some northern steel in the team.

On debut, the portents for Stewart's White Hart Lane career looked shaky. He'd been forced to sit out the opening weeks while serving a suspension carried over from the previous season. When he did make his belated bow from the bench in a home game against Manchester United, he insisted on taking a last-minute penalty to win the game, impetuously shoving spot-kick specialist Terry Fenwick out of the way. Stewart's resulting effort pounded the crossbar, and a section of the Tottenham support immediately got on his case. Stewart is virtuously diplomatic when asked about his relationship with the home crowd. 'I loved the Spurs fans and never had any problems with them. When you come for a big fee and don't hit the ground running, you know you'll get some stick. But that was ok by me.'

Those detractors Stewart had within the fanbase were often influenced by aesthetic concerns. He wasn't the archetypal Tottenham striker. His primary gift was prodigious physical power rather than a dainty deftness of touch. Stewart compares and contrasts his mentality to Lineker's, who he was regularly partnered with in attack. 'I was lucky to play with Gary. Whenever he had a chance, you just knew it would be a goal. He'd be thinking, "Where am I going to put this?" Whereas someone like me was worrying, "What if I miss?" He had such great confidence that even if he did miss, it would be someone else's fault. He wasn't the type to chase around, either. If we didn't have the ball, he'd be out on the touchline filing his nails! But what a finisher and a nice guy. Players like that have something natural that your ordinary ones don't.'

Venables had stuck by Stewart during the striker's stuttering first two Spurs seasons, and the regard Stewart holds for his manager has only grown in the intervening years. 'Terry was a master at managing players, the best I played for. He was years ahead of his time. He wouldn't ever hammer you in front of everyone, and I can hardly ever remember him swearing. His office at Mill Hill was upstairs in the old stately home. He'd call you in there to go and see him if you'd made a mistake. A bit like going to see the headmaster. He'd give you a chance to recognise what you'd done wrong in a game. If you didn't, he'd have the video out and show you. He never missed a thing.'

Rather than considered design by Venables, however, necessity proved the catalyst for rejuvenating Stewart's wilting Spurs career. 'People talk about Terry's masterstroke of moving me into midfield, but it came about because of Nayim and Pat Van Den Hauwe's sendings off against Luton.' Stewart was pressed into midfield action, and ironically, given how hard he'd found goals to come by, scored either side of half-time to complete a come-from-behind win. Stewart revelled in the role, and Venables had the sense to recognise he was on to a good thing. Tottenham would flood the midfield with five men and leave the lethal Lineker alone to lead the line. 'I thought to myself "this is a great gig",' says Stewart. 'From then on, I just had to win the ball, give it to Gazza and watch him do his magic. All of a sudden, people are writing "Paul Stewart is a player", "Stewart is man of the match", "Stewart for England".'

Christmas Day fell three days after the Luton match, and John Sheridan has particular reason to remember that festive season. Fenwick, who'd spent the start of the season on loan at Leicester following injury, was recalled to bolster the numbers in Venables's dwindling camp.

'Things had become very tight. There was a specific rowing machine Terry Fenwick requested, and there wasn't the money for it. I even remember Terry Venables buying the Christmas turkeys for the players and staff that year out of his own pocket. That's the sort of man he was.'

'I'd forgotten about the turkeys,' laughs Gudni Bergsson. 'That was well played by Terry because footballers still love a bit of a freebie – even if they come off the back of a lorry or whatever. We really appreciated that Terry did that for us.'

But as the festive season drew to a close, the only things being handed out to Spurs on the pitch were three consecutive beatings at the hands of Coventry, Southampton and Manchester United. The last of those games, played on New Year's Day, was particularly painful. Just 24 hours earlier, shareholders – including those newly aligned to TISA – had convened at White Hart Lane for the eagerly anticipated Annual General Meeting, not least because the club had recently communicated that ticket prices would be raised for the second half of the 1990/91 season. If delaying the meeting to the last possible day of the year and hosting it during the holidays had been designed to discourage attendance, the Tottenham board were sorely disappointed. Around 200 shareholders – boosted by a sizeable press presence – were determined to extract answers.

Having barred admission to the journalists, acting chairman Douglas Alexiou ignored calls from the floor and an overwhelming show of hands in opposition to the only item on the agenda – a motion brought by the board to immediately adjourn the meeting. The microphones in the room were then turned off. Whatever lingering empathy remained for the board among shareholders – if any existed – was now utterly spent. As fan Stephen Pinner reflected, 'Everybody is pretty disgusted at the way the meeting was handled. The mood was angry and hostile. As an information exercise it was a non-event.'

Irving Scholar's decision to decline a seat at the top table with the PLC contingent led to some speculation that he had ducked the abortive AGM. However, in an interview screened during half-time of ITV's live coverage of the United match, the football club chairman confirmed he'd been discreetly present in the room. He refused to be drawn on how negotiations with Robert Maxwell were progressing; but he went on to intimate that proposals as to who would have the controlling stake in Tottenham would be put before shareholders in the 'next couple of months where they will decide the future ownership of the company'. When asked if he would still be at White Hart Lane, Scholar confidently asserted with a smile, 'I sincerely hope so,' while also vowing to resist 'under any circumstances' all attempts to sell Gascoigne and Lineker.

With Scholar's red lines further escalating the tensions at Tottenham, it was fitting that deep into the second half, two streakers momentarily halted play while parading themselves and a banner calling for peace. However, their intended target was not those belligerently prowling White Hart Lane's corridors of power, but the UN Security Council who had set Saddam Hussein a deadline of 15 January to withdraw his forces from Kuwait. Had they made their increasingly blue-skinned bolt from the Paxton Road a little earlier, they might have spared Gascoigne the straight red card he'd received for an ill-considered outburst at referee Vic Callow. A miserable night for Spurs became even worse when Brian McClair plundered a United winner with the game's final attack.

As sections of the media ripped into Gascoigne in the match's aftermath, Terry Venables rallied to his player's defence. 'I don't think anyone understands the pressure he's been under … press men are outside his house every day driving him mad. That shouldn't be allowed.'

Chapter Five
The North Wind Doth Blow

THE BLEAKNESS of Tottenham's winter left few fans
relishing the prospect of an FA Cup third round excursion to
bottom-tier Blackpool's Bloomfield Road. While practitioners
of Spurs' unique strand of numerology could take solace from
the new year's fourth digit ticking over to a one, coming a
cropper in a January 'David versus Goliath' tie like this formed
as much a part of the cup's lore and lexicon as did mention
of Wembley's fabled 'Twin Towers' or '39 steps' come May.

Indeed, none of Terry Venables's three previous tilts at
the competition as Tottenham manager had endured long
enough to reach February. Losing at White Hart Lane to
Southampton at this stage a year ago had been painful. But at
least Saints were a top-flight side with an emerging talent like
Matthew Le Tissier in their ranks. Weighing more heavily on
those setting out on the M1 for the Fylde coast were memories
of the abject cup defenestrations at Vale Park in 1988 and
Valley Parade in 1989. The Bradford defeat rankles with Paul
Walsh to this day. 'Argh. Embarrassing. Afterwards, we got
on that great big Holsten double-decker bus. We've just lost
to Bradford, and the wine waiter comes down the aisle to
take our orders. I'm thinking "fucking hell". At Liverpool, it
would have been a quick stop at the chippy for a fish supper.
I remember there were a load of fans giving us shit as we sat
there on that bus, and it felt like we didn't deserve to be on
there when we'd just been beaten like that.'

Jonathan Pearce recalls the overwhelming trepidation that accompanied Spurs to Lancashire on the first weekend of 1991. 'I'd done the radio commentary for Capital Gold at Bradford – what a terrible performance that was, by the way – and Bobby Moore and I went up to Blackpool fearing, almost expecting, the story of the weekend would be Tottenham getting knocked out.' The impending sense of doom was exacerbated by the onset of weather blown straight from the pages of the Old Testament. Pearce picks up the story. 'Ahead of the game, Bobby and I went out for a bit of a recce. Even though we were a good few roads back from the sea, there were all these sandbags and police. It was like, "What's all this? Are the Germans invading?" A policeman said to us, "It's a surge tide. If we take the sandbags away, there'll be no football."'

As the intrepid 3,000 travelling Tottenham supporters sought in vain for refuge within Bloomfield Road's Spion Kop, they were entitled to ponder whether the realities of Blackpool's present might be a window into Spurs' future. Peter Ball of *The Times* described the ground as 'one of the most dilapidated in the [Football] League'. The extent to which the club was on its uppers was reflected by the actual rather than metaphorical lack of a roof over the heads of the exposed visiting fans. It had been removed from the crumbling stand – which was now permitted to hold only half its capacity – a decade earlier, having been condemned on safety grounds by the local authority.

The club's latest custodian, Owen Oyston – described in Ball's match preview as 'ebullient and charming' but who, in years to come, proved himself to be one of the most despicable characters in English football's long and often grubby history – anticipated a bumper home crowd. 'With the success in the World Cup, Lineker and Gazza have created an awareness of the game that hasn't been there for a number of years, and the prospect of them playing here has brought an enormous interest among people who haven't previously been committed to the game. It means we'll make a profit for once. We've been making a loss of £12,000 a week. And that's without expenditure on meeting the requirements of the Taylor Report or on new players.'

But beyond the undoubted draw of seeing England's Italia 90 idols in the flesh, Tottenham's visit also allowed Tangerines fans to wistfully reminisce over happier times. In the immediate years after the Second World War, Blackpool were a fixture in the upper echelons of the First Division, boasting two bona fide superstars of their own: the Stanleys, Matthews and Mortensen. Consequently, Blackpool became the biggest box office draw in the golden age of Football League attendance. Matthews's quest to fulfil an oath sworn on his father's deathbed to win the FA Cup became almost a national obsession between 1946 and 1953. Three times Blackpool reached Wembley in that period, overcoming Spurs at Villa Park in both the 1948 and 1953 semi-finals.

Blackpool's cup exploits also heralded a new sub-culture in English football – the 'ultra', long before that term was coined. A group of fans, making light of the perilous geopolitics that were dividing the world along ideological lines and threatening nuclear armageddon, adopted the monicker of the Atomic Boys. Their escapades in first wearing tangerine-dyed jackets to Blackpool's Cup games, then graduating to elaborate fancy dress costumes 'borrowed' from the town's Louis Tussauds waxworks had for a time made them almost as famous as the team's players.

Soon, the troupe's inimitable leader, Syd Bevers, was bringing a live duck – also dyed in Blackpool's tangerine colours – named Puskas out on to the pitch before kick-off. When the team reached Wembley in 1951, his flouting of a ban imposed on the duck made the front page of the *News of the World*. The paper led with a picture of Bevers diving around the national stadium's pitch in hot 'pursuit' of Puskas, whom he'd smuggled through the turnstiles in a carpet bag and then let loose on the turf. Had he been around back then, it would doubtless have been the sort of japery of which Paul Gascoigne approved. Blackpool lost the final 2-0 to Newcastle, compounding the 4-2 defeat they'd suffered in the 1948 final, which had handed Matt Busby a first trophy as Manchester United manager.

Even actor Douglas Fairbanks Jnr – every inch a Hollywood A-lister in his day – was drawn into the Atomic Boys' madcap support of the Seasiders. While filming a satirical Cold War comedy in England about a duck that laid atomic eggs and was thus invaluable to NATO in providing the material needed for the nuclear weapons required to rival the Soviet Union, Fairbanks Jnr presented the Atomic Boys with a replacement duck. Puskas had expired after a cat breached his pen.

Bevers saved his finest feat for the occasion of Blackpool contesting their third FA Cup Final in 1953. On the morning of the game against Bolton, dressed as an 'Eastern potentate' in a flowing tangerine robe and silver headdress, he blagged an invite inside 10 Downing Street. Passing through the country's most famous threshold, he produced a 7lb stick of tangerine and white Blackpool rock. Stamped all the way through it were the words 'Sir Winston'. Even Churchill, it seemed, had become an honorary Atomic Boy.

The 1953 'Matthews' FA Cup Final, won 4-3 by Blackpool, perhaps above all others, elevated the status of the competition to its position as the pre-eminent annual sporting fixture, but also a national event. Stanley Matthews finally winning the Cup coincided with the coronation of Queen Elizabeth II a few weeks later. Many Britons bought their first-ever television to witness this double-header. In most of the country's households over the next four decades of the 20th century, watching the FA Cup Final live on the BBC or ITV was sacrosanct.

From that high-water mark of 1953, Blackpool's footballing decline mirrored the town's dwindling fortunes. In

Terry Venables's playing days, a trip to the Fylde coast evoked the excitement of a cheery British summer seaside holiday. Back then, there was even a dash of glamour about Blackpool, owing to its golden beaches, fabled tower and illuminations. Ensconced inside the away dressing room as they prepared to run out and face the brutal wintery elements, such notions must have seemed inconceivable to Venables's Tottenham charges of 1991. None of them would be planning an end-of-season return with their families or team-mates for some 'R and R' now that sunshine breaks to the Mediterranean or Florida were *de rigueur*.

During the warm-up, all eyes inside Bloomfield Road were trained on Paul Gascoigne. Perhaps in a nod to 1953 and his new-found status as a national hero, he was presented with a giant stick of rock by Tango, Blackpool's gorilla-suited mascot. The Atomic Boys' brand of harmless frivolity hadn't survived the Seasiders' descent down the divisions or the hooliganism that plagued English football in the 1970s and 1980s. For Syd Bevers, however, Spurs coming to town was an opportunity too good to miss. He donned his tangerine regalia for the first time in a long time. Duck clasped in one hand, turban held in place against the blowing gale with the other, he strode out toward the Bloomfield Road centre circle and took his bow. Regrettably, Stanley Matthews had other commitments which prevented him from accepting an invitation to attend the game as a guest of honour.

Before referee Philip Wright rang the bell, calling the players to assemble in the tunnel ahead of being led on to the pitch, Venables imparted a cautionary tale. David Howells, deployed at centre-back that afternoon as the manager made-do and mended, recounts the gist of it. 'Terry told us about this famous matador who was in a bullfight in a small village. He got complacent and switched off. The bull ended up killing him. We all understood the moral of the story. Don't underestimate anyone.'

Teamsheet
Bloomfield Road
Saturday, 5 January 1991

Blackpool	Tottenham Hotspur
Colours: tangerine shirts, white shorts, tangerine socks	Colours: white shirts, navy shorts, white socks
1. Steve McIlhargey	1. Erik Thorstvedt
2. Mike Davies	2. Terry Fenwick
3. Alan Wright	3. Justin Edinburgh
4. Trevor Sinclair	4. Vinny Samways
5. Gary Briggs	5. David Howells
6. Ian Gore	6. Gary Mabbutt
7. Tony Rodwell	7. Paul Stewart
8. Phil Horner	8. Paul Gascoigne
9. Paul Groves	9. Paul Moran
10. Andy Garner	10. Gary Lineker
11. Dave Bamber	11. Paul Allen
(Subs)	(Subs)
12. Gary Brook	12. Gudni Bergsson
14. Chris Hedworth	14. Peter Garland

Given the meteorological levelling of the playing field, there was little danger of Tottenham taking Blackpool lightly. Ask any Spurs player involved in the tie what their abiding memory of it is, and you'll get the same response; 'That wind.' Hugh McIlvanney memorably described it in *The Observer* as being sufficiently wild to lift 'a medicine ball over the stands'. With no hi-tech base layers manufactured with yet-to-be-invented synthetic materials, the best kit-manager Roy Reyland could do for the players in his care was to start doling out the thermal vests he'd purchased from a camping supplies shop. 'I used to buy them deliberately to fit tight so they'd hug and keep the lads warm,' chuckles Reyland, 'but even then, you'd get some of them who'd insist on wearing short sleeves.'

Gudni Bergsson grimaces and then laughs as he recalls the 70mph squall that tore across the stadium. 'I'm from Iceland, so I should be able to cope. But that was not the weather to be playing football in.' Vinny Samways – asked to do a job on the left wing in Nayim's absence – remembers exchanging a worried look with rookie left-back Justin Edinburgh just before the referee blew to allow the game to commence: 'I was thinking this is outrageous. You couldn't tell whether it was an advantage to be playing into it or against it. I don't know how windy it is in Blackpool usually, but that was an experience and a half.'

Any nerves Edinburgh was feeling were understandable. Since his summer move from Southend, he'd made only one league start, secure in the confines of White Hart Lane against Sunderland. But with Pat Van Den Hauwe's suspension, he was pitched from the relative comfort afforded to a fledgling first-team 'prospect' into the ruthlessly testing environment of an FA Cup away tie against lower-league opposition. Every conceivable opportunity to 'put it on top of him' would be taken as Fourth Division players he'd only just left behind now strived to make their name at his and Spurs' expense.

Erik Thorstvedt's anxiety had been heightened when he alighted from the team bus. 'When I played back home for Stavanger, you'd sometimes arrive at the stadium and hear the ding ding ding of the ropes being blown against the stands. I just knew it was one of those days at Blackpool! As a goalkeeper, you dread conditions like that. Everything you've learned about judging the flight of the ball goes out the window.' But swirling crosses weren't the extent of the jeopardy for the Norwegian. One attempt to launch a goal kick upfield failed to cross even the 18-yard box before being blown back with interest over his head. To his eternal relief, the ball narrowly cleared the crossbar at the expense of a corner. 'Erik didn't have the most powerful kick,' jokes David Howells, 'a bit of a spoon foot, but that was unbelievable.

'I don't think it's disrespectful to say,' continues Howells, 'that the difference between teams like us and them is in terms of technique; you're better than they are. They might be able to match you for fitness, but you're able to move it quicker and be more clinical when chances come along. But when you can't trust the ball and the conditions don't let you pass it, that negates the advantages you have. You end up trying to do the same thing as the opposition: get it into areas further up the pitch and protect your goal. As soon as we set foot on that pitch at Blackpool and felt the wind, we would have definitely taken a draw there and then to get them back to White Hart Lane.'

Terry Venables, herringbone coat buttoned up protectively around his throat, sat pensively on the bench as Blackpool weaponised the conditions to pin Spurs back. Gary Mabbutt chased an optimistic up-and-under back into his own area only to find an ill-timed gust diverting it away from him as the ball bounced. The angular figure of striker Dave Bamber – who'd had to send for his boots having arrived at the stadium unsure whether Hull, owner of his registration, had deigned to allow him to play – found himself with a shooting chance seven yards from goal. Only a desperate Howells block prevented Blackpool from drawing first blood. The visibly rattled Spurs rearguard was fortunate to escape again moments before the interval when Andy Garner left Terry Fenwick trailing on the wing and centred for Bamber. Clambering over Edinburgh inside the six-yard box, he directed his header in the only place Thorstvedt could save it, directly at him.

At the beginning of the second half, the referee was the next of the game's protagonists to bail out the perturbed visitors. Trevor Sinclair cushioned a pass that invited Mike Davies to whip one in first time. Yet again, the wind provided the telling assist, suddenly diverting the ball's trajectory. Tony Rodwell strong-armed the over-balanced Paul Allen at the far post before firing a low shot that eluded Thorstvedt. Bloomfield Road's raucous celebrations were curtailed by the award of a foul best described as generous in the extreme.

Soon afterwards, Rodwell bewitched Allen near the corner flag before sending an inswinging cross to the back stick. Edinburgh slashed at it with his right boot and could only look on aghast as the ball flew across the helpless

Thorstvedt's goalmouth. Thankfully, its velocity meant Paul Groves, standing no more than three yards out, had insufficient time to direct his header downwards. Spurs could add lady luck to the club's ever-lengthening list of creditors.

'I remember we were right under the cosh,' says Paul Moran. 'Then I won a free kick out on the right wing.' Blackpool manager Billy Ayres claimed post-match that Spurs' stand-in number nine had duped the referee, having jinked inside Groves on the right touchline. Nowadays, the lunge that felled Moran would have unquestionably warranted a yellow card. Fenwick, making his first Tottenham appearance in 15 months, spotted the ball up and prepared to get it launched. But before he could start his run-up, Gascoigne supplanted him in the conduction of proceedings. It was to be the first of a thrilling catalogue of game-defining interventions the midfielder staged during Spurs' FA Cup campaign.

An assiduous review of the replay only enhances the beauty of the arching cross he shaped into the Blackpool box. Just as Gascoigne pulled back his foot to strike through the ball, it began revolving as it was blown back towards him. Fortunately, Mr Wright had failed to notice, and no command was forthcoming that the free kick be retaken. Having run his marker under its flight, Gary Lineker ducked in behind. Eyes locked on the ball, the striker looked set to volley home from close range. Before it reached him, however, Lineker lost his footing. With split-second improvisation, as he fell, the England captain somehow feathered the ball down with his heel to where Paul Stewart was stationed. Stewart's immediate left-foot shot from six yards – bounced down into the Bloomfield Road turf – was sufficiently paccy to beat the dive of the blue tracksuit-bottoms-wearing keeper, Steve McIlhargey.

Stewart, the former Blackpool apprentice, had burgled a precious lead for the visitors. Happily, the custom of performative 'non-celebration' of goals against an ex-employer had yet to take root in English football, allowing a beaming

Stewart to wheel away, leap from the ground and jubilantly punch the air before Vinny Samways tethered him in a loving headlock. The players had to make the most of their on-pitch celebrations as any noise from the remote band of Spurs fans behind the opposite goal was lost to the ether.

Match of the Day commentator Tony Gubba recognised the result was far from secure as Sinclair tried to burst beyond Edinburgh on the flank. The full-back slid in with a fine challenge before inexplicably conceding a corner when attempting to knock a square pass for Thorstvedt to gather. 'You do get the feeling Blackpool are capable of scoring here. They've certainly shown that in the second half,' Gubba opined. He was in danger of becoming a scourge for Spurs on these harrowing occasions. He'd provided the BBC commentaries of the aforementioned Port Vale and Bradford humblings. Sinclair's resulting set piece died on the wind, dropping chest-high to Andy Garner. The lay-off by the Seasiders' skipper was cushioned across the box where Rodwell nodded into the goal. Again, though, a blast of referee Wright's whistle came to Spurs' rescue, this time for a handball by Garner.

Inside the last ten minutes, Lineker had the chance to allay any further need to fret. Gascoigne dropped his shoulder and drove infield. Swapping passes with the striker, he raced to reach the return before the sprawling McIlhargey. The ball broke loose to Moran on the right side of the box, who looped it over the marooned goalkeeper. There, unassailed, five yards from a gaping net, Lineker pushed a header meekly wide. The forward's bowed head and the derisive jeer from the home crowd – the type exclusively reserved for the rare occasion of a truly great player erring – conveyed the wretchedness of the miss.

On a highlights programme of the match for the nascent British Sky Broadcasting, Martin Tyler attempted to ascribe the error to the inclement conditions. His co-commentator, Andy Gray, was having none of it. 'I think you're being kind to him. I think a man of that class and of that quality will be absolutely disgusted with himself at missing that.' Paul

Moran strikes a much more conciliatory tone, recalling the astonishing moment three decades on. 'It's one of those bloopers that's been on telly, but we've all missed them, so I won't say too much. And to be fair, Gary didn't miss too many, did he?'

In the embers of the game, Blackpool failed to mount an attack capable of punishing Lineker's uncharacteristic profligacy. His relief upon hearing the full time whistle was mirrored by the travelling supporters. They had endured rather than enjoyed a quintessential third-round FA Cup tie but had seen their team live to tell the tale. In his post-match remarks, Terry Venables, acutely aware of how close his side had come to disaster, proved incapable of focusing on the upside of this unsafe passage into round four. 'It's just a lottery. Games should not be played in those conditions. The spectators don't get value for money.'

Nor did the *Sunday Mirror*, for whom it had been a disappointingly expensive afternoon. The professional lip reader they'd sent along to Bloomfield Road, hoping to skewer Gascoigne for any repeat of the verbals that had precipitated his expulsion against Manchester United, was left unfulfilled. 'Only once was the Tottenham ace even slightly out of order. As he was upended by a Blackpool defender, he muttered "S***" – but strictly to himself.'

Heaven forbid.

The result did allow the Blackpool *Evening Gazette* to indulge in one of the FA Cup's most cherished traditions; the unashamedly partisan match report of a local newspaper's football correspondent. Tony Durkin did the honours, writing that 'star studded Spurs ... headed back south thanking their lucky stars it was they who got the lucky break ... the only difference between the sides on the day was the clinical finishing of Paul Stewart – and we all know where he learned that.'

While McIlvanney's write-up was also fulsome in its praise of Blackpool's worthy efforts, he identified the real point of divergence. Gascoigne, who 'unmistakably outstripped every other talent on the field', was the 'man apart, forever giving the storm a still centre of excellence'.

The stark reality that Tottenham's prospects were now so inextricably intertwined with Gascoigne made the assessment of the club 'insider' quoted in Jeff Randall's Sunday column all the more dismaying. 'Tottenham cannot expect to trade its way out of trouble. It needs to attract new funds or sell one of its biggest assets. It's either "Hello sugar daddy" or "Bye-bye Gazza."'

Few of a Spurs persuasion could countenance that things were becoming so difficult the club's survival might soon necessitate both.

Chapter Six

Magic and Madness

ELSEWHERE ON third-round weekend, other potentially epic FA Cup scripts moved closer to being green-lit or were dispatched to the shredder. Where, thankfully for Spurs, Bloomfield Road had failed to produce a desired giant-killing, the Hawthorns delivered in spades. Those reporting non-league Woking's sensational bouncing of the Baggies from the competition filled their boots and match reports with compulsory mentions of 'the magic of the cup'. And with good reason. Having been too nervous to eat before the match, Surbiton-born, 29-year-old computer operator Tim Buzaglo rattled in a 14-minute hat-trick to transform a 1-0 half-time deficit into a 4-2 victory for Woking. Buzaglo, who also represented Gibraltar at international cricket, was later rewarded with a nomination for the FA Cup Team of Heroes – compiled in 2006 to celebrate the competition's 125th season.

If Woking's wonders upheld the best of the FA Cup's vaunted traditions, the beginnings of the momentous changes for English football in the decade ahead – for better or worse – were visible at Old Trafford. Cup holders Manchester United's progress in the world's oldest cup competition was screened live to barely a handful of UK homes via all-new satellite technology. That the game against Queens Park Rangers kicked off at 8pm on a Monday night only added to the novelty. Recognising the potential threat this development posed to the hegemony of one national institution, if not yet the FA Cup itself, Des Lynam told *The Times*, 'The BBC's position is being slightly eroded. Sooner or later, the great British public may wake up and see just what they have lost. They do have this underlying expectation that if it is big and it's sport, then it should be on the BBC.'

At Highbury, George Graham's Arsenal, ominously unbeaten in the league, took a first furtive step toward a possible double with a 2-1 defeat of Sunderland. It was a game notable for a sublime lobbed own goal by David O'Leary, the first such indiscretion in his 690-game Gunners career.

Nottingham Forest's tie at Crystal Palace was framed by the Nottingham *Evening Post* as the potential start of a farewell tour with a Wembley Stadium culmination for English football's most beloved contrarian, Brian Clough. Palace, Clough told the paper, 'Will have an almighty cross to bear if I get knocked out. It will mean I'll be staying around for another year to have another crack at winning the cup ... and I wouldn't wish that on my worst enemy.' Clough, who had improbably marked Forest's promotion to the top flight in 1977 by immediately winning the title and the League Cup and had then produced an impossible encore of two European Cup triumphs in consecutive seasons and three further League Cups, yearned to complete the set. Forest had twice reached the semi-finals of the FA Cup during his tenure but lost out to Liverpool in both 1988 and 1989.[7]

While many assumed retirement talk was little more than Clough's latest ruse to remind the British footballing public of his unparalleled brilliance, the sudden passing in October 1990 of Peter Taylor – the collaborator with whom he'd achieved so much – was a bitter jolt. Clough may have 'walked on water', but he wasn't immortal. The pair had never reconciled after animosity caused by Taylor's decision to come out of retirement for an ill-fated spell managing Derby; this

---

7   Regrettably, in his first autobiography, Clough parroted many of the lies popularised by the Murdoch press about the 1989 Hillsborough disaster before belatedly setting the record straight.

had become outright hostility after Taylor poached John Robertson from Forest without consulting Clough. The fall-out led to Clough branding Taylor a 'rattlesnake' and threatening to run him over if he ever saw Taylor broken down on the A52 between Nottingham and Derby. However, reflecting on a relationship described in his first autobiography as 'unique', Clough lamented, 'I never imagined him dying at all. I wish he hadn't … I had lost my pal. I had lost any chance of ever healing the rift that had been allowed to separate us for seven years … Peter's death put everything into perspective.'

Clough's identification of the FA Cup as the final flourish he craved before drawing down the curtain on his stellar career perhaps explains the scale of the eccentricity he exhibited in its pursuit. Even by his exultant standards, 1991 was a bountiful year. As nervy as Spurs' progress to the fourth round had been, it had at least taken only 90 minutes. Forest and Palace's tussle would span four weeks before a resolution was reached.

The original match in what became a Homeric contest was shown live on BBC One from Selhurst Park. The resulting 0-0 draw was less memorable than Jimmy Hill's on-air assertion that Clough should retire come what may at the end of the season. Terry Venables, also on punditry duty and doubtless aware any comment could be worked up into a tabloid storm, wisely declined to wade in.

Control of the replay at the City Ground fell to veteran referee Roger Milford. Given the indelible mark the Bristolian official would make at the climax of Forest's cup run, it was rather fitting he was there at its start. The first date of five eventual schedulings of the fixture fell foul of a waterlogged pitch. Game off. A week later, that water had frozen solid. Game off for a second time.

The turf had thawed sufficiently by the following midweek for studs to bite. Palace striker Ian Wright's belting second-half volley finally brought a goal to the tie. With 15 minutes remaining, Terry Wilson's deflected shot forced extra time. Following a typically bludgeoning surge into the box,

Stuart Pearce, finishing sweetly from close range, propelled Forest into the lead. With seconds remaining, however, they yielded their winning position, as 19-year-old Roy Keane under-hit a ball which drew his keeper, Mark Crossley, from his box. These were the end days before the prohibition on goalkeepers handling back passes from their team-mates, so Crossley, like most of his contemporaries between the sticks, wasn't particularly adept with the ball at his feet. His feeble clearance offered neither height nor distance, falling to John Salako. The winger took one touch to kill it before looking up and pinging a shot over the helplessly back-pedalling keeper's head: 2-2, and yet another replay required.

In his post-match utterances, Clough was phlegmatic. 'Keane got it wrong and is devastated, but he will be ok … It was a superb game. And I thought we'd got it, but Palace are a formidable side because they are so athletic. We'll have it all on to beat them again.' Such affected stolidity belied the fury he had unleashed behind closed doors.

In his 2002 autobiography, Keane recounts the scene that unfolded. 'When I walked into the dressing room after the game, Clough punched me straight in the face. "Don't pass the ball back to the goalkeeper," he screamed as I lay on the floor, him standing over me. I was hurt and shocked. Too shocked to do anything but nod my head in agreement.' It cruelly punctuated Keane's staggeringly polished first six months in the English game following his anonymous £47,000 arrival from Cobh Ramblers.

It is likely Clough's capriciousness in attacking Keane and placidly addressing the press owed much to a toss of a coin that, in the meantime, had determined the City Ground rather than Selhurst Park would host the replay of the replay. Clough had grown to loathe long coach journeys, particularly to London, a city at odds with his blend of socialism and social conservatism. This aversion to away travel could partly be attributed to the state of the Forest team bus. There was no double-decker luxury to be found in the City Ground car park. In the mid-1980s, the club had run into financial difficulties of its own after several costly transfer market missteps and the refurbishment of the stadium to include a grand Executive Stand newly built at Clough's behest. This had left Forest reliant on unearthing low-cost gems like Keane while serving up an austerity diet of bread and soup aboard the team bus. In his brilliant memoir of Clough, *Provided You Don't Kiss Me*, Duncan Hamilton recalls the Forest manager wryly quipping the coach was 'so old we could enter it into the London to Brighton rally'. Hamilton also once observed Clough 'pummelling his fist into the headrest of his seat' while raging, 'If I have any more soup, I'm going to look like a fucking tin of Heinz. I am a fucking European Cup-winning manager, and here I am going to a match on soup and sandwiches and a bag of chips on the way home. What the fuck am I doing here?'

A first attempt at take three of Nottingham Forest versus Crystal Palace was postponed when thick fog from the River Trent enveloped the City Ground. Referee Milford was in danger of becoming a bête noire to Forest folk. More on that later. A sixth and mercifully – as it turned out – final date to determine who progressed to the round of 32 was arranged for 28 January. A second-half salvo of three goals in 11 minutes saw the Reds finally down the Eagles. It also permitted Clough to indulge in some pre-final-whistle point-scoring. Steve Hodge was withdrawn from the fray with seven minutes to play, leaving Forest to voluntarily play out the match with ten men. Milford was at a loss to explain it. 'I've been refereeing for 18 years – and I've never seen anything like it.'

Some observers in the press box hypothesised it was a pretext for Clough to deliver a surreptitious v-sign aimed at Palace's muscular brand of football. Forest assistant manager Ronnie Fenton's summation that, 'Quite simply, football triumphed over the long ball game', appeared to bear their theory out. Indeed, Hodge confirmed years later that Clough told him he'd done it to take the 'piss out of Palace'. However, it seems probable Hodge himself was at least his manager's dual target. Ostensibly, after the match, Clough claimed he had been protecting Hodge from injury. But his none-too-subtle musings that made print as to whether '[Hodge] would ever get off the injury table' – a series of injuries had hampered the England international's season – made the gesture seem witheringly pointed.

The fourth-round draw had long since been made by then. Forest would board their 'vintage' coach to St James' Park. Woking's good deeds were handsomely rewarded as they were paired with Everton. The Surrey outfit quickly decided to cash in their chips rather than spin the wheel in search of further glory by switching the tie to Goodison Park. Arsenal would host the First Division's coming force, Leeds.

Fate conspired to bring the Robert Maxwell-affiliated Oxford United, vanquishers of Chelsea, to White Hart Lane. Having avoided the fancied First Division sides, Gary Lineker, excited by Spurs' cup prospects, couldn't resist the temptation to invoke the power of one. 'Tradition is on our side … More trophies have followed in the first year of every new decade, so look out!'

Before the fourth round came around, however, Operation Desert Storm had commenced. Britain was at war with Saddam and Iraq.

Chapter Seven

Best in the World

ANY FLEETING respite bestowed on Spurs by the FA Cup dissipated amid more financial gloom. On 16 January, perhaps seeking an opportunity to bury bad news beneath the outbreak of hostilities in the Gulf, Tottenham Hotspur PLC released its long overdue annual figures. A further loss of £2.6 million for the year to May 1990 and an auditor's note that the accounts were qualified 'due to uncertainties as to whether there is sufficient finance to enable the group to continue as a going concern' did little to soothe the suits in the Midland Bank's intensive care unit. Small shareholders were no less vexed. As one told *The Guardian*, 'The incompetent way things have been run threatens to destroy the club. Team policy is being dictated by the bank.'

Recognising the current iteration of the board had run out of road, trusted City man – and lifelong Spurs supporter – Nat Solomon was sworn in as chairman of the PLC. His emulsifying presence precluded the Midland from taking the fatal step of withdrawing its support, at least for now. Solomon's task was starkly plain: bring in capital and do it double quick.

The appointment coincided with press reports that police had been called in by the club to investigate a 'hoax' letter, drafted on an official THFC letterhead and sent to national newspapers stating that as soon as Spurs were eliminated from the FA Cup, Paul Gascoigne and Gary Lineker would be sold.

The prospect of Robert Maxwell making good on his earlier promises looked increasingly remote as, four days later, Spurs trekked to Derby County for their next league game. Terry Venables's side were depleted by injury to Gary Mabbutt – who would require frequent pain-killing injections to battle through to the end of the season before surgery on a worsening hernia – and the start of Gascoigne's suspension.

Captain Bob had turned the money-tap off at the Baseball Ground, and Derby County – the Maxwell name emblazoned on their shirts – were currently tanking. Derby fans were understandably incensed by their absentee owner's parsimony, contrasted with the largesse he'd shown Irving Scholar over the Lineker loan. They'd been further antagonised that morning by breaking news. Maxwell, having publicly stated he was seeking a buyer for his shares, had rejected a £3 million bid he deemed insufficient from a local businessman.

A glassy-eyed Brian Clough gave Rams fans' discontent a sympathetic hearing as he joined Elton Welsby in a studio overlooking the pitch for ITV's live match coverage. Jauntily wearing a 'Number 1 Grandad' badge on his lapel, Clough's sardonic response to Welsby's question about the strength of feeling toward Maxwell was, 'He's not very popular, but that's the way it goes.'

His remark was accompanied by a chorus of 'He's fat, he's round, he's never at the ground, Maxwell, Maxwell' from the Derby fans. (Maxwell had honoured the Baseball Ground with his presence on match days for a grand total of 53 minutes over the past season and a half.) That pithy tune soon morphed into a burst of 'We want Maxwell out', receiving a warm ripple of applause in solidarity from the travelling Spurs support. Before the afternoon was out, hundreds of Derby fans peacefully took their protestations on to the pitch.

Lineker rubbed Deep Heat into Derby wounds by bundling home the game's only goal midway through the first half. Clough's forthright assessment at full time was that Derby's Arthur Cox and Terry Venables had two of the Football League's most 'rotten jobs'. In light of newspaper speculation linking Venables to the USA national team, Clough posited, 'It wouldn't surprise me if Terry got the first plane out to America. If I was him, I would do it. But he's his own man, and he'll make his own mind up.'

Venables, however, remained steadfast in his desire not to cut and run. But speaking candidly in a press conference on the eve of a League Cup quarter-final replay with Chelsea, he underlined that his reserves of resilience weren't infinite. 'I don't have trouble sleeping – waking up is the problem. We have just got on with the job all season. No one has complained. [But] of course, it is hard to dismiss all the other things that are going on around the club ... No one has control, not even the directors ... Someone has got to do something to sort it out.'

On the morning of the Chelsea game, the *Daily Mirror*'s back-page banner headline read 'CRISIS'; the text, for effect, was fragmented like broken glass. Beneath was a picture of a decidedly weary-looking Venables, accompanied by a 'Spurs in a shambles' sub-header. Bookmakers William Hill responded by making Ossie Ardiles the 5-2 favourite to replace Venables as Tottenham manager. Whether they would refund bets if the club went under was unclear.

Venables's most recent exasperation seemed to have been triggered by the Tottenham board's attempt to sell Vinny Samways from under him. Before the turn of the year, Samways, frustrated by a lack of games, had been quoted in newspapers as wanting to join Nottingham Forest. But following swingeing cuts to the playing staff, Venables now considered the player an integral part of his squad, and Samways had started three of the last four fixtures. Despite this, in the three days following the Derby match, Tottenham accepted an £800,000 offer for him from Aston Villa. Desperately trying to placate Venables, given the volume of injuries and suspensions he'd been juggling, Irving Scholar negotiated with Villa chairman Doug Ellis that the deal would only be completed after the game against Chelsea. This gave Villa manager Jozef Venglos one final chance to run the rule over his potential new recruit from the comfort of White Hart Lane's West Stand.

Samways doesn't recall any of this being relayed to him: 'There was speculation, but I didn't know if there was any truth in it.' However, the implication in Scholar's book is that Venables's calculation in replacing the midfielder with Nayim midway through the second half concerned the bigger picture rather than trying to salvage that night's result. In Scholar's view, Venables, 'who had expressed objections to Samways going', used the substitution to 'put a spoke in the deal'. Venglos left the match early, and Villa reneged on the deal the next day.

Scholar's memory of that Chelsea match – a dispiriting 3-0 defeat which could have been even more damaging had the arm Gascoigne thrust into Andy Townsend's face been spotted by the referee – was heightened by what unfolded after the final whistle. According to the account given in Scholar's book, club secretary Peter Barnes entered the directors' room with a policeman in tow. The detective informed Scholar that word had reached the police that he would be shot on his way out of the ground. The threat was deemed sufficiently credible for Scholar to be smuggled out of the stadium and to his car through a side exit. From there, he was flanked by an armoured police vehicle for 20 minutes until clear of Tottenham.

Less than 72 hours later, John Motson's preamble for Tottenham's fourth-round FA Cup tie with Oxford felt entirely apposite. 'It may sound an exaggeration to say this is one of the most important games in Spurs' modern history, but after all the rumblings and rumours behind the scenes this week at White Hart Lane, it's vital they win this to keep their season alive.'

Teamsheet
White Hart Lane
Saturday, 26 January 1991

Tottenham Hotspur	Oxford United
Colours: white shirts, navy shorts, white socks	Colours: red shirts, red shorts, red socks
1. Erik Thorstvedt	1. Ken Veysey
2. Terry Fenwick	2. Les Robinson
3. Pat Van Den Hauwe	3. Garry Smart
4. Nayim	4. Martin Foyle
5. David Howells	5. Steve Foster
6. Gary Mabbutt	6. Andy Melville
7. Paul Stewart	7. Jim Magilton
8. Paul Gascoigne	8. Les Phillips
9. Paul Walsh	9. John Durnin
10. Gary Lineker	10. Lee Nogan
11. Paul Allen	11. Paul Simpson
(Subs)	(Subs)
12. Justin Edinburgh	12. Mark Stein
14. Steve Sedgley	14. Mike Ford

Nayim, for whom Oxford was an FA Cup bow, can still vividly recall the feverish grip the competition held over his team-mates' imaginations. 'Even before I came to England, I knew that the FA Cup had all this tradition and was known around the world. But to an English player, it meant everything. It was crazy.'

That was undeniably true in Oxford's ranks, too. Their only non-English starters were Cardiff-born Lee Nogan and Northern Ireland's Jim Magilton. The U's, buoyed by their shock victory at Stamford Bridge, immediately set about Spurs. The 'exotic' pair combined to cleave through the home defence. Nogan's first touch from Magilton's lofted pass bounced up invitingly for him to swivel and hit from the edge of the box. Erik Thorstvedt plunged full-length to his right to palm away a shot destined for the bottom corner.

It was an even better stop than the acrobatic one he'd made earlier in the season against Aston Villa.[8]

Having been so comprehensively pinned back by the Division Two side, Spurs belatedly found an escape route through Paul Walsh. The striker slid a ball down the left touchline for Nayim, who drove into the penalty area. 'I remember that player,' Nayim laughs when reminded of Oxford's vast centre-back Steve 'the headband' Foster. Following a lightning-quick stepover that bamboozled the U's skipper, Nayim toppled over Foster's imprudently outstretched leg. There was no visible contact, but that didn't stop the Spurs man from shooting a beseeching look the referee's way – even as Foster gave him both barrels. It was the vanguard of the cultural differences in football that would confront the hitherto parochial English game across the next decade as the influx of foreign talent accelerated.

Nayim recalls the occasion of his first match at Anfield in the season before. 'Always in Spain, we were told football is for clever guys, and that's why you tried to win a penalty or get a yellow card for an opponent by doing things that in England weren't accepted. In that match, I dived – the player never touched me. Gary Mabbutt came over and told me, "Get up, get up". I said "ok". At half-time, Terry Venables said, "Stay in the dressing room. You're coming off. I'll talk to you after the game." I remember his words afterwards, "Here in English football, you can't do this. It's going to be a big problem for you. You're going to get a bad reputation. From now on, if you feel something, stay on the floor. But if you don't, get up and keep fighting."' Nayim considers the moment to have had a transformational effect on him. 'I never dived again. After that, I was a football player.'

---

8 A stunning photograph capturing 'Erik the Viking' in full flight making that save later made the mighty goalkeeper the cover star of an early edition of EA Sports' wildly popular FIFA computer game series. Thorstvedt ruefully smiles when recalling that 'two reps came to the training ground to ask my permission but I never received any payment'. The image was also featured in a promotional poster for the 1992 Barcelona Olympics.

Given the debt of gratitude all Spurs fans owe Nayim, not only for his time with the club but also for 'that' goal for Real Zaragoza against Arsenal – and as he is as warm and gracious a person as you could wish to meet – it seems only proper to afford him the benefit of the doubt over his Oxford tumble. He must indeed have felt 'something' as he evaded Foster. Despite no penalty being awarded, Trevor Brooking's take on the incident during that night's *Match of the Day* wasn't quite so magnanimous.

The relentless flux buffeting the club made Gary Mabbutt's dependable excellence all the more precious to Venables. It was the skipper who opened the scoring against Oxford after eight minutes. Walsh took a short corner that certainly wasn't a faithful reproduction of whatever had been choreographed on the training ground. His pass forced Gascoigne back towards his own goal. A quick shimmy to right his course saw him progress to the edge of the box, where Lineker gainfully offered himself for the one-two. Before Gascoigne could get on to the return and unleash a shot, an Oxford defender went to ground with a challenge. The ball rebounded off Gascoigne in a perfect parabola, which Foster wafted an injudicious jumping karate-style kick at. As Foster crashed down to earth, Mabbutt nudged the ball beyond the defender's now prone body and skimmed a right-footed shot from just inside the box beyond Oxford keeper Ken Veysey. It was a moment of déjà vu for Veysey. As a youngster, he'd served as a ball boy retrieving balls that had eluded two of the most esteemed Spurs goalkeepers, Pat Jennings and Ray Clemence, in that same goal.

Gascoigne's effervescence aroused the type of feedback he so relished extracting from opposing fans. A growing chorus of boos from the heaving Oxford end greeted his every touch. They were unwise to feed the beast. Spurs' second goal, arriving in the 20th minute, illuminated an underrated facet of his game. Thorstvedt's up-and-under was routinely headed into the safety of midfield by Garry Smart, but Gascoigne was the first to react. He propelled himself above Lee Nogan and butted the ball beyond the Oxford defence for Lineker to race on to. Lineker opted for explosive power over finesse, thrashing a shot into the roof of the net.

Before John Motson could articulate the old truism about 2-0 being a dangerous scoreline, Martin Foyle delivered a swift riposte to Spurs. The striker wearing the number 4 shirt – perhaps an act of subterfuge in these pre-squad number days of 1–11, where defenders were expected to don the low numerals, attackers the high – escaped a home defence caught horribly square to latch on to Paul Simpson's through ball. He then sauntered around Thorstvedt's dive before stroking the ball into the exposed net. Game on.

As the second half flowed wildly from end to end, Terry Venables cut an agitated figure, white-knuckled hands clasping the edge of the dugout from where he'd vacated his seat. Oxford's threat continued to be aimed at the heart of the Spurs backline. Mabbutt attempted to intercept a through ball but could only divert it into Nogan's path. Thorstvedt threw himself at the Oxford man's feet as he jostled with the recovering David Howells. But the goalkeeper's victory in collecting the ball ahead of Nogan proved pyrrhic. Howells winces at the memory of the collision. 'Erik came flying out with his studs up and caught me on my left knee. I had to be stretchered off and needed seven stitches in this great big gash.' It was cruel on Howells, who'd valiantly been putting off surgery to correct a persistent problem with his right knee in service to the floundering Tottenham cause. His ferocious commitment to putting his head – or whatever else was required – in where it hurts had already seen him twice knocked unconscious in matches that season. Venables was shorn of one of his most trusted lieutenants until mid-April. Steve Sedgley was rushed into action from the bench, replacing Howells beside Mabbutt.

Sniffing the growing threat, Gascoigne immediately set to work quelling it. Paul Allen pushed a cautious pass back to Terry Fenwick on the halfway line. No sooner had he controlled it than Gascoigne charged towards him, demanding possession of the ball. He turned infield and drove forward with his potent blend of swagger and purpose. Bouncing the ball off the obliging Walsh, the midfielder stormed through four Oxford defenders, rode Foster's lunge and from an ever-diminishing angle, somehow calculated precisely what was required to slip his shot inside Veysey's near post. Motson's speed of thought – and turn of phrase – was almost as impressive as he excitedly marvelled at the goal in his commentary. 'Gascoigne has turned an attack that was going into a cul-de-sac into one that may drive Tottenham down a main road into the fifth round of the cup. It was an absolutely outstanding piece of individual play.'

Oxford manager Brian Horton may have been rueing his pre-game promise not to detail one of his players with the sole duty of attempting to nullify Gascoigne. In fairness to Horton, the man in his ranks potentially most suited to fulfilling this onerous task, Steve McClaren (yes, *that* Steve McClaren), had been indisposed by a knee ligament injury sustained during a midweek fixture with Ipswich. Horton's team did make good on his other vow, 'to keep having a go' at Spurs. Oxford's cavalier approach bore fruit in the 79th minute. Simpson chipped a pass over the disorientated Sedgley, who seemed to lose its flight in the air. Les Phillips, sneaking in behind the substitute, nodded the ball down to Foyle. The striker trapped it on his chest, allowing him to sweep home an emphatic volley: 3-2. Game on. Again.

With sleeves everywhere in the White Hart Lane stands being furiously yanked up to reveal watches that disappointingly confirmed the interminably slow passage of time, Gascoigne finally settled the contest with three minutes to play. Allen skirted across the face of the Oxford box, probing for a gap into which he could poke a pass. Gascoigne, playing with the poise of a man who'd received an advance copy of this script, found space amid the attentions of four

Oxford defenders. Two swift touches with his celestial right foot shifted the ball on to his left, with which he ripped a shot past Veysey high into the net. Gascoigne against Oxford, like more recently Gareth Bale versus Inter, is a memory that any Spurs fan who had the distinct good fortune to witness it live will take to their grave.

Speaking to the press at full time, Horton was effusive in his praise for the undisputed match-winner. 'Gazza's performance was an education to my players. They've been in with the best in the world ... You can't stop Gascoigne in that form. The man has sheer brilliance. We would have needed 12 players even to try to stop him. With talent like his, I just hope we don't ever lose him to the continent. That would be tragic for the supporters, for his team-mates, and even for the people like us who have got to play against him.'

Rather than the cerebral analysis of a coach, Venables brimmed with the infectious enthusiasm of a fan in his assessment of Gascoigne's uniquely superlative display. 'Over the years, you can always compare a current player with somebody from the past. A player always reminds you of somebody. But in the case of Paul Gascoigne, I don't know anyone who plays like him. He has the attitude of Dave Mackay towards the game, the hunger for it ... Also, his football is as good as anybody's, and he has that great ability to run with the ball. He has that upper body strength – just like Maradona, enabling him to hold opponents off.' Mackay and Maradona – commendation doesn't come any higher.

Gascoigne's virtuosity was all the more remarkable given Venables's subsequent revelation that the player had been hampered by injury. 'He's had a groin problem for two or three months. It's not a big thing, but before Oxford, he required an injection ... We've got to keep an eye on it. But with rest, he should make it through the season.'

The veneration of Gascoigne was matched by the excoriation of football's authorities. The *Sunday Mirror* was among several papers taking the game to task 'for failing to make a public statement of support for our troops in the Gulf'. In its preview for that night's Super Bowl between the Buffalo Bills and the New York Giants, the paper championed an initiative to adorn the players' helmets with Stars and Stripes and for the teams to turn out with yellow armbands. Ahead of the outstanding fourth-round ties, the FA's head of external affairs, Glen Kirton, meekly confessed in response to this confected outrage, 'I have not heard of anything especially patriotic being planned.' 'Why not?' boomed *The Mirror.* 'Are we too macho to wear our emotions on our sleeves? … We know that our footballers, like all of us, have thought privately about the boys in the Gulf. But what it needs is a public display. They have until next Saturday to do something to show the world they care as much as the Americans.'

In a rare success for Tottenham's beleaguered PR department, the club won some credit, with Terry Venables dispatching 500 copies of his *The Manager* board game to the front line. Gary Mabbutt supplemented this gesture by writing letters of encouragement to troops.

For those elements of the press enthralled by the bellicose climate, Guy Whittingham's FA Cup sharp-shooting for Portsmouth proved manna from heaven. The striker remained on the army reserve list, having bought his way out of the military for a reported £450 to pursue professional football. After a prolific spell in non-league, army coach Chris Eade recommended him to Pompey, where he'd become a firm favourite and been affectionately anointed 'Corporal Punishment'. Whittingham followed up a hat-trick against Barnet in the third round with a four-goal blitz of Bournemouth, delivering the Fratton Park club into the last 16 of the cup with a flourish. The fifth-round draw paired Pompey with Spurs. Arsenal, Liverpool and Nottingham Forest were all taking circuitous routes to join them.

Ahead of Arsenal's televised tie with Leeds, Bob Wilson talked up his old club's chances of emulating the 1970/71 side he'd served in goal with such distinction. 'I'm convinced victory over Leeds would launch Arsenal towards another double ... But this tie looks as if it might take more than one game to decide – in fact, it could easily go to two or three matches.' He was wrong, but only just. It took four.

Despite Des Lynam's best efforts on the BBC, the first game, drawn 0-0 at Highbury, had very little to recommend it. The replay three days later was drawn 1-1 at Elland Road. Reflecting on marginal calls by the officials that had denied Leeds two seemingly good goals, Venables, a BBC studio guest for their highlights programme, was compelled to voice an early advocacy of VAR. 'This year, I think we've had a lot more controversial decisions. There are a lot of people pushing for some kind of summit to make some changes. There is a problem there, and something has got to be done about it ... If it's a decision that's going to change the game one way or the other, it's so important. We're not in a hurry. We can take ten seconds to give us a decision [using video]. They do it in American sports. And there's no reason why it shouldn't happen here.' Suffice it to say, it wasn't the last time in that season's FA Cup that contentious refereeing dominated the discourse.

The 'three-peat' of Arsenal versus Leeds, 0-0 at Highbury, failed to conclude the saga. Those who took their seats for 'Take Four' at Elland Road were entitled to wonder if they'd been caught up in a football-inspired reimagining of Samuel Beckett's *Waiting for Godot*. Paul Merson and Lee Dixon found the path out of purgatory, giving the Gunners a 2-0 half-time lead. Leeds roused themselves with a Lee Chapman goal – the striker was not long recovered from a horrifying facial injury sustained in a drawn league game at White Hart Lane – but Arsenal held on, preventing an unwelcome fifth instalment of the flagging franchise. Unsurprisingly, in the wake of this odyssey, the FA moved to cap all ties in the competition from the next season to one replay with extra time and penalties – the first of the FA Cup's endearingly impractical idiosyncrasies had given way to the demands of the 'modern game'. Arsenal looked a safe bet to make further progress, having been drawn at home to Shrewsbury for a place in the quarter-finals.

Kenny Dalglish's Liverpool seemed to be the most likely candidates to thwart the Highbury outfit in becoming the first to do the 'double-double'. A blistering start to the league campaign for the Reds – 12 wins and two draws – had many observers crowning them champions in December. However, their momentum had been checked by a patchy Christmas period. There was nothing between them and Arsenal at the summit of the First Division when tier-two Brighton visited Anfield in the fourth round. The quick-fire concession of a two-goal lead in the last 20 minutes of the match (although not fatal, as Liverpool won the replay by the odd goal in five) was the first tremor of the seismic shock soon to shatter Liverpool's domination of English football.

Despite the clamour for 'Cloughie' to sign off in style at Wembley, Forest came perilously close to being pitched out by Newcastle at St James' Park. Snow on the terraces prevented the game from being played on the original Monday night date – costing Forest the cool £60,000 they'd been due to bank from BSkyB. When the teams belatedly faced off 48 hours later, Clough saw his out-of-sorts side ship two goals inside 13 minutes to their lower-league opponents.

In his first autobiography, Roy Keane recalls how Stuart Pearce's insatiable desire to salvage the situation proved a formative experience in his own career. 'He was an amazing warrior, relishing every moment of our fightback, relishing too, I noticed, his reputation as a man it didn't pay to mess with. Most opponents "bottled it" when Pearce was on their case. That cup tie taught me an important lesson. Willpower and desire mattered. Indeed, the mental strength to out-battle the opponent was more important than mere technical ability.'

Pearce had resuscitated his listless colleagues by converting Keane's low cross early in the second half. He then dragged Forest to an equaliser, which arrived in the game's dying seconds, Nigel Clough administering the telling touch to Terry Wilson's pass. According to Steve Hodge's memoir, Brian Clough spared his players the rod as they shuffled back into the dressing room. Instead, his words were, 'Well done, number 9 [as Clough senior insisted on calling his scion], you've helped keep us in the cup tonight.'

Redemption wasn't to be squandered. Newcastle were battered 3-0 in the City Ground replay, punching Forest's ticket for a fifth-round trip to Southampton.

Chapter Eight

The Pompey Chimes

TO USE modern parlance, preparations for Tottenham's visit to the south coast for their Portsmouth cup tie were sub-optimal. Word reached the tabloid press of a skirmish at a nightclub on the Tuesday evening ahead of the game involving several Spurs players. This was later worked up into a front page 'scoop' deemed worthy of such great public interest as to knock the Gulf War from *The Mirror's* front page. 'SPURS STARS IN BRAWL SHAME'.

David Howells, convalescing at the time following his knee surgery, recalls what unfolded. 'Quite a few of us had gone out into Hoddesdon for a lads' night, which we often did when we'd been given the day off. We'd gone into this wine bar called Bumbles. It was £1 entry. We'd just walked in and not paid, which was a bit out of order, but that was that. Some of the lads were a bit chirpy to the doorman [reportedly a former weightlifter] – not me, by the way, as was said in the press. He ended up really unhappy and got very aggressive. I wasn't even looking, and he punched me. We left after that. It wasn't until the next morning when I woke up that I thought, crikey, this still hurts.'

Paul Stewart smiles at the memory of the 'Bumbles Brawl'. 'That was a fairly typical night out for us back then. Nothing that happened came as much of a surprise. I remember David telling me the next day, "Stewy, I think my jaw is broken." I said, "You'd better go and tell the boss."'

'Terry asked me what had gone on,' recounts Howells. 'When I told him, he just said, "These things happen in life, but I'd have been fuming if it had meant you'd missed games. Learn from it." It was a horrible couple of weeks. I had to have my teeth wired together, and all my food had to be liquidised. I must have lost about a stone and a half – and there wasn't that much of me to begin with!'

In addition to the long-term absence of Howells, Terry Venables had to reconfigure his side for Fratton Park without Stewart, who was serving a suspension. Paul Walsh's participation was jeopardised by a knock that, despite intensive treatment, failed to clear up sufficiently for him to be passed fit on the morning of the game. And then there was Paul Gascoigne's troublesome groin. He had cut a forlorn figure when forced to limp from the field during England's recent Wembley friendly with Cameroon. The specialist who examined Gascoigne briefed the press that it was a new injury likely to require surgery. Given the extent to which Spurs' future was wedded to Gascoigne, the story of what transpired at the team hotel on the eve of the cup game that has since seeped out is all the more ludicrous.

Having dispatched his players to their beds, Venables had turned in. Waking in the morning, he was greeted by the glum face of his assistant manager Doug Livermore. 'I've got some bad news. Gazza was playing squash for an hour last night.' Venables later recalled that his concern was more for Gascoigne's opponent, 'who'd be shattered' than his talisman. Livermore was sent sleuthing, but Gascoigne wouldn't give up the name. Walsh remembers being wrongly outed in print years later but corrects the record. 'I was injured. It was John Moncur.'

In his autobiography, Gascoigne further indicts himself, admitting the squash session was actually '11 games over the course of two hours … On the coach to Fratton Park, I could hardly move. My legs were so sore. I tried to do some press-ups when no one was watching to get them going.'

It was symptomatic of Tottenham's 'crisis club' status that *The Times* dedicated space in its business pages to previewing the tie. City editor Michael Tate quipped, 'Spurs' fifth-round FA Cup match at Portsmouth is likely to attract almost as many bankers as football supporters, with Tottenham Hotspur PLC's survival possibly depending on Gary Lineker's shooting form.'

At least the moneymen could expect a decent share of the gate receipts. Gascoigne's presence ensured a bumper 26,000 Fratton Park crowd, swelled to capacity by 7,000 travelling supporters. The ground was notorious among away fans for its raucously hostile atmosphere. Spurs lifer, Terry Deller, remembers making the journey down from north London with his then-girlfriend, now wife Penny. 'I vividly remember it was a crisp, bright day because I was wearing sunglasses in the middle of February, and there was a lot of piss-taking about that. The turnstile was incredibly narrow, and there was a crush going in. That was football back then. We were stood behind the goal [in the Milton End] on a sheer terrace close to their main stand. You could see their fans were really, really lively before kick-off.'

Annelise Jespersen, who'd also journeyed south that morning, recalls: 'It felt tasty once we got inside. Old school. What you might expect Portsmouth to be like in those days. When a bigger club from the First Division came to play, it wasn't just seen as a challenge for the home team, it was also one for the home fans – how could they make things "welcoming".'

Colin Farmery, chair of the Pompey History Society, who was among the Pompey crowd, concurs. 'It reminded me of 1971 when we played Arsenal here in the fourth round on their way to the double. And the fact Gazza was in the team elevated it even more. We were well up for it. It was a proper FA Cup pitch, too. We always liked a bit of mud on it against First Division teams to make things interesting.'

Portsmouth were not a club shy of FA Cup tradition. They had won the final staging of the competition before the outbreak of World War Two in 1939.[9] Pompey upset the odds to beat Wolves 4-1 at Wembley in a game sensationally billed as the 'monkey-gland final'. This was a reference to the attempts of both sides to seek 'marginal gains' by ingesting a supposedly performance-enhancing elixir made from the glands and testicles of primates.

Now, 52 years later, it was Gascoigne's groin causing a similar stir. He emerged on to the Fratton Park pitch for the warm-up sporting long black cycling shorts – a novelty worthy of ridicule in 1991 – made all the more conspicuous as the navy Hummel hot pants masquerading as the Spurs shorts barely covered them.[10] Seeing that English football's headline act wasn't in top working order bolstered the fervour of the home support's belief that Tottenham were there for the taking.

At least Gascoigne came through the warm-up sufficiently unscathed to start the match. The same could not be said for the luckless Terry Fenwick. Having leapt to head a ball, an awkward landing on the furrowed Fratton Park pitch left the Tottenham right-back with a broken ankle. It was particularly cruel on Fenwick as he'd only had four games back in the Tottenham first team since recovering from a broken leg sustained at Old Trafford in an early round of the previous season's League Cup. How's your luck! (On that occasion, though, he'd been culpable. Following a stray arm from Mark Hughes, seeking retribution in a fit of pique, Fenwick had gone in two-footed on the Welsh striker, only to damage himself in the process.)

It was yet another blow to Venables, who'd faithfully taken Fenwick from Crystal Palace to QPR in the early stages

---

9 With the FA Cup not resuming until 1946, Portsmouth 'held' the trophy for a record seven years.

10 The cycling short innovation was not well received in some quarters. FIFA's director of communications Guido Tognoni remarked at the time, 'This undesirable fashion trend must stop. Some players look like clowns.' A directive was subsequently sent to member associations insisting the garments must at least be the same colour as the team's playing shorts.

of his managerial career before coming back in for him at Spurs. Paul Walsh recounts how it was a running joke among the players to refer to Fenwick as 'son of Terry' such was the esteem Venables held for the player. 'The lads would say after training, "What are you and your dad having for dinner?"'

It's fair to say the Spurs fans didn't share the manager's view. Steve Davies, who also made the trip to Fratton Park, elaborates. 'Fenwick wasn't a popular player, although he'd been good enough to play for England in a World Cup. I remember him scoring in a League Cup tie against Southend before he broke his leg the first time. It was when the East Stand was closed again in 1989, and he made a point of going to celebrate with the empty stand.'

As it happened, it was in that tie with the Shrimpers that Justin Edinburgh first came to Terry Venables's attention as a potential Spurs player, and it was his name Venables added at left-back as he furiously amended his starting XI in the Fratton Park referee's room, with Pat Van Den Hauwe shunting over to the right-back slot. Edinburgh was instantly no longer 'one for the future'. His time as a first-team regular had arrived.

'Terry Fenwick's injury was fate,' reckons Paul Stewart. 'No disrespect to him, but he was more of a centre-back than a full-back. Justin came in and did great. He offered more in that position, so it didn't weaken us. I don't think Justin had expected to break into the team. I think the plan was for him to develop over a few seasons, but he took his chance.' It's clear as Stewart rounds off his thoughts that he hasn't quite come to terms with the loss of Edinburgh. The youngster of the 1991 team died in 2019, aged only 49, having suffered a sudden cardiac arrest. 'He was just such a lovely lad.'

Having recalibrated the defence, Venables was short of options to fill the subs' bench. Walsh's injury saw Mitchell Thomas drafted into a starting berth in a five-man midfield, so John Moncur, (un)fresh from his clandestine squash marathon the night before, was elevated to the number 12 shirt. The other substitute eventually named was young forward Philip Gray.

Gray's progress at Spurs had been stymied in shocking circumstances. Having made only three senior appearances, Gray was the victim of a deliberate and random hit-and-run incident in Enfield while walking his girlfriend home.

Jonathan Pearce explains how Capital Gold – who were providing live commentary from Portsmouth for its burgeoning London audience – always had the inside track on late-breaking team news. 'Bobby Moore would just wander down on to the pitch from our commentary position as the teams came out. It's Bobby Moore – who's going to stop him? He'd then come back up and say "so and so is in for so and so".'

Teamsheet
Fratton Park
Saturday, 16 February 1991

Portsmouth	Tottenham Hotspur
Colours: blue shirts, white shorts, red socks	Colours: white shirts, navy shorts, white socks
1. Andy Gosney	1. Erik Thorstvedt
2. Warren Neill	2. Justin Edinburgh
3. John Beresford	3. Pat Van Den Hauwe
4. Warren Aspinall	4. Steve Sedgley
5. Graeme Hogg	5. Nayim
6. Lee Russell	6. Gary Mabbutt
7. Steve Wigley	7. Vinny Samways
8. Martin Kuhl	8. Paul Gascoigne
9. Colin Clarke	9. Mitchell Thomas
10. Guy Whittingham	10. Gary Lineker
11. Mark Chamberlain	11. Paul Allen
(Subs)	(Subs)
12. Shaun Murray	12. John Moncur
14. Darren Anderton	14. Philip Gray

Within minutes of the kick-off, several Spurs players' numbers were illegible. Upon first contact with the abysmal playing surface, their pristine white shirts were decorated earthy brown. Gascoigne, pronouncedly reserved in his willingness to dribble, instead showcased his exquisite passing range. So different in character and temperament to Lineker, there was a symbiosis to their football. They had developed a series of unspoken signals that dictated where Gascoigne would deliver a pass to the striker. A nod of the head towards the opposition goal by Lineker conversely meant he wanted to come short. Whereas a spinning gesture of the index finger meant he'd fake to drop deep and then dart in behind the defence.

The Portsmouth rearguard struggled to decode this as Lineker hared after a flighted pass from Gascoigne that, post-match, would have Venables drawing comparisons to Glenn Hoddle. Lineker's resulting low shot was well fielded by home goalie Andy Gosney. The pair combined again from a free kick awarded against Graeme Hogg, who had felled Vinny Samways with a scandalous raking tackle down the midfielder's Achilles. Gascoigne's devilish centre found Lineker unmarked in the six-yard box. But the striker's skimming header was directed wide of the post.

Such was the audacity of Gascoigne's next dead ball – a low curling shot from improbably far out that narrowly whistled wide – John Motson couldn't suppress an involuntary gasp in his commentary.

'Oh, I say!'

'You just don't quite know what he's going to do next from free kicks.'

These were prophetic words for a day yet to come.

However, with further chances spurned, four minutes from the interval, Tottenham's defensive frailties proved their first-half undoing. Warren Aspinall roved from the halfway line to the edge of the box unassailed by anyone in muddy white. Weighing up his options, he elected for an unrefined bash towards Erik Thorstvedt's goal. His shot posed little threat until it ricocheted off Steve Sedgley's calf – the defender had committed the cardinal sin of turning his back – straight into the advancing Mark Chamberlain's path. The former

England winger gleefully accepted this good fortune, shaping to fire across Thorstvedt, before bouncing a shot into the turf and inside the near post. Cue Pompey pandemonium in the Fratton Park stands.

Spurs had played well enough to dissuade Venables from ringing the changes at half-time. And, with only the two little-known youngsters on the bench, the recovery job would have to be piloted by those already on the pitch. The one notable change to the Tottenham side that kicked off the second period was that Gascoigne had dispensed with his cycling shorts.

Business was about to pick up!

Shortly after the industrious Paul Allen had been denied by a fine double save from Gosney, Gascoigne took possession inside the shallows of his own half from Thorstvedt's throw-out. Dropping a shoulder to escape Martin Kuhl and attracting Aspinall towards him, he dribbled through the Fratton quagmire, releasing the ball into Mitchell Thomas's lolloping path. Thomas measured a crafty ball into Samways, who welcomed it in with his left foot, span 180 degrees in the D of the Portsmouth box and fed the ball into the right-hand channel for the onrushing Allen to centre first time. The unadulterated pleasure broadcaster Danny Kelly takes in describing what happened next is undiminished even after all these years. 'It wasn't enough for Gascoigne to head the equaliser. He had to make himself into a sort of human missile to meet the ball.' The score was 1-1; 30 minutes to play.

The intensity of his celebrations gave notice that Gascoigne's work was far from done. Not by a long way.

Another brutishly balletic dribble – all torso and pumping arms – carried him to the edge of the Pompey area. With panicked defenders converging upon him, he flicked a pass to Allen with the outside of his boot, leaving the winger with only Gosney to beat. Allen's first touch forced him wider than he would have wished. His second was a shot skewed outside the keeper's near post. Allen's apologetically raised hand acknowledged the calibre of the chance. The same combination – Allen being the beneficiary of another Gascoigne marauding run and perceptive pass – drew a diving save from Gosney. A humming expectancy, even from the home support, now greeted his every touch of the ball.

Having done all he could to lay on a winner for his team-mates, Gascoigne resolved to attend to the matter himself. With six minutes to play, Van Den Hauwe volleyed a ball deep into Portsmouth territory, where he'd spotted the midfielder charging into space. As Gascoigne bore down on goal, the last man in blue, Lee Russell, played the percentages. He attempted to shepherd the juggernaut down the line while cutting off the passing lane to the unmarked Lineker. But by now, Gascoigne's mastery of a football was so complete that such barriers were of little consequence. Russell was sent for a lollipop by the midfielder's whirling feet. As the defender tried to regain his equilibrium, Gascoigne drilled a left-foot shot through his legs and beyond Gosney: 2-1.

The Milton End convulsed, with a handful of Spurs fans spilling on to the pitch. Gascoigne squatted in front of them, fists clenched in jubilation at what proved to be the winning goal. For some of the Pompey faithful, this proved too much to bear. 'As soon as he scored,' recalls Terry Deller, 'they started pelting us with coins. They were furious it was him. All these coins were rattling about. I turned around, and Penny had shot 20 rows back.'

'I really didn't like it,' explains Penny. 'I was scared because I could see people in the front row of the Portsmouth stand we were close to saying, "Come on, let's jump over and storm them."'

David Lacey described the scenes in his report for *The Guardian*. 'The match was held up for two minutes while police and stewards cleared a corner of Fratton Park of rival fans who had begun to cut across the pitch to get at one another. The situation was defused quickly and compared to the worst hooligan scenes of the Seventies and Eighties, the incident was trifling. Nevertheless, it was a stark reminder of the reason that the perimeter fences now out of favour following Hillsborough were originally installed.' One apoplectic Pompey fan hectored those in the press box. 'Gascoigne's responsible, make sure you write that!' While referee Terry Holbrook did see fit to quietly usher Gascoigne back to the safety of the centre circle, in Lacey's assessment, attempts to link his celebrations with the conflagration on the terraces 'was stretching things a little'.

There was no doubting, however, in terms of the result, yet again, Gascoigne had been the difference-maker. 'He mined that victory – I can't think of another word for it – out of the hardest, coldest, most unpromising clay,' asserts Danny Kelly. 'That was the point where people started saying "we could go all the way here with Gascoigne playing like this".'

Any needle is long forgotten for Pompey chronicler Colin Farmery. 'I'm currently editing the club's 125th-anniversary history. There's a great picture of Gazza heading his goal towards all the Spurs fans in the Milton End, and it's a very strong contender to go in the book. An iconic display by an iconic footballer. It was a privilege to be beaten by him – if you know what I mean? That is how the game is remembered in Portsmouth, seeing one of the greats of the English game at their peak.'

In the Spurs dressing room after the match, Gascoigne refused to take all the credit. The usually menacingly brooding Van Den Hauwe was thrilled when Gascoigne described the full-back's pass for his winning goal as one of the best he'd ever received. Although in his autobiography, Van Den Hauwe ruefully recounts how 'a week later, [Gascoigne] said exactly the same thing to Vinny Samways and the following week to Walshy. I began to think mine hadn't really been that special.'

Although the fan experience of Portsmouth had been fraught, Penny and Terry Deller laugh at their final memory of the day. Released from Fratton Park, they began the walk back to their car. The couple simultaneously did a double take as a familiarly athletic figure sprinted past them in a Spurs tracksuit before diving into a waiting car that sped away. 'The next day,' says Penny, 'we saw in the papers that Pat Van Den Hauwe had been papped with Mandy Smith in a Portsmouth nightclub.'

While this budding relationship gave the tabloids a dry run at generating 'content' from the romantic liaisons of footballers and celebrities a few years before the hysteria caused by 'Posh and Becks', Gascoigne's fame was transcending the confines of the British Isles. *The People*, reporting the morning after this latest bravura performance, said that Tottenham were braced for imminent bids from Serie A. Roma and Napoli were named as the player's principal suitors. While in *The Mirror*, Diego Maradona was quoted as saying, 'When you are talking about who is the heir to me, then I must say it could be him. I'm crazy about Gascoigne.'

Gascoigne would be afforded the opportunity of further staking his claim to El Diego's world's best crown live on the BBC following the FA Cup quarter-final draw. Notts County would visit White Hart Lane in the last eight. Having beaten Hull City and Oldham in rounds three and four, Division Two County, and the club's loquaciously opinionated young manager, Neil Warnock, had upset Manchester City to progress this far.

Across the River Trent, Brian Clough's Forest continued to live dangerously. Playing their sixth FA Cup match of the season already, room in the calendar had to be found midweek for their tie at The Dell. Forest, in their changed strip of white shirts and shorts, came close to being enveloped by the descending fog and ejected from the cup after Neil Ruddock had given Southampton the lead within two minutes. With worsening visibility and the ball seldom approaching his goalmouth in the second half, Saints keeper Tim Flowers might have begun to wonder if the game had been abandoned without his knowledge. Then, with ten minutes left to play, a

Mitre Delta whacked by Stuart Pearce from 35 yards whizzed out of the gloom and crashed off Flowers's post. Roy Keane was first to react and guided the ball to Steve Hodge to slot home the equaliser from inside the six-yard box.

Forest survived an injury-time scare – Rod Wallace belted a half-volley against Mark Crossley's crossbar – to force the replay. They would now require a seventh FA Cup match to reach round six. Brian Clough was irritated by suggestions that his side were fortunate to get another crack at Southampton as he listened to the radio report on the team bus on the long journey back to Nottinghamshire.

A knee injury to goalscorer Hodge, which had forced him from the field for the final five minutes, had a similarly antagonising effect on the manager. 'The specialist told me to sit out for six weeks,' wrote Hodge in his autobiography, 'but after seven days, Cloughie was asking if I'd be training tomorrow. Two and a half weeks later, I was still injured and walking around the training pitch. "Harry [Clough's nickname for Hodge], do you want to join in?" he called to me ... "Mind you don't get pneumonia, won't you."'

Despite the midfielder's absence, Forest made easy work of the replay. Striker Nigel Jemson scored a hat-trick in a 3-1 victory that set Forest up with a quarter-final tie against Norwich – who had deposed holders Manchester United – at Carrow Road. Jemson, like Hodge, would find his goals didn't hold much sway with the manager as Wembley came closer into view.

Unquestionably, however, the biggest story of the fifth round played out on Merseyside. Liverpool welcomed Everton to Anfield in apparently rude health, three points clear of Arsenal with 24 games played. Everton, by contrast, sat 12th and were banking on Howard Kendall's second coming – he'd replaced Colin Harvey in November – to bring an uptick in their fortunes.

The clubs had last met in the FA Cup in the 1989 final. That was perhaps the most emotionally charged and poignant occasion in the competition's history. After the horror of Hillsborough, the whole city of Liverpool had come together in grief and defiance. Beyond the confines of Anfield's famed Boot Room, the disaster had no discernible effect on the team. Kenny Dalglish's side won that compelling all-Merseyside final in 1989 and, just a few days later, missed out on the league title by a matter of seconds – 'it's up for grabs now' and all that – in the most thrilling climax ever to an English season. They roused themselves from the tragedy, trauma and sporting disappointment of 1989 to win the league the following season by nine points. Dalglish had added a third title as Liverpool manager to the five he'd won at Anfield when exclusively a player.

The widespread assumption after their 0-0 draw with Everton, played on 17 February 1991, was that Liverpool would win the replay at Goodison three days later and then make their customary surge to the end of the season. Perhaps they'd even crown it with another double to add to the one achieved by Dalglish in 1986. King Kenny, however, was desperate to abdicate.

By the turn of the year red blotches had begun to swarm across his body and Dalglish was receiving almost daily injections from the team doctor. In his 1997 autobiography, he recalls lying on his hotel bed before the Everton replay and deciding, 'I had to get out. The alternative was going mad … Liverpool needed somebody who was going to be authoritative, somebody who could make a decision. I couldn't do that anymore.' Four times, Liverpool took the lead in the replay. Four times, they relinquished it, to draw 4-4.

Within 48 hours of the final whistle, journalists scrambled to attend a hastily convened press conference. They sat open-mouthed as Dalglish announced he was stepping down.

That Dalglish's departure came as such a bolt from the blue is indicative of football's utter lack of awareness – let alone understanding or compassion – toward mental well-being. Dalglish had attended funeral after funeral for Hillsborough's immediate 95 victims. He'd also provided unquantifiable support to the victims' families and other survivors while continuing to perform one of the highest-profile, most pressurised jobs in British society. How could it not take its toll on him? Even someone as emotionally intelligent as Terry Venables seemed incapable of empathising with Dalglish. Doubtless with no malice at all intended, Venables facetiously name-checked Dalglish when discussing the tribulations that season had wrought on White Hart Lane. 'I've gone past the Kenny Dalglish stage. I've gone potty, and I'm coming back again.' The joke made light of the harsh reality of elite football management. That very month, one of Venables's successors at Barcelona, Johan Cruyff, required bypass surgery, having suffered a heart attack.

With Ronnie Moran in temporary charge at Anfield, Everton won the second replay 1-0 to set up a last-eight tie at Upton Park. Liverpool's cup exit was sandwiched by back-to-back league defeats to Luton and, critically for the destination of the championship – Arsenal. George Graham's side had by then relinquished their unbeaten league start, but with only 12 goals conceded from 26 games, the title was now theirs to lose. The Gunners made unfussy progress into the last eight of the cup, winning 1-0 at Shrewsbury on a pudding of a pitch, thanks to Michael Thomas.

The match marked a return to first-team football for Tony Adams. He'd recently completed a 57-day stint in HMP Chelmsford, having crashed his Ford Sierra into a garden wall while three times over the legal drink-drive limit. Adams, noticeably unkempt, upon his release explained he'd been unwilling to entrust his hair to the prison barber, a Spurs fan.

David Dein, then vice-chairman, has since recounted how some within Highbury's marble halls had called for Adams to be sacked following his conviction. George Graham – ill-equipped, unwilling or unable to address Adams's grim descent into alcoholism – remained resolute that he would retain him as captain. Buttressed by Adams and drawn at home to Division Three Cambridge in the quarter-finals, Arsenal were upbeat. A song began to be heard on matchdays in Islington's pubs, to the tune of an old 1964 Righteous Brothers hit.

'We've got that double feeling
Woah that double feeling
We've got that double feeling
Now it's on on on.'

Chapter Nine

Assets and Liabilities

A WEEK on from Portsmouth, 'loving feeling' was the last thing Tottenham Hotspur PLC's embattled directors were receiving from the club's incandescent fans. The season's nadir arrived at Plough Lane.

Cut apart by injury and the fire sale of squad players, Terry Venables threw together a team to play Wimbledon using all the warm bodies he could find. With Paul Gascoigne now being regularly omitted from league action to spare him for the cup, Spurs got a chasing.

Restored to the line-up, having been left out in the winter cold, it's an afternoon seared into Gudni Bergsson's memory for all the wrong reasons. 'Wimbledon back then had the slopey pitch, elbows flying, and they were bang up for the fight. But we were Spurs at our worst. I scored when we were 2-0 down – a good finish, you know – and felt upbeat that we could get back into it. But we were all over the place after that and got hammered 5-1. It was probably the worst performance I ever took part in, and after that, I dropped out again and didn't get to play a lot.'

The pain caused by the heft of the scoreline was exacerbated by Venables's conspicuous contempt for the opposition's footballing philosophy. In comments that were no doubt pinned to the wall in the Dons' dressing room whenever they faced Venables's Spurs, he'd bristled, 'Wimbledon are killing the dream that made football the world's greatest game. I could take any non-league player and turn him into a Wimbledon player in a matter of weeks.'

As a support act, the pounding at Plough Lane had set a suitably black mood for the main event, the delayed AGM held three days later. TISA had been urging fans to attend en masse, distributing hundreds of postcards ornamented with an image of Gascoigne and Gary Lineker overcome by the ecstasy of scoring a goal. The pithy accompanying caption read, 'Want them to stay? Have your say!' More than 700 shareholders answered the call by making their way to White Hart Lane's Chanticleer Club on Tuesday morning for what promised to be a spicy early kick-off against the PLC board. Anticipating aggro, a uniformed presence from Tottenham police station was deployed at the entrance. But it was brickbats rather than bricks and bats that shareholders came armed with. Pun-heavy placards addressed the board's fiscal incontinence. Some read '£22m DEBT IT'S HUMMEL-IATING'. Another, bearing portraits of Irving Scholar and Gascoigne, asked, 'SHOULD TOTTENHAM DISPOSE OF ITS ASSETS OR ITS LIABILITIES?' While others took a more route-one approach: 'GAZZA GOES – WE GO', 'BOARD OUT', 'WHERE'S THE MONEY GONE?' and 'SAVE OUR CLUB'.

Inside the meeting, board members were heckled from the floor by fans accusing them of 'financial hooliganism' and demanding that they 'fall on their letter openers'. Annelise Jespersen recalls that TISA had tacit recognition from the club that they spoke on behalf of the wider Spurs fanbase. Having opened the meeting and dealt with the formalities, PLC chairman Nat Solomon gave way to TISA, allowing them 20 uninterrupted questions – submitted in writing in advance – before turning to other shareholders. Steve Davies, who was responsible for formulating the questions, explains TISA's strategy. 'It was not so much about the board's answers but more aimed at shining a light on what they'd done wrong.' As Jespersen puts it, 'We'd spent a lot of time preparing for the AGM, so it wasn't like we were going to turn up with no clue of what we wanted to ask. That's why directors should never underestimate fans.'

By contrast, the board's lack of preparedness was thrown into sharp relief when new chief executive Ian Gray could only answer, when asked to confirm the current state of the debt, that he did 'not have the figures to hand'. Shareholders had to content themselves with the figure released in January for the year up to May 1990, which showed Spurs £22.9 million in the red. Gray was having a torrid time of it. When asked if Martex – the loss-making textile subsidiary – was successful, his reply, 'It was when we bought it', raised an unintentional laugh.

Mirth was fast replaced by anguish as the agenda turned to Lineker and Gascoigne. Solomon, looking suitably doleful, prepared to confirm Spurs supporters' worst fears. 'After 55 years supporting the club, I have not accepted the chairmanship in order to preside over the demolition of the company.' So far, so good, Mr Chairman. Although, it was apparent to the entire room an almighty 'but' was coming. 'We fervently hope that we can find a solution to our current financial position that would not require those players to be sold. However, if we receive an offer we cannot refuse, the board will have an inescapable responsibility to consider it.'

With lip service to 'trying to keep Gazza' paid, Solomon unholstered his pricing gun. 'I don't want to help buyers by giving an indication, but if a club comes in with a figure above £10 million, then I shall have to take it very seriously.' One fan received thunderous applause from the floor as he responded with a heartfelt clarion call. 'All we have heard is that if we receive the right offer for Paul Gascoigne he will be sold. Let me say right now that there is no right offer for Paul Gascoigne. And there never will be. Sell the other companies. Ask the fans to help. Do anything before you sell Gazza.'

The problem for Solomon was that with Scholar and Paul Bobroff still bunkered in their intractable feud and with the

Midland Bank calling the shots, there were precious few other levers available for him to pull. So while publicly Solomon's pronouncements only reluctantly invited offers for the Koh-i-Noor in Tottenham's slipping crown, privately, the club actively sought them out.

Solomon asked Scholar how to organise the sale. Scholar says in his memoir that he was only prepared to discuss the transfer of Gascoigne as a last resort to avoid placing Tottenham into administration or receivership. The company was fast reaching that point.

Even faced with this alarming reality, Scholar played for time. He recommended to Solomon that the board engage the doyen of football agents, Dennis Roach, to hawk Gascoigne around to Europe's leading clubs. Roach would receive 1 per cent of any transfer fee up to £7 million and 1.5 per cent of anything exceeding that. Roach's terms were of little concern to Scholar – he was counting on them never being paid. In a move worthy of Machiavelli, Scholar's championing of Roach had been designed to scupper any deal for Gascoigne. Scholar had failed to divulge to Solomon that there was a deeply felt enmity – bordering on hatred – between Roach and Gascoigne's representative, Mel Stein. As Scholar put it in his book, 'If [Roach] couldn't sit in the same room as Gascoigne's adviser, how could the transfer details be arranged?'

Extraordinarily, it appears that no one at the club deemed it necessary to discuss the matter with Gascoigne. He would later write, 'I was upset that Tottenham had even contemplated selling me behind my back without talking to me first about any of it. I began to feel like a piece of baggage, just another load of goods for sale.'

Intriguingly, parallel to near-daily bulletins about Gascoigne's future, Harry Harris had begun to drip-feed *Mirror* readers the details of a paradigm-shifting development. 'It has been an open secret for weeks that Venables and director Tony Berry have spoken to parties interested in buying Spurs.

Venables has been promised boardroom power, fulfilling an ambition to become managing director of a club.'[11]

Harris – seemingly taking his line directly from Scholar – was at pains to make clear this wasn't necessarily something Spurs fans should welcome. 'New investors might arrive with grandiose claims of saving Gazza and Lineker. But reality could soon set in, and they might eventually have to consider: the sale of White Hart Lane; the sale of Gazza; the sale of Lineker and other top stars. A vision of Spurs in 18 months' time could be a nightmare. No Gazza. No Lineker. No Spurs FC chairman Irving Scholar ... no ground. No trophies ... no hope.' That the potential loss of Scholar was ranked above concerns about White Hart Lane and the club's ability to stock its trophy cabinet said much about the provenance of this story.

Having been responsible for bringing Terry Venables to Spurs, Irving Scholar was damned if he was going to be ousted from the club by him. Shots were soon fired in Venables's direction.

Whereas Alf Ramsey – raised on the same Dagenham streets a generation before Venables and the right-back in Spurs' 1950/51 championship-winning side – had taken elocution lessons to buff away any trace of his working-class accent, the Tottenham manager remained proud of his roots. While the authenticity of his communication was undoubtedly one of his great strengths, it also triggered a section of the press to disdainfully mock him for harbouring ideas 'above his station'. They wished him to fail.

Two days before Tottenham's FA Cup quarter-final, Michael Bowen took a dim view of Venables's corporate aspirations in his self-styled 'Outstanding and Outspoken' *Mirror* column. 'He's a clever lad. Clever enough to use the financial troubles which have beset Tottenham as a

---

11 In 1984, as Venables's managerial contract expired at QPR, he'd explored a deal to buy the club from chairman John Gregory. The proposal would have seen Gregory retain Loftus Road, with Venables, as owner of the football club, leasing the stadium for home fixtures. According to Venables, as he sought the means to finance his takeover, Gregory backed out. Venables was then approached by Barcelona.

smokescreen for the fact that his footballing balance sheet is looking equally sick. Shrewd enough to be the link man for a consortium with ambitions to take over the club – despite the fact that this might involve a conflict of interest. But no amount of moaning at his board to sort out the bank debts ... can disguise one absolute fact. Venables has spent over £9 million to assemble a team at White Hart Lane which has won nothing. Which will win nothing ... It's generally believed that a team is often a reflection of their manager's personality. I would be the last person to accuse Venables of being brittle and lacking in class. With the glowing exception of Gazza, that is what Spurs are ... if Tel Boy gets past Notts County on Sunday – as I suspect he will – there will be tests his team will not survive.'

Venables's best efforts to keep focus on the football ahead of the last-eight tie were dealt another blow as he was forced to respond to reports emanating from Italy. *Gazzetta dello Sport* asserted that Lazio had reached an agreement over a £7 million bid for Gascoigne. 'If he is going to Lazio then I don't know anything about it.' Solomon's milky attempt to dismiss the news as 'pure speculation' proved all the less convincing when it emerged club officials had met with their Lazio counterparts as early as 20 February, a whole week before the AGM had taken place.

Acknowledging the unsettling effect this speculation was having on Gascoigne, Venables's primary concern was whether the midfielder – who he rated a 50/50 chance – would be fit enough to start the game. 'Every time he plays, he aggravates [the groin] further and the recovery time is definitely getting longer.' Gary Mabbutt attempted to put a brave face on things. 'All we can allow ourselves to think about is the footballing side, not the financial side of Tottenham Hotspur PLC ... The approach to Sunday's game will be the same as if the club had millions in the bank. We are determined to win for our own ambition.' 'Humour' was Mabbutt's answer when asked about the squad's coping strategy for the White Hart Lane perma-crisis: 'That is basically how the players react. All the talk hasn't demoralised us nor has it had a detrimental effect on the spirit. I can promise you that.'

While Venables was tied up fighting fires mostly of Spurs' own making, County manager, Neil Warnock, was free to indulge in the more traditional pre-game managerial arts. The FA Cup had propelled Warnock on to the national stage for the first time, and observers quickly noticed his proclivity for stirring the pot. 'Listening to the interviews with one or two of their players, they're already in the next round, planning ahead that they "might get into the final" and this, that and the other. I just take things one step at a time. If we lose, we lose. But we'll have given it a shot, and we have gone further than Liverpool and Manchester United.'

Warnock vowed to take the game to Tottenham, joking in his press conference, 'I thought at one stage about playing with a sweeper and trying to get a draw. But then I thought, "What the hell." Our natural game is suicidal football, with everyone charging forward, and it wouldn't be fair to ask the lads to change.'

Such soundbites had resulted in the BBC inviting him to join the *Match of the Day* punditry panel. On the evening before the biggest game of his career to date, Warnock travelled to London to join Des Lynam and Trevor Brooking in the studio – and was the undoubted star turn. Looking totally at ease, having given his assessment of the two quarter-finals played that day, he then joshed that he was planning to mark Gascoigne – who he fully expected to play – with three men. No sooner had the *Match of the Day* end credits rolled than he made the journey under cover of darkness back to Nottingham – only to venture down to the capital on the County team bus in the morning.

Brian Glanville, in his *Times* preview of the fixture, pinpointed the likely determining factor. 'Victory will largely depend on Paul Gascoigne. But how far, these days, can he be depended upon? Will his groin injury bother him? Will he get himself sent off? Those wild, erratic challenges, often made early in the game without provocation are going to elicit a red card one day.'

From his vantage point in White Hart Lane's Paxton Road end terrace, Terry Deller was equally fretful. 'I remember it vividly, Gazza out on the pitch warming up and I kept saying "he's not fit". My thinking was, "If he's not at it, we're losing this," because he was carrying the whole thing by this point. For that to be my mindset against a team like Notts County is not a good place to be.'

Stadium announcer Willie Morgan was doing his best to stir belief among the apprehensive home crowd that they could very soon be on their way to Wembley, pumping out over the tannoy a classic medley of Chas & Dave from bygone cup final glories. Following his trademark greeting – 'Welcome to White Hart Lane, the world-famous home of the Spurs' – he announced the teams. His confirmation of who was wearing the white number 8 shirt elicited a full-throated cheer around the ground as the players emerged from the tunnel.

Teamsheet
White Hart Lane
Sunday, 10 March 1991

Tottenham Hotspur	Notts County
Colours: white shirts, navy shorts, white socks	Colours: sky blue shirts, sky blue shorts, sky blue socks
1. Erik Thorstvedt	1. Steve Cherry
2. Justin Edinburgh	2. Charlie Palmer
3. Pat Van Den Hauwe	3. Paul Harding
4. Steve Sedgley	4. Craig Short
5. Nayim	5. Dean Yates
6. Gary Mabbutt	6. Don O'Riordan
7. Paul Stewart	7. Dean Thomas
8. Paul Gascoigne	8. Phil Turner
9. Mitchell Thomas	9. Kevin Bartlett
10. Gary Lineker	10. Gary Lund
11. Paul Allen	11. Mark Draper
(Subs)	(Subs)
12. Paul Walsh	12. Tommy Johnson
14. Vinny Samways	14. Alan Paris

As the match got underway, for several minutes there were more tackles than passes as County got wired into the hosts. Mark Draper was foolhardy enough to leave one late on Pat Van Den Hauwe, undaunted by the 'receipt' surely forthcoming from the Spurs man as soon as the referee turned his back. Dean Yates left Lineker curled up in the fetal position on the halfway line with a knee-high challenge that never entered the same airspace as the ball. Referee Peter Foakes deemed the perpetrators of these assaults as deserving nothing more than a stiff talking to. Nayim was next to be chopped down, by Charlie Palmer.

Despite Gascoigne's remonstrations to the referee – and a primitive attempt at off-the-ball retribution – play was waved on. Dean Thomas took a few steps forward with the ball. Confronted only by open grass, he advanced further still. By the time Mabbutt identified the danger, Thomas had already lined up his shot. His skimmer from 35 yards took a hideous bounce on the exposed brown turf of Erik Thorstvedt's six-yard box and looped over the keeper's dive. Spread-eagled, all Thorstvedt could do was swivel his neck to watch the ball cannoning off the post to safety.

It was only by the breadth of Thorstvedt's fingertips that Tottenham survived County's next attack seconds later. With barely six minutes elapsed, Gary Lund seized on a heavy touch in the Spurs midfield and slipped a pass beyond Mabbutt and Steve Sedgley to the prodigiously rapid Kevin Bartlett. The forward toed the ball to the right as Thorstvedt threw himself at his feet. But harnessing every millimetre of his 6ft 4in frame, the Norwegian managed to lay a glancing pink Uhlsport-gloved touch on it, which waylaid Bartlett long enough for Mabbutt to retreat into the goalmouth and head the delayed shot off the line.

'Spurs are rattled!' screamed John Motson in his commentary for BBC1's live match coverage, 'They're really rattled back there.' Mabbutt, as if underlining the accuracy of this assessment, immediately massaged the air with his left palm to implore his team-mates to remain calm.

Unable to exert any influence on the proceedings, Gascoigne looked worryingly combustible. Paul Harding was the primary source of his vexation. Harding was less than six months removed from grafting on a London building site while turning out in the Vauxhall Conference for Barnet. Now, he was tasked with harassing the most celebrated player in the First Division – an assignment he was performing admirably well. In the 11th minute, as Gascoigne tried to wriggle down the line, Harding strong-armed him to the ground. The intensity with which the Spurs man got to his feet, chest pumped forward, shoulders menacingly square, suggested trouble. But much to the relief of the Spurs fans looking on from the front rows of the West Stand, the right-hand Gascoigne thrust towards Harding delivered a handshake rather than a haymaker.

The first time Gascoigne escaped the attention of his marker, chiselling some space near the touchline with a gorgeous Cruyff turn, Spurs should have taken the lead. His surging dribble was halted by a pincer of County tackles. The loose ball found its way to Mitchell Thomas on the edge of the box, who attempted a give-and-go with Lineker. The makeshift midfielder's attempt to reach the return was seen off by Yates. As the defender hesitated, hoping an avenue to his goalkeeper would appear, Thomas pinched back possession and presented Lineker with a shooting chance: 12 yards out and in the centre of the goal, the England captain only had time to put his weaker foot forward and failed to best Steve Cherry.

The lesson for Paul Harding was abundantly clear. Even impaired, Gascoigne was a cut above and required cutting down. Again, anger contorted the Spurs midfielder's boyish face as he picked himself up from Harding's latest transgression – not least because Yates had taken the opportunity to torpedo him with the ball while he lay prostrate. Again, at the last second, Gascoigne suppressed the urge for reprisal, opting to tousle his oppressor's hair instead. Wound up and wounded, as the half wore on, Gascoigne took up a post as an auxiliary centre-forward alongside Lineker. The discomfort emanating from his groin prohibited him from doing much else.

Frustration at his plight contributed to County establishing a deserved lead four minutes from half-time. Sedgley conceded a corner with a desperate challenge to halt Bartlett's progress into the box. Bar Lineker, every Spurs player came back to defend it. County skipper Phil Turner's outswinger was soundly met by Nayim's forehead. Gascoigne brought the ball under his spell on the edge of the area and, seeing Harding haring towards him, decided to exhibit his class rather than lump it to safety. Harding read it. His interception inadvertently teed up Don O'Riordan for a shot that stayed hit. But for the net, it would have troubled the foundations of the tired Park Lane end stand. Thorstvedt had no chance.

So exuberant were the County players' celebrations that O'Riordan had to have a gash on his head bandaged before the game could restart. Jubilant team-mate Craig Short had accidentally nutted him.

During the interval, Jimmy Hill, in the BBC studio, launched into a diatribe on Gascoigne's unhappy first 45 minutes, advocating Venables administer the half-time hook. 'If I had a groin injury, I wouldn't want to play against Notts County today. They are a hard, determined side … A player of his calibre, when he's an asset, he's a wonderful asset. When he's off, he's a liability. And that's the trouble.'

In the bowels of White Hart Lane, Venables dispensed with the tactical observations he'd been carefully jotting down as the tide had turned against his side and instead went for broke. The rousing address he gave his crestfallen players is recounted in his first autobiography: 'They're beating us in every phase. They are first to the tackle and first to the ball. We've got to show the same attitude. What's worth having is worth fighting for. You have no choice, you just have to go for it. Forty-five minutes, that's all it is. If you don't do it you're out, and that's the end of it.' The wider implication beyond the FA Cup of that closing remark was lost on no one in the home dressing room.

When play resumed, the galvanising effect of the manager's oratory was immediately apparent. Paul Stewart began to dominate proceedings with his blend of muscular creativity. A lovely shimmy saw him escape down the right wing, where he stood a ball up to the back post. Lineker's downward header from inside the six-yard box was smothered by Short, while a combination of Cherry and Palmer on the goal line repelled Nayim's follow-up. If Gascoigne's ailment had shorn him of a yard or two, Stewart, full of running, made good on the deficit. His perfectly weighted switch of play invited Lineker to charge infield. Rather than admiring the precision of his pass, Stewart galloped forward in support of the striker. Taking back possession, Stewart attempted to surge beyond Yates into the County area. Under extreme duress, the defender coughed up a welcome corner in the 51st minute.

Nursing his groin, rather than swirling one under the bar, Gascoigne side-footed it to Nayim, who'd ambled undetected to the edge of the box. Shaping to shoot with his right, Nayim cannily dragged the ball inside on to his left and thrashed a low shot that, in truth, looked destined for the corner flag before a hapless intervention from Short diverted it on to the far post and into the net.

'It was my goal,' laughs Nayim as he recalls the moment. 'They gave it to the guy who got the deflection. I didn't worry about goal bonuses, which was good because I didn't score that many in my career! But the ones I did score, like against Notts County, were important.' Venables permitted himself only the briefest of clenched fists in celebration. The game needed winning here and now. A midweek replay at Meadow Lane – almost certainly without the pained Gascoigne – looked a treacherous prospect.

Just after the hour, Gascoigne's simmering resentment at Harding's limpet-like attentions finally erupted. Before Paul

Stewart's short throw-in on the halfway line had even reached Gascoigne's foot, Harding was pawing at his back. Seeking an escape from this stifling embrace, Gascoigne dropped a shoulder to the right but could find no way out. He then dipped back the other way and momentarily looked to be in the clear, until Harding yanked him back in a waist-lock. The midfielder's exasperation may have been understandable, but the vicious elbow he smashed into Harding's face was indefensible. Knowing the blow he'd landed was red-card worthy, Gascoigne dropped to the floor, hoping to divert the referee's attention. Several County players made a beeline for Mr Foakes to demand action; others took Gascoigne to task as he skulked away from the scene of the crime. With Harding laid out flat on his back, Gascoigne's protestations that the County player had tugged his shirt seemed utterly trivial.

Thankfully, after a few minutes of treatment, Harding stirred. The ugly purple-black contusion already gathering under his left eye provided irrefutable evidence of Gascoigne's guilt and the violence of the blow. That Harding managed a smile and even accepted the sheepish cuddle of apology offered by Gascoigne was a testament to both his fortitude and just how much he was relishing the scrap. With referee Foakes keeping cards of both colours clamped inside his top pocket, Trevor Brooking on co-commentary was left to ruminate, 'With the wrong referee at the wrong time, he'll find himself taking an early bath.' On this occasion, such laissez-faire officiating worked to Gascoigne's – and Tottenham's – advantage. A day was rapidly approaching when it would prove almost ruinous for his career.

More cautious managers might have withdrawn Gascoigne from the fray in self-preservation. Venables's faith, however, never wavered. Paul Walsh and Vinny Samways were sent on for Thomas and Nayim. Gascoigne would have to see the match through, come what may. Samways, a midfielder born and bred in Bethnal Green but with a poise more in keeping with Barcelona, immediately started spraying penetrative passes out of keeping with the midfield maelstrom he stepped into. Stewart, Lineker and Walsh were all presented with shooting chances. But all found Cherry an insurmountable barrier. County continued to pose their own threat, with Bartlett persistently probing Spurs' offside trap for a fissure. The one time the striker got clear, he looked certain to re-establish the visitors' lead – until Sedgley, trailing in the foot race, managed to snake out a long limb and divert the ball safely to Thorstvedt.

With six minutes remaining, Sedgley was released from thanklessly chasing Bartlett to make his way forward for a corner industriously won by Walsh. Samways raised both arms to signal his intention to send the ball to the far post. Mabbutt and Sedgley took up their positions accordingly but were no match in the air for Yates, who powered a header well clear of danger. Justin Edinburgh scurried to retrieve and looped the ball back into the County box, where Yates was again toweringly dominant. Gathering possession, Sedgley wisely sought a low route forward into Mabbutt. Mabbutt flicked the ball into Walsh, who – in turn – nimbly nudged it beyond the massed ranks of the County defence. Sedgley gave chase, but before he could reach the ball, Gascoigne stole in to plant an irresistible shot into the corner of the net. Absorbed in the euphoria of the moment, Gascoigne tore away from his team-mates, pointing an approval-seeking finger toward his father in the West Stand. It was the first unencumbered sprint he'd made in the entirety of the afternoon, and was only halted when he was ensnared beneath a joyous white-shirted pile-on. Capital Gold's Mick Lowes perhaps underplayed the broader significance of the goal in his instantaneous assessment. 'Gascoigne has kept Spurs' season alive.'

Within minutes of the final whistle, Ray Stubbs pinned Gascoigne and Lineker down in the White Hart Lane boot room for a post-match interview. Stubbs's line of questioning centred as much on Gazza's errant elbow as his match-winning right foot. 'I just want to say I didn't deliberately do it. It was an accident, you know. Definitely,' said Gascoigne before his subconscious – and some clever probing from Stubbs – lulled him into saying the quiet part out loud as he was shown a replay of the incident. 'About five or six times he was pulling on my shirt. I wanted to get away from the guy.' Realising his mistake, he offered an unconvincing addendum. 'It looks there like I deliberately did it, but, honestly, I definitely didn't.'

When Stubbs enquired why Gascoigne's performance had been laced with such emotion, Lineker interjected ironically, 'Makes a change.' Gascoigne's answer revealed the vulnerability that had endeared him to the nation in Turin and served as a timely reminder of his tender age, still just 23. 'My dad was up there, and he doesn't come to see us much, so I was pleased to get a goal in front of him. Really pleased.'

Spurs physio John Sheridan divulges what happened when the BBC cameras stopped rolling. 'I had to make the case for getting him operated on straight after the game. I could see he was in pain and struggling. He went directly from White Hart Lane to the hospital. It wasn't a popular decision, but it was clear to me he couldn't make it to the end of the season, which had been the original plan. Thankfully Terry and the doc went along with me. The window was so tight that even a day or two's delay would have ruled him out of the semi-final.'

Sheridan was able to leverage a family connection in Tottenham's latest hour of need. 'We had a network of surgeons, but when it came to groins, Jerry Gilmore was the top man.' Sheridan isn't overegging it. Such was Gilmore's repute he came to have a condition, 'Gilmore's groin', named after him. Observant visitors to his celebrated clinic would notice the plush carpet bore a pattern made of his initials, JG. Gascoigne was in safe hands. 'My daughter was Jerry's secretary,' explains Sheridan. 'He went out of his way to help us by operating on Paul first thing on the Monday morning.'

The race to get Gascoigne fit had become all the more pressing in the wake of the semi-final draw. Those tuning in to the BBC's newly launched Radio 5 heard a suitably plummy voice from Lancaster Gate announce: 'Arsenal ...' 2-1 victors over Cambridge United in their quarter-final, 'will play ... Tottenham Hotspur.'

West Ham (having beaten Everton 2-1), and Nottingham Forest (triumphant over Norwich via a strike goalscorer Roy Keane marked with a vivacious roly-poly which in turn earned him a bollocking from Brian Clough) had little choice but to accept second billing. While Villa Park was swiftly allocated to host their match, a suitable venue for what the tabloids inevitably dubbed a 'Right North London Knees Up' had to be found.

As Spurs captain, Gary Mabbutt implored the FA to dispense with tradition in light of this unprecedented pairing. 'Wembley makes sense. No neutral ground is suitable. Is it wise to have both sets of fans travelling up the same motorway?'

* * *

The Tottenham skipper had more reason than most for being acutely attuned to sensitivities surrounding the selection of semi-final stadiums. It was only 24 months since Mabbutt had received correspondence from the family of Andrew Sefton, a 23-year-old security guard from Skelmersdale near Liverpool. Sefton had resisted the pull of the trophy-laden Merseyside clubs on his doorstep and had instead opted to follow Spurs. As a boy, he'd lovingly hung a Tottenham pennant above his bed. And when he got engaged to his fiancée, Helen, he joked: 'I'm only marrying you because you've got legs like Gary Mabbutt.'

On 15 April 1989, Sefton had accepted a ticket from a group of his Liverpool-supporting friends for the semi-final at Hillsborough. He happily volunteered to drive them down to Sheffield in his mum's car on that deceitfully beautiful spring morning. Sefton never made the return journey. He was one of those carried lifelessly on a makeshift stretcher from the mangled 'pen 3' of the Leppings Lane terrace. In his 1989 autobiography, *Against All Odds*, Mabbutt recounts attending

Sefton's funeral and being asked to read a bidding prayer by the priest. He also relays the heart-rending request of a family bereft. They wished to bury their son in a Spurs shirt bearing Mabbutt's number 6.

In 1989, Spurs fans had been uniquely placed to understand the horrors that unfolded at Hillsborough and debunk the disgraceful smear put about by South Yorkshire Police – wilfully swallowed and regurgitated by the Thatcher government and *The Sun* newspaper – that Liverpool fans were to blame for the disaster. Eight years earlier, 38 Spurs fans had been injured amid a crush in Leppings Lane during Tottenham's FA Cup semi-final with Wolves. The terrace's capacity that day had been exceeded by up to 335 people. Several fans were taken to hospital with broken bones. Loss of life was prevented because around 200 Spurs supporters escaped the terrace by scaling its fences and sitting down around the perimeter of the pitch. Lethally for Sefton and the Liverpool fans who lost their lives at Hillsborough eight years later, the lessons of 1981 had gone unheeded.[12]

Within 24 hours of the semi-final draw in 1991, Glen Kirton, the FA's head of external affairs, announced that Tottenham versus Arsenal would be staged at Wembley on Sunday, 14 April. Adding to the novelty, the kick-off was set for 12 noon. The rationale for the decision laid bare how the Taylor Report into the Hillsborough disaster had belatedly shaken the reluctant authorities from their culpable complacency.

'We don't like breaking with the tradition of the FA Cup. It's a great competition, and it's stood the test of time. But when you've got two big London clubs and no other ground in the London area available, you've got a choice of two

---

12 Disgracefully, the fight for justice for Hillsborough's victims would continue for a further 25 years. Following an inquest, in March 1991, a jury had returned a verdict of accidental death. Finally, in April 2016, this was quashed when a second inquest ruled those who died had been unlawfully killed due to gross negligence and manslaughter. Footage of Spurs fans escaping Leppings Lane in 1981 was shown as part of the proceedings.

things. You go to Wembley or you take 40,000 supporters 120 miles up the motorway. Neither we, nor the police, nor the supporters would have been particularly happy with that so we've chosen Wembley and one of the fortunate by-products of it is it will be a good payday for the game of football.

'We've always put the tradition of the FA Cup first. I think we've now moved into an era where we have to put the safety and the convenience of the supporters first with the tradition of the competition coming a very close second. Wembley will be able to take all of the fans from Arsenal and Spurs who want to see the game. And they won't have too far to travel to see it.'

Bert Millichip, chairman of the FA, made it abundantly clear his hand had been forced by a unique circumstance. '[Tottenham versus Arsenal] is the only conundrum that would enter the consideration as to why we should move to Wembley. And I believe it is a one-off situation. I think it is quite unlikely it will be repeated. Now, having made that statement, perhaps something will happen, and it will occur again. But, at this moment in time, I can think of no other reason why we should go to Wembley for a semi-final.'

Smarting from the criticism they'd received at the outbreak of the Gulf War, the FA rushed to mark the liberation of Kuwait and the cessation of hostilities by ensuring the media were thoroughly briefed that 2,000 complimentary tickets for the match would be issued to the armed forces.

Brian Clough – never shy in giving the game's governing body an often thoroughly deserved bashing – voiced his support of playing the game at the national stadium and dismissed concerns that the victors would have an advantage come the final.[13] 'It's only logical to take them to Wembley.

---

13 Most contemporary observers did believe the experience of playing at Wembley in the semi-final would prove an advantage for the victorious team come the final. Justin Edinburgh, for example, had never set foot in the national stadium – even as a spectator – before lining up there to face Arsenal.

No one wants Spurs and Arsenal to play outside London. I don't care a jot that it's being played where we might have to face the winners. All I'm bothered about is getting there myself on May 18.'

Chapter Ten

Larry Who and Lazio

THE MONTH between the quarter- and semi-final was a time of perpetual anxiety for Spurs fans. As if the prospect of facing all-conquering Arsenal at the national stadium wasn't enough to churn stomachs, the futures of Terry Venables and Paul Gascoigne hung in the balance. The chatter about Venables being involved in a consortium had been proved right, as had the assertion that he was intent on swapping the hard bench of the dugout for a cushioned swivel chair in the boardroom. Four days after Notts County, Venables refused to fully break cover but acknowledged he was 'involved in discussions, and that's all I really want to say at this stage. I know the fans are anxious – that's why we are trying to sort something out quickly, but these things take time.'

Few people beyond Scotland had heard the name Larry Gillick before he'd been pictured in the posh seats at White Hart Lane during the quarter-final. In truth, few people had heard of him north of the border either. Suddenly, however, he was thrust into the spotlight as the financier of the £20 million takeover that offered hope of Venables and Gascoigne remaining inside the Tottenham Hotspur big top.

If solid information was scarce, there was a surfeit of speculation. Who was Gillick? And how did he come to have £20 million spare to buy Spurs? Intriguingly, boxing promoter and Arsenal box-holder Frank Warren was identified as the interlocutor. Warren had been enduring the roughest of rough patches. In 1987, he'd launched the 12,500-capacity London Arena in Docklands. Following its opening two years later, Luciano Pavarotti and Frank Sinatra were among those to perform there. The problem was that the drawing power of such stellar names was offset by the cost of refitting the arena to comply with safety recommendations arising from the Bradford City stadium fire and Hillsborough. Furthermore, the dismal transport links to the Isle of Dogs did little to recommend the venue to audiences. With interest rates rocketing, debts began to spiral. Warren needed funds to refinance the venture.

Warren's timing couldn't have been worse. In late November 1989, he arrived in Barking to attend a boxing show he was promoting. As he alighted from his chauffeur-driven car, a man in a balaclava shot him in the chest. Despite losing half of his lung, Warren survived. One of his former fighters, Terry Marsh, was charged with the crime but was acquitted following a trial at the Old Bailey. Journalist Lynn Barber, who attended the trial as a fascinated observer, later wrote, 'The defence strategy was to say: "Look, there are all sorts of people who might want to kill Frank Warren for the following reasons," and they were so convincing that by the end you expected to see rows of rival hitmen jostling for a chance to pick him off.' Aside from nearly costing Warren his life, the assassination attempt was a calamity for the London Arena. As Warren once memorably remarked, 'That bullet cost me £14 million ... because banks don't like it if you get shot.' That's why he was forced to seek alternative sources of capital.

Enter 44-year-old Larry Gillick, operating out of a well-appointed Harley Street office while heading up Occidental Financial and Holdings. Warren and Gillick embarked upon negotiations over a £20 million sale and lease-back deal for the London Arena.[14] Warren suggested to Venables that Gillick

---

14 Gillick proved incapable of bailing out Frank Warren. The London Arena went into receivership in May 1991. A subsequent investigation by the DTI saw Warren banned from being a company director for seven years.

might be worth sounding out about a similar rescue package for Spurs. In his first autobiography, Venables describes Gillick as a 'genuine football man'. No doubt this was a nod to Gillick's illustrious ancestry. Larry's father Torry was a free-scoring winger who, having won league titles with Rangers and Everton before the outbreak of World War Two, was considered one of the finest British players of his generation. Gillick Junior had been a promising footballer himself. He'd reportedly trained with Rangers reserves before inheriting his father's scrap metal business. From there, he entered the world of 'property deals', an opaque cocoon where many businessmen metamorphosed into 'respectability'.

Irving Scholar's first impression was not favourable. Writing of Gillick, this was his assessment: 'He resembled an out-of-work gangster. Everything from his clothes to his looks suggested that. The dark suit, white shirt, bright fish tie, the very portly, thick-set appearance with shortish crinkling hair and a thinning, receding hairline.' However, such reservations were set aside as Scholar and Paul Bobroff considered the Gillick/Venables proposal, which was being championed by Tony Berry. An anodyne statement confirmed, 'The board of Tottenham Hotspur PLC announce that an approach has been received which may or may not lead to an offer being made for the whole of the issued share capital of the company.' Behind the scenes, Scholar was driving a hard bargain. He set three conditions for the sale of his shares:

- The retention of Gascoigne
- Evidence the consortium would have funds to build the team
- A fair price for shareholders (Gillick was asked to up his offer from 90p per share to 95p)

Scholar seemingly kept Harry Harris fully apprised of negotiations. Harris continued to cast Scholar in the best possible light, peppering his copy in *The Mirror* with reminders that Scholar was a 'lifelong Tottenham fan' and acting in the 'best interests of the club'. Venables and Gillick weren't to be outdone in the battle for hearts and minds. Word reached the press of their intention to make Bill Nicholson life vice-president.

On 15 March, *The Mirror*'s back page proclaimed 'SPURS ARE SOLD'. This apparent salvation was all the sweeter for Spurs fans because, according to Harris, 'On the insistence of outgoing Spurs chairman Irving Scholar, a world-record bid of £8.5 million by Lazio of Rome for Paul Gascoigne was thrown out yesterday.'

But the headline proved premature. While Brown Shipley, the club's new financial adviser, verified the receipt of a formal bid, proof of the consortium's funds was, as yet, unforthcoming. David Buchler casts his mind back to that time. 'I vividly remember a meeting where Tony Berry kept saying over and over to Larry Gillick "show me the money, show me the money, show me the money".'

Those in the Tottenham boardroom were understandably twitchy. It was less than two years since Manchester United chairman Martin Edwards had been left embarrassed by the Michael Knighton affair. Edwards had accepted a bid for his shares from Knighton – whose origin story bore more than a passing resemblance to Gillick's. Things had been allowed to go so far that Knighton had even been permitted to indulge in a spot of full-kitted keepy-uppy in front of the Stretford End before his inability to pay his way was exposed.

Worse still, newspapers in Scotland had started to do some digging. Gillick – one-time owner of a fleet of Rolls-Royces, two Jaguar coupes and two Mercedes saloons – looked an increasingly unpromising proposition. He'd relocated to London after being made bankrupt at Glasgow Sheriff Court following an 'injudicious property development'. Injudicious is perhaps a mild adjective to describe a greyhound stadium venture that went bust without running a single race and had the subsequent misfortune of being damaged in a fire. The *Daily Record*, dedicating a front page to 'THE CASH

SECRET OF SHY TYCOON', quoted Gillick's brother Billy as saying, 'I have no idea how Larry is doing this Spurs deal. I have not a clue where the money is coming from.'

Intriguingly, Gillick intimated to the Tottenham board that he was fronting the deal on behalf of the rulers of Abu Dhabi – a full 17 years before their investment in Manchester City irrevocably stratified English football – as Sheikh Zayed bin Sultan Al Nahyan wanted to keep a low profile. Yet how serious any Middle Eastern interest in Spurs was is debatable. It certainly seems to have cooled quickly. Even after renegotiating his offer downwards, Gillick proved incapable of supplementing promises with pound notes. Venables attempted to intervene and buy Gillick more time, briefing the press that if the consortium's bid failed, 'The future of the club won't be too good, and that's putting it mildly.' Asked if this meant receivership, he replied, 'You'll have to draw your own conclusions.'

Despite this sober warning, matters came to a head when a deadline imposed on Gillick by Brown Shipley came and went. 'The board has received certain limited information on these matters from the offerer's financial advisers but has not received the detailed assurances and information which it requires ... the board has therefore terminated discussions with the proposed offerer and its advisers.'

Such a clean break seemed unlikely, given that one of the 'offerers' was still responsible for trying to field a winning team! A task that, in the First Division, was proving increasingly difficult. A day on from the board's statement, Spurs played out a dour 0-0 draw with QPR to extend a run of form that yielded a paltry two wins from 14 league games. The only excitement stirred in the White Hart Lane press box during the match was caused when Venables left the dugout midway through the second half and headed up the tunnel. Rumour quickly spread among journalists that he'd quit on the spot, and Scholar had gone too. David Lacey joked in his match report, 'Given the club's debt of £18 million, we knew he could not have gone to spend a penny.' But the unfolding 'scoop' was squashed when Venables reappeared a few minutes later.

Gary Lineker made it clear in a post-match interview that the febrility of the boardroom was now infecting the dressing room. 'Players are not stupid. We are aware that something is going on. The whole thing is a hell of a mess. Nobody knows what is really going to happen. That is bound to put doubts into people's minds. The sooner it is resolved, the better for everybody. The players are sad about the mess the club has got itself into.'

Venables quickly deployed his rare gift as a communicator to rally the Tottenham fanbase behind him and firm up his flagging consortium. There's no doubt he could do wisdom and wit with the best of them. 'I was very surprised by the board's statement on Friday … I still can't see why there has to be a deadline … What I'm trying to do is vital to the club's survival. I've never known anything like it, it's been murder … I've never worked so hard in my life. The crowd wants something to be done. It's bad for the players and for the supporters. There's 100 years of history here, and people are concerned.' His rejoinder to one reporter's attempt to pin him down with the killer question, 'Have you got the £20 million?' nearly brought the house down. 'No, not on me, no. But I can assure you we have it.'

Outflanked by Venables and unable to break the stalemate between Scholar and the PLC board, the pressure on Nat Solomon to satisfy the Midland Bank intensified. The self-tagged 'Listening Bank' had had its fill. They wanted £8 million wiped off the debt before the semi-final. What's more at their insistence, Tottenham Hotspur PLC was forced humiliatingly to apply for an extension of its overdraft facilities at fortnightly intervals, accruing a £50,000 charge each time for the privilege. And that wasn't the end of the indignity. Crystal Palace reported Tottenham to the Football League for welching on £31,905 due to the Eagles in ticket sales.

The situation had become so desperate that agents reportedly acting on behalf of the club had sounded out AC Milan owner Silvio Berlusconi. If they hoped he'd be discreet they were left doubly disappointed. Martin Samuel quoted the garrulous Italian in *The Sun*: 'Representatives of Tottenham contacted me and wanted me to buy the whole club with the stadium included. The price and conditions were £10m in cash with a further £10m to pay off the bank overdraft ... I was very flattered, but I have enough on my hands running Milan.'

With Milan a bust, the eternal city looked the board's best bet. Lazio president Gianmarco Calleri gladly accepted an invitation to meet Solomon and Scholar in London, and even amid Spurs' vapid official denials, confirmed to the Italian press that Gascoigne would be playing his football in Rome next season. His surgery had done nothing to temper Lazio fans' excitement. For a match against Cagliari, the Curva Nord – home to the club's *Irriducibili* ultras – was decorated with a giant illustration of a frothing pint glass accompanied by warm words of welcome, 'IT'S READY FOR YOU GAZZA'.

As fate would have it, the surge of excitement about Gascoigne's rising star in Italy now intersected with Maradona's sorry, rather squalid decline. That same weekend, the Argentinian tested positive for cocaine ahead of Napoli's fixture with Bari. The ensuing 15-month ban curtailed his captivating Serie A career and ended his undisputed reign as the world's finest player.

Chapter Eleven

The North London Cup

FINDING SANCTUARY in the Portakabins of Tottenham's Mill Hill base, Paul Gascoigne stoically blocked out the incessant chatter swirling around him about the gilded future awaiting him away from north London. Instead, all his frenetic energy was thrown into defying the odds in order to be passed fit to play against Arsenal. The unanimous verdict of football writers and fans alike was that for Spurs to stand any chance, Gascoigne had to play. 'Paul worked so hard to try and make it,' recalls physio John Sheridan. 'We knew if he was going to be there, he needed a run-out before the semi-final. Our target was the league game at Norwich in the midweek before Wembley. I remember counting it was three weeks and six days between his double hernia operation and Carrow Road.' Regular briefings from the club to the press downplayed his prospects: '50/50' and 'doubtful' were the party line.

Sheridan smiles at memories of football's much-practised art of misdirection. 'It's funny the tricks you'd get up to. That was all part of the game. If a player had a knee injury that the opposition knew about, sometimes you'd strap the other knee up!' So well-guarded was news of Gascoigne's progress that even those frequenting the boardroom were left guessing. David Buchler recalls attending a league match at White Hart Lane shortly before the semi-final, with his then-girlfriend. For the purposes of the story, he makes clear that she was a beautiful, well-spoken woman. 'We walked into the West Stand and were getting the lift up to our seats. By chance, Gazza was coming the other way, and she politely enquired, "Mr Gascoigne, how's your groin?" Just as the lift doors closed, Gazza grinned and replied, "All the better for seeing you, pet!"'

Gascoigne was not the only player who'd pinpointed Carrow Road as a staging post for a high-noon comeback at Wembley. Following his knee and jaw surgeries, David Howells was back in training. 'It was great to have the target of Arsenal. I'd been willing the lads through each round, and Gazza and I rushed back from our operations. We were probably pushing miles ahead of where we should have been in our rehab, but I couldn't miss out. Terry already had his plan for Arsenal. And he told me my role in the team if I got through Norwich. I knew I couldn't hold anything back at Carrow Road, and I think I played the full 90 minutes there, which gave me a real confidence boost even though we lost 2-1.'

Sheridan can still feel the tension of that night in East Anglia. 'I was working as the consultant physio by then, so I was based at Mill Hill rather than travelling to away games with the team. But for Norwich, Terry said, "You'd better come with us, John." I told him, "Paul needs to play the first half, and then if he's ok, he can have another quarter of an hour at the most, but then he's got to come off." I sat in the stand watching the game with my son. Gazza was getting visibly stronger as the match went on, and by half-time, he was buzzing. When he came out for the second half and was straight back into it, I'd seen all I needed to know he'd be fit for Wembley. But then the minutes were ticking by, and I started to worry that they wouldn't take him off. I raced down to the bench and asked Terry and Dave [Butler, the physio who travelled with the team], "What's going on?" Terry said to me, "He's doing fine." So, I grabbed the board with the number 8 to hold it up for a substitution. "Listen, Terry," I said, "If you want him fit for the semi, get him off now. This game isn't important." Thankfully, that's what happened.'

Gascoigne, captain for the night of a side comprised of reserve players and young prospects like goalkeeper Ian Walker and forward John Hendry (scorer of the Spurs goal), left the field to hearty applause from both sets of fans. Canaries manager Dave Stringer reflected the abiding sentiment. 'A lot has been said about Gazza's clowning. I wish Norwich and England had 11 clowns like him. The man is brilliant.'

That Gascoigne had come away from Carrow Road unscathed had a transformative impact on Tottenham's *esprit de corps*. 'It gave us such a huge lift,' reflects Vinny Samways. 'A fit Gazza enhances any team, whoever you're playing against.' Paul Walsh expresses the sentiment in much starker terms. 'Without Gazza, we were never going to beat Arsenal.' An irrefutable belief that the Arsenal players were all too aware of.

George Graham moved quickly to downplay the Gazza effect. Speaking with the air of a man who'd suspected Gascoigne would line up against his team all along, he said, 'He'll play against us without a question. Now that he's going to be in, he'll be a factor in my selection and team tactics. I always do my homework on the opposition, but the important thing is to get our game in order. And if we play like I know we can, whatever system they play will be immaterial.' It may have sounded like hubris, but Graham's claim was built upon solid ground. With five games remaining, Arsenal sat five points clear at the First Division's summit. This lead would have been seven but for a two-point deduction imposed after December's 'Battle of Old Trafford' – a match where the Gunners had demonstrated literally that they'd scrap it out for the title against all comers.

Behind this bravado, however, Gascoigne loomed large over Graham's thoughts. In the week of the match, at Arsenal's London Colney training headquarters, Graham gathered his squad around him. Players so used to being dictated to – the nickname 'Gaddafi' given to Graham by John Lukic in the early days of his autocratic Arsenal rule had well and truly stuck – were spooked to find their boss taking a collegiate approach. Gunners striker Alan Smith recalls the scene in his autobiography: '"Lads, I want to know what you think." Straight away, this was unusual. Normally, the gaffer couldn't give a monkey's about our opinion ... "I'm wondering whether we should man-mark Gazza, get someone to follow him wherever he goes." This, too, was virtually unprecedented. I couldn't remember the last time he had even considered such drastic action, never mind implemented it.'

Aside from subscribing to the well-worn 'wisdom' that form had little bearing on the outcome of derby matches, another explanation as to why, from such a position of strength, Graham fretted about the opposition was his bond with Terry Venables. Jonathan Pearce, who grew close to both men while working at Capital Gold, explains: 'It was unique that relationship they had between a Tottenham and Arsenal manager. I can't envisage how it could ever happen again.' The connection could be traced back to their playing days in the early 1960s, when they were young team-mates at Stamford Bridge. Both had graduated to lift silverware as players in north London – Venables was part of the Spurs side that beat Chelsea 2-1 in the 1967 FA Cup Final. Famously in September of that year, he was best man when Graham was married at Marylebone registry office, even though four hours after the nuptials had been completed the pair lined up against each other in the north London derby at Highbury. Arsenal romped home 4-0.

Venables made Graham one of his first signings as a manager at Crystal Palace and when Graham called time on his playing career it was Venables who convinced him to take up coaching and gave him his start with the Palace youth ranks. Indeed, it was Venables's tutelage of the offside trap – drilling the back four by tethering them to each other with a rope on the training pitch to synchronise their movements –

that Graham had stultifyingly perfected with Messrs Dixon, Adams, Bould and Winterburn. If anyone could find the combination to unlock Arsenal, Graham could count on it being his old mate.[15]

Remarkably on the eve of the game – given their dire league form and grave quotes in the press that morning from Venables, stating, 'We're in a bigger spot than any club in history' and that trophy talk was 'ridiculous when we're in the hole we are' – optimism abounded among the Spurs players as they checked into the Royal Lancaster Hotel near Hyde Park. They were in for a long night. Paul Gascoigne was bouncing off the walls.

Word had reached the Tottenham players that their Arsenal counterparts were expectantly decluttering their mantelpieces to make room for an FA Cup medal. The incendiary effect was immediate. Paul Stewart recalls the first of two fantastical rumours: 'I can't remember where it came from but we'd heard Arsenal had already recorded their cup final song. I remember being really angry – I've got absolutely no idea if there is any truth in it, by the way, but it definitely wound us up.'

Spurs fan Willie Morgan, whose career as a record promotions man had led him to become the stadium announcer at both White Hart Lane and Highbury by 1991, is well placed to dispel the myth. (He's keen to stress that he only took the job with Arsenal because he was going through a costly divorce and 'needed to earn money wherever I could'.) 'There was certainly no Arsenal record made. I would have heard of that in my professional capacity.'

Morgan can uniquely attest to the motivational power of a perceived disrespectful slight. The last time Spurs and Arsenal had faced off in a semi-final had been in the 1987 League Cup, which was settled via a replay at White Hart Lane. With Tottenham 1-0 up at half-time and no other time to broadcast

---

15 To the surprise of many, when Highbury's refurbished Clock End was opened ahead of the north London derby in January 1989, Venables accompanied Graham in performing the unveiling ceremony.

ticket arrangements for the final, Morgan was asked to read a note from the club secretary over the tannoy telling Spurs fans how to buy their Wembley tickets. 'I remember saying to him, "I can't do this, it's ridiculous. I'll get slaughtered if we now lose." But I was given no choice.' The story goes that Arsenal winger Perry Groves, who wasn't playing in the match, heard the announcement and headed straight for the dressing rooms to let his team-mates know that Spurs were taking liberties. Inevitably, Arsenal came back to win the match, with virtually the last kick of the game. 'Mea culpa,' says Morgan, 'but it was definitely done under severe coercion.'

Four years on, as if the alleged premature cup final song recording wasn't enough to fan the derby flames in the Tottenham camp, such was Arsenal's supposed arrogance, their squad were said to have been measured for their cup final suits. Or so the Spurs players were willingly encouraged to believe. 'I hated them,' says Stewart playfully. 'Still do! Coming from Manchester, I didn't really appreciate the intensity of the rivalry but as soon as I got to north London it was drummed into me: you have to beat Arsenal.'

Nayim was another outsider who'd come to embrace the parochial passion of the derby. 'We had players in the first team [David Howells, Steve Sedgley and Vinny Samways] who were Spurs supporters as kids. It was like at La Masia when I was young, playing for Barcelona against Real Madrid. You felt it the whole week before any game with them. But the semi-final, of course, it was even more.'

Erik Thorstvedt recalls his early indoctrination. 'I remember being told by the club when I signed that I could never buy a red car. I was bloody nervous before the semi-final. While it was about us getting to the final, Arsenal were winning the league, so it was also about stopping them from doing the double. I've spoken to so many fans since who say that's what they really cared about.'

So where had the song and suit rumours come from? Stewart's best guess is the manager. 'Maybe it was Terry being a bit clever.' Howells agrees that Venables was the likely culprit. 'Yeah, it was probably Terry just putting it out there and mucking about. He could be a bit mischievous like that. Listen, I don't think we really believed it. They wouldn't have been daft enough to do anything like that. But maybe, subconsciously, it helped.'

There is no confession in either of Venables's autobiographies. Tellingly, though, he does recount a story from early on in his coaching career while working under Malcolm Allison at Third Division Crystal Palace. During Palace's run to the FA Cup semi-final in 1976, the team were on the train when the fourth-round draw was made. Allison observed a fan approaching the carriage whose gloomy expression suggested Palace had been given a tough assignment. [Mighty Leeds United of the First Division, away.] Venables and Allison quickly cooked up a plot. When the supporter told the assembled Palace squad the outcome of the draw, Venables jumped from his seat. Punching the air, he spuriously told the Palace players how Elland Road had always been a lucky ground for him. The unfancied Eagles went on to win the game 1-0.

Perhaps he was trying a similar shtick in 1991 and identified the perfect vessel for delivery. Days before the semi-final, the *Daily Mirror* had attributed the following quote to one Paul Gascoigne: 'I've heard a few things that Arsenal have been up to lately, and once I tell the lads what's been happening, I am sure they will be fired up for this game.'

In the posh Royal Lancaster Hotel, the fire was in danger of burning itself out. As the hour drew late and the players became keen to head for their beds, Gascoigne remained implacably hyped. He was eventually sedated at 11pm following the intervention of the team doctor, who administered an injection to, as Terry Venables later put it, 'knock Gazza out' and 'let him and the rest of us get some sleep'.

With the players down for the night, John Sheridan, exhausted from the strain of nursing Gascoigne and Howells back to fitness, decided to relax with a well-earned glass of red at the hotel bar. Sheridan picks up the story. 'As I get up, out of this Georgian chair – being the Royal Lancaster all the furniture was fancy – the whole arm falls off. I thought no one was watching, so I banged it back in on its dowels. The next morning, at the pre-match meal before we head off to Wembley, Terry is about to give his team talk.

'Just as he's ready to start, the hotel manager comes in. He was a posh-looking guy, dickie-bow and everything. He's carrying an envelope and says, "Mr Sheridan, this is for you." I open it, and it's a bill for the chair. I'm trying to be discreet and quietly tell him, "Can I square this up later?" but he's not having any of it. The players are, by now, all over me, "What have you got there John?", that sort of thing. One of them then says, "Oh dear, we'll have to have a whip-round for John." I've gone bright red. I can see Terry Venables staring at me. It's my absolute worst nightmare. Then, after what felt like ages, I clock Roy Reyland quietly grinning in the corner. It turned out he'd seen the chair come apart the night before and put the hotel manager up to it. It was a brilliant stitch-up. Terry was laughing, and I think it helped break some of the tension everybody was feeling.'

Moments of levity were scarce for Penny and Terry Deller as they made the short trip, like 80,000 others, across north London to Brent. 'I'd been pleased when Wembley was chosen,' says Penny. 'My first thought was we'd easily get tickets because unlike the final there wouldn't be loads of corporates and dignitaries. We'd queued for hours to get them. But then travelling there and seeing all those Arsenal fans, the reality dawned on me. When you live where we do absolutely everyone is either Spurs or Arsenal. So the thought of facing their fans if we lost – especially as they knew they'd be going on to win the league – was unbearable. There was no way we were going to enjoy it.'

'I didn't sleep the night before,' says Terry, 'I was feeling so sick at the prospect of them doing the double. That was the big thing. We'd both done it once and I just couldn't be having them doing it again.'

Broadcaster Danny Kelly sensed that sentiment extended to neutral fans. 'In those days the double was still an extraordinarily rare event. That Arsenal team was accelerating to the title and was expected to win the game fairly handily. Lots of people across the country wanted Spurs to stop it happening.'

Jonathan Pearce, who was at Wembley providing radio commentary, remembers the occasion 'for London football' as being 'like when *Eastenders* does a Christmas special. You had everything there. Terry and George, Gazza, the Arsenal back four ... just wonderful. Chris Tarrant, who had millions of listeners to Capital's breakfast show was cutting in clips from our commentaries to build up to the game. I think that was the first time that happened for a club game. It was the biggest football match since Italia 90 and the build-up was feverish. Getting there on the day, it felt like a cup final occasion, and there was never any danger of there being any trouble.'

Football writer and Arsenal aficionado Jon Spurling, a student at the time, remembers setting off for Wembley from Hertfordshire. 'The trains were utterly rammed but I seem to remember the atmosphere being a good one.' That's Steve Davies's recollection too. 'There'd been some violence when we'd played Arsenal in the late Seventies. But when you get that number of fans, fortunately, it dampens it down. There are 40,000 of us and 40,000 of them so I don't remember there being any real prospect of hooliganism.' The spiciest it got on Wembley Way was a brief exchange of droppings, scooped up from behind the police horses and 'playfully' used as projectiles.

In the cavernous Wembley dressing rooms, Paul Gascoigne picked straight up where he'd left off the night before. Venables describes the scene in his book: 'Gascoigne was so hyped up going from player to player that I could hardly get a word in. I was talking but he was drowning me out and I didn't need to do any motivation on the team because Gazza did it all for me. I could not have got a word

Happier times. Irving Scholar welcomes Terry Venables to White Hart Lane in 1987

PRE-MATCH MEAL REQUIREMENTS

	SATURDAY	MID WEEK
P ALLEN	Roast Chicken	
NAYIM	Lasagne	
G BERGSSON	Spaghetti Bolognese	
K DEARDEN	Ham & Mushroom Omlette	Roast Chicken
J EDINBURGH	Roast Chicken	
M EDWARDS	Cheese Omlette	
T FENWICK	Dover Sole	
P GARLAND	Breast of Chicken	
P GASCOIGNE	Lasagne (and cornflakes)	
I GILZEAN	Cheese Omlette	
P GRAY	Roast Chicken	
I HENDON	Lasagne	
J HENDRY	Roast Chicken	
S HOUGHTON	Plain omlette & baked beans	
P VAN DEN HAUWE	Beans on Toast	Spaghetti Bolognese
D HOWELLS	Macaroni Cheese	
G LINEKER	Spaghetti Bolognese	
G MABBUTT	Ham & Cheese Omlette	Roast Chicken
D McDONALD	Fish in Breadcrumbs	
J MONCUR	Roast Chicken	
P MORAN	Lasagne	
A POLSTON	Ham & Cheese Omlette	
M ROBSON	Roast Chicken	
V SAMWAYS	Plain omlette (& Baked beans)	
S SEDGLEY	Lasagne	
K SMITH	Eggs on toast	spaghetti bolognese
N SMITH	Breast of Chicken	
B STATHAM	Roast chicken	
P STEWART	Lasagne	
M THOMAS	Plain omlette & baked beans	Spaghetti bolognese
E THORSTVEDT	Mixed sandwiches	spaghetti bolognese
D TUTTLE	Breast of Chicken	
P WALSH	Roast Chicken	
I WALKER	~~Beans on toast~~ Roast chicken	

STAFF:	TV	Roast Chicken
	DOUG	Roast Chicken
	ROY	Roast Chicken
	DAVE	Roast Chicken
	JOHN	Dover Sole (off the bone)
	CLEM	Fillet Steak (medium)
	PB	Fillet Steak (well done)
	DOC	Dover Sole

Anyone for lasagne and cornflakes? The squad's pre-match meals in 1990/91 (Courtesy of Tottenham Hotspur Archive with thanks to Sian Allpress and the OOF Gallery)

Neither the 70mph wind nor the Blackpool defence can stop Gascoigne on third round weekend

Gascoigne's two goals against Oxford turned a fourth round cul-de-sac into an FA Cup highway

Gascoigne's 'human missile' header against Portsmouth in front of the Spurs fans in round five

Erik Thorstvedt to the rescue vs Notts County

Best mates. Venables and George Graham share a laugh before Wembley's first-ever semi-final

'Is Gascoigne going to have a crack? He is you know'

Jumping for joy after 'the best ever' free kick at Wembley

Gary Lineker territory – the striker prods home Spurs' second in the semi-final

Paul Stewart restrains Gascoigne against Arsenal as north london derby passions boil over

'And David Seaman will be very disappointed with that!' The Arsenal keeper is consoled by Gary Lewin and David Rocastle

We're off to Wembley 'cos we beat the Arsenal

The Tottenham Independent Supporters' Association calls for action (courtesy of Annelise Jespersen)

in edgeways even if I wanted to … I do not think I have ever seen a player so hyped up for any game. The other boys caught the fever from him, and we were really flying in that dressing room like nothing I had seen before.'

Roy Reyland remembers watching on in awe. 'Gazza was circling the table that was in the middle of the room screaming at each of the boys, "C'mon, we've got to do these lot." I remember Terry trying to tell him a few times to sit down and be quiet, but he had no chance. In the end, he gave up and said, "Just all bloody kick it the same way!"'

As the two teams lined up in the tunnel, the Arsenal players were taken aback by the intensity of the battle cries from those in white and, as they made their way on to the pitch, more than a little confused by the principal attack line of the Spurs trash-talk. 'I remember Paul Stewart saying to them, "What are your suits like? What colour are they?"' chuckles John Sheridan. Alan Smith recollects Gascoigne was just as vocal, though as he records in his book, 'We didn't know what he was talking about.'

Teamsheet
Wembley Stadium
Sunday, 14 April 1991

Arsenal	Tottenham Hotspur
Colours: red and white shirts, white shorts, red socks	Colours: white shirts, navy shorts, white socks
1. David Seaman	1. Erik Thorstvedt
2. Lee Dixon	2. Justin Edinburgh
3. Nigel Winterburn	3. Pat Van Den Hauwe
4. Michael Thomas	4. Steve Sedgley
5. Steve Bould	5. David Howells
6. Tony Adams	6. Gary Mabbutt
7. Kevin Campbell	7. Paul Stewart
8. Paul Davis	8. Paul Gascoigne
9. Alan Smith	9. Vinny Samways
10. Paul Merson	10. Gary Lineker
11. Anders Limpar	11. Paul Allen
(Subs)	(Subs)
12. David O'Leary	12. Paul Walsh
14. Perry Groves	14. Nayim

'There was a rumour on the morning of the game that Gazza wasn't fit,' says Jon Spurling. 'So it was a bit of a downer from an Arsenal perspective to see him come out on to the pitch. These were the days before fat-shaming was frowned upon – even Jimmy Greaves would call him "Fat Boy Bamber" on *Saint and Greavsie*. He was getting loads of stick from the Arsenal fans – "Give us your Mars bar" and stuff about his girlfriend. Not very mature or something to have pride in.

'David Hillier suffered a nasty gash on his leg against Southampton midweek leading up to the game. He's not a player who'll live long in many people's memories, but he was a good tracker. Had he been fit I think George Graham would have put him on Gascoigne instead of Michael Thomas. That said, and being totally honest, as the game got underway, I couldn't see any reason why we wouldn't win and go on and do the double.'

The last time Spurs contested an FA Cup semi-final, in 1987, they'd faced a goalkeeper in Watford's Gary Plumley making his one and only appearance for the club. Having retired from football, Plumley was managing a wine bar in Wales when his dad, the Watford chief executive, got on the phone. Due to a goalkeeping injury crisis at Vicarage Road, the only solution for the Hornets, given that the transfer deadline had passed, was to sign the rusty keeper as an unattached free agent. The story goes that after letting in four goals to Spurs, he spent his semi-final appearance fee on a new fridge for his business. Arsenal's David Seaman – firmly establishing himself as the best goalkeeper in the First Division – posed an entirely different prospect. The England international had conceded the absurdly miserly tally of 14 goals in 33 league games.

'He was in incredible form,' testifies Spurling. 'That was the best Arsenal team I'd seen, perfectly built for the early 1990s. They weren't beloved by outsiders – always in referees' faces and the offside trap of the legendary back four. But we adored them. The midfield was very adept. Alan Smith was in outstanding form up top, with Paul Merson a brilliant foil for him. And, for the first half of the season, Anders Limpar had been as good as anyone in the country.'

'They were an incredible team,' says David Howells. 'But we fancied it anyway. We'd drawn 0-0 with them in both the league games that season. At White Hart Lane, David Seaman had had one of those days where he'd saved everything, but we'd battered them. So we kicked off the semi with a lot of confidence. Terry had been planning how we could beat them for ages, and we all knew our roles inside out. The plan was to negate their full-backs, who created a lot of goals for them.'

Venables had been sedulously studying videos of Arsenal and deployed Howells on the left of midfield with Paul Allen on the right. They were instructed to start from deep and draw Lee Dixon and Nigel Winterburn on to them, disrupting the unity of Arsenal's impregnable back four and allowing their team-mates to exploit the space created in behind. The satisfaction is apparent in Howells's voice all these years later. 'It worked to a T.'

No sooner had referee Ray Lewis – in a delightful piece of nominative determinism hailing from Great Bookham – blown for the kick-off, than Spurs tore into Arsenal at a ferocious pace. Gary Lineker – rejuvenated having been sent by Venables on a sunshine break to Tenerife in preparation for Arsenal – looked full of running in the lone striker role. Within two minutes he'd harried Winterburn into a mistake on the touchline and then slipped Allen through with a delicate lay-off. Allen's progress was only halted by a desperate last-ditch tackle by Tony Adams. Gascoigne seized upon the loose ball, shooting narrowly wide from an unpromising angle.

The verbal barrage he aimed at the linesman, who'd had the temerity to raise his flag, was indicative of the adrenaline coursing through his body. It was about to surge to unprecedented levels. In the fourth minute, Paul Stewart tried to spin one with the outside of his boot to Howells on the left wing. The pass cleared Howells's head and flew out of play, but Mr Lewis had blown for a Limpar foul on Stewart. A conservative estimate would mark the infringement as taking place 30–35 yards from Seaman's goal. David Howells takes up the story.

'I heard the referee's whistle so I went to retrieve the ball and kind of spotted it up for Gazza, so it's almost like an assist for me! Gazza started fiddling about with the ball and I asked him, "What are you going to do?" and he said "I don't know," so I told him "Just smash it." So it's definitely my assist when you think about it! If you look at a replay, Gary Lineker also jogged back and asked Gazza "What's the plan?" He told him to smash it too.'

Having paced backwards from the dead ball, Gascoigne began a run-up so long it would have enabled a 747 sufficient time to take off and clear the Wembley crossbar. Fortunately, it also afforded BBC commentator Barry Davies the chance to formulate a burst of words destined to become immortal as the Tottenham number 8 bore down on the ball. 'Is Gascoigne going to have a crack? He is, you know … Oh, I say, brilliant! That is Schoolboys' Own stuff!!'[16]

Roy Reyland laughs uproariously as he recalls the rapidly evolving dialogue on the Spurs bench. 'I was sat one along from the gaffer. As Gazza puts the ball down, Terry is shouting "Don't shoot, don't shoot, don't shoooo … Great goal Gazza!"' Nayim beams as he recalls his view from the side of the pitch. 'When Gazza took it, I thought that's normal for Paul, no problem. That happened every day in training! It was the same as what it must be like for Messi's team-mates who get to watch him all the time doing these things … What a free kick, blooming hell. Gazza was a genius. Different class.'

Gascoigne barely broke stride as his right-footed shot arrowed into the top corner of Seaman's net. He was off on

---

16 It's worth noting Davies is a Spurs fan, although he worked very hard to downplay his allegiances throughout his illustrious commentary career to avoid accusations of bias.

an ecstatic tear to the side of the pitch, his feet seemingly disconnected from terra firma. Vinny Samways was the first to give joyful chase. 'I don't have a clue what the words coming out of his mouth were but I could just hear him screaming … It never crossed my mind he was going to shoot. It was a worldie. To score from there was ridiculous.'

Venables later revealed what Gascoigne had been saying as he wheeled away. 'As he reached the bench, Gazza put his arms around my neck and laughed in my ear: "The silly bastard only tried to save it, didn't he!"' Seaman for his part told his team-mates on the pitch that his attempt to keep it out – he'd got fingertips on the ball – had been encumbered by his studs getting caught in the ground. A likely story.

He was soon extracting the ball from his net a second time. A series of meaty challenges had ensured there was no plateau in the ferocious pace of the play nor the noise cascading down from the stands as the game entered its tenth breathless minute. Stewart jigged past Paul Davis in the shallows of the Arsenal half, before sliding a pass wide to Gascoigne, who'd crept into space on the right. He played a delicious one-two-three with Allen – both of Gascoigne's insouciant touches delivered first-time. Allen scampered toward the byline and fizzed a low ball across the face of goal, which Alan Smith – who'd retreated in defence of an earlier free kick – could only divert into the middle of the six-yard box. Or as it was known in 1991, Gary Lineker territory. There he was, uncoiling a tanned leg, to toe it over the line: 2-0.

Arsenal's venerated defence was being annihilated. Annelise Jespersen recalls the unbridled celebrations in the Spurs half of the ground. 'I was hyperventilating after the second went in. I couldn't believe what was happening. I went with three guys, two of them were smoking – not cigarettes – and the other was on crutches. I couldn't tell you whether he managed to keep hold of them both. There were limbs everywhere.'

Indicative of how thoroughly the Arsenal players' brains had been scrambled by the Tottenham *blitzkrieg*, Dixon ploughed into two unhinged challenges on Justin Edinburgh and Howells, the latter drawing a yellow card from the referee and an acerbically disapproving 'Dear, dear' from Barry Davies: 'That really was an awful tackle from an international full-back.'

The only threat to Tottenham's supremacy lay in Gascoigne's volatility. Michael Thomas attempted to wrestle the ball from his grasp to take a quick free kick. Gascoigne's hackles were immediately up. Thankfully Paul Stewart was primed for such danger and snatched his team-mate away in a textbook full-nelson until his anger subsided. Even Pat Van Den Hauwe came over to preach restraint. Approaching the half-hour, Davies felt compelled to relay to viewers, 'Tottenham are on top in every area of the field at the moment … quicker to the ball, the defence hasn't been troubled. Their ideas are much more inventive. Arsenal, not to put too fine a point on it, are not really in this semi-final yet.'

Moments later Gascoigne dribbled around the toiling Dixon, who couldn't resist having a little nibble at his ankles. Gascoigne, embodying both bull and matador, rounded on him before dribbling past him again. 'That's one of my main memories of playing with Gazza,' says Erik Thorstvedt. 'He was at his peak and he'd have these personal battles with the other team's players – sometimes more than one at the same time. He'd receive the ball and you could actually see him waiting for someone to get close to him before he'd start to run with it. You'd see him running back and forth with the ball with these two guys around him trying to chase him down. It was as much about him showing the opposition "you can't touch me". I don't think you could do that in football today, but he could.'

Barry Davies was struggling for superlatives. He couldn't resist contrasting Tottenham's effervescent play to the thud and blunder of the recent Wembley international between Graham

Taylor's turgid England and Jack Charlton's unsophisticated Ireland. 'Well, in the light of the last match we saw at this stadium ... it's interesting to see a side proving that you can get players forward from midfield, it doesn't always have to be knocked long.'[17]

'Spurs have been a delight,' cooed Trevor Brooking. 'Knocking it through the midfield ... just shows we do have players capable of playing in that manner.' For all his foibles, here was Gascoigne – ably abetted by the outstanding Samways – being presented as the panacea for the British game's stylistic ills. The unspoken question was where would English football and the national team be without him?

With seconds remaining before the interval, it was a goal very much of the First Division's dominant style in its conception that pulled Arsenal back into the contest. Winterburn's long punt out of defence pinballed around players until Kevin Campbell brought it under control. He set back for Dixon to swing over an immediate deep cross. Smith towered above Gary Mabbutt and steered a fine header into the bottom corner. David Howells still chastises himself for not cutting off the supply. 'I couldn't quite get out to Dixon quick enough. I was knackered and just didn't have that little metre in me to affect the cross. I was a bit disappointed as that was my role, to snuff those situations out. You can't stop everything.' In the dressing room, Venables called for calm. 'We'd have taken 2-1 at half-time a few days ago, wouldn't we? So don't let your heads drop.'

Terry Deller sums up the abiding sentiment among the Spurs contingent in the Wembley stands as the second half got underway: 'I was absolutely shitting it.' Arsenal weren't messing about. Any and every opportunity was taken to pump high balls up to Smith and Campbell to use their height and power against the valiantly game Mabbutt and Sedgley. In

---

17 Adding to the dismay caused by the limitations of both nations' play were the 68 arrests made on a thoroughly depressing night for English football.

the 53rd minute, Sedgley denied Campbell a certain equaliser underneath the crossbar, diverting the ball with a telescopic left leg into Thorstvedt's relieved embrace just as the Arsenal striker cocked his foot to ram it in. Minutes later, Mabbutt and Campbell battled to get their heads on Dixon's hoick. Under severe pressure, the Tottenham captain couldn't get any distance on the ball and, to his evident horror, Winterburn had set off in anticipation. The galloping Arsenal left-back flicked the ball over Van Den Hauwe's attempted sliding tackle, and as it began to drop, nudged it on beyond the penalty spot with his head. Thorstvedt charged from his line, flinging himself courageously at Winterburn's feet. There was no prospect of him getting to the ball first, but his intervention forced Winterburn to try to lob the bouncing ball over the keeper's dive. His effort narrowly cleared the crossbar, but Venables recognised the need to stem the red tide.

As at Norwich, the fatigued Gascoigne was withdrawn with an hour played. Arsenal fan Jon Spurling with grudging humour acknowledges he'd witnessed greatness. 'I wouldn't bring myself to say I was pleased to have seen Gascoigne at his peak that day. But I do remember it well. Let's leave it at that!'

Nayim explains his mindset as he came on in Gascoigne's stead. 'I was nervous on the bench when Terry told me to get ready. It was my first time playing at Wembley. It was crazy to be playing there, all of its history. One of the most important stadiums in the world which I'd only ever seen on TV back home. But once I got the ball I calmed down and tried to play my football.'

Through Nayim and Samways, Spurs found a modicum of the control they'd had before Smith's goal. And with Gascoigne – now sat on the bench – finding his second wind, they had an unrelenting cheerleader roaring them on.

Mabbutt flattened substitute Perry Groves with a blockbuster tackle on the left corner of the Tottenham box that drew a cheer worthy of a goal. He then showed rare coolness amid the din to scoop the ball over Thomas, eliciting a purr from Barry Davies. Mabbutt's next contribution would tee up the commentator for another of his most celebrated soliloquies. Lineker surrendered possession dangerously in the centre circle. Momentarily, Paul Davis and Campbell looked menacingly primed until Edinburgh reclaimed the ball with a timely sliding challenge. Mabbutt took over, steering the ball on to Lineker, who immediately played it back to him before darting off into the space vacated by Davis. Mabbutt threaded a pass between two onrushing Arsenal players and suddenly Lineker was away. Cue Barry Davies. 'Nayim to the left. Samways ahead. And Lineker uses him by not using him ... Good try ... Scores! And David Seaman will be very disappointed with that, it seemed to go through his fingers.'

Lineker lay in exhausted ecstasy on the Wembley turf, arms outstretched, like a child making snow angels. Samways was again the first to reach the goalscorer, and soon Lineker's body disappeared beneath those of his team-mates. Samways's enduring memory of his all-important decoy run? 'That Wembley pitch was just outrageous. You know in your legs the next day that you've played at Wembley, that's for sure.'

Danny Kelly relishes repeating Davies's line 'And David Seaman will be very disappointed with that.' Not because he bears Seaman any ill will, far from it. But as the editor of the *NME* in April 1991 he was about to witness a synergy of his two great passions, Tottenham Hotspur Football Club and indie music. A supergroup called the Lillies comprising Spurs-supporting members of bands Lush, Moose and the Cocteau Twins released an original composition called 'And David Seaman Will Be Very Disappointed With That'. Aside from sampling Davies in full commentary flow, the only discernible vocal on the track is singer Miki Berenyi chanting 'Three-one'. 'I've still got the little flexi-disc,' says Kelly, 'which I treasure to this day.'

'It was only after the third went in that I allowed myself to think we might actually win this,' recalls Terry Deller. Not that Arsenal resigned themselves to their fate. With ten minutes remaining, Groves hurled a long throw into the Tottenham area. After various failed attempts to clear, Steve Bould headed the ball down to Campbell, who swivelled goalside of the penalty spot and blasted a shot against Thorstvedt's bar. And still Arsenal came. But for the Norwegian goalkeeper's excellent right-handed save from Campbell's low drive, the Tottenham fans' agonised longing for the final whistle might have proved intolerable. When referee Lewis finally granted their wish, Gascoigne and Venables immediately shared a passionate embrace. And then Gascoigne was off. Sprinting to each of his team-mates in turn and leaping with abandon into their arms.

By contrast, David Seaman cut a lonely figure, leaving the field in tears. He later described the ordeal as 'the semi-final I turned up for but never played in'. Erik Thorstvedt speaks in solidarity. 'I was friendly with David. I thought he was a really good guy and a top, top goalkeeper. I remember the next day hearing on the radio this joke: "What do Michael Jackson and David Seaman have in common? They both wear gloves for no apparent reason." That's the plight of us goalkeepers. It was so tough on him. Here's this incredible guy who'd done so well for them that year ... but he just had one of those days we all have.'

Paul Gascoigne was less conciliatory in his BBC post-match interview. Pointedly, given all the pre-game scuttlebutt, he told Ray Stubbs, 'I'm now away to get my suit measured ... YES.' Stubbs followed up with, 'What about your start to the game?' To which a gurning Gascoigne cheekily replied, 'It wasn't bad, was it? HEEE,' before running off. When he eventually found John Sheridan, he tenderly peeled the number 8 shirt – worn in scoring one of the most instantly iconic goals in Tottenham's history – from his back. It was a gift to the man who'd made his performance possible.

The shirt wasn't the only treasure born of Gascoigne's free kick. It later emerged the excitement of the goal had caused Spurs fan Joanna James to go into labour. New father David

Baker explained to the press how the couple's shortlist of baby names was immediately ripped up following the arrival of their 7lb 6oz son, Paul Gascoigne Baker.

A positively giddy Venables described Gascoigne's strike to Des Lynam as 'the best ever seen here … What can you say? He's the only guy capable of doing something as good as that … I'm very, very pleased for the supporters. You don't know how pleased I am. They've had a very difficult year with all the problems we've had … we're trying to sort it out [but] at least we know what's going on. With the supporters, it's the not knowing and I've felt for them. And it's something wonderful sometimes in life when you have all the problems we've had, the uncertainty and the grief that's involved, that something wonderful like this comes along and makes it very special.'

With media duties complete, the Tottenham players eventually reassembled on the pitch to share their triumph with the fans. They were garlanded with navy blue and white scarves and bobble hats that rained down from the stands. The Arsenal end was by now all but empty. Jon Spurling ruefully recalls the song he'd heard striking up among the Spurs support to send them on their way:

'You've lost that double feeling
Woah that double feeling
You've lost that double feeling
Now it's gone, gone, gone.'

Chapter Twelve

34th Time Lucky?

THE MIDDAY kick-off meant the night, or more accurately afternoon, was still young for those Tottenham players keen to extend their buzz. 'I remember we went back to White Hart Lane,' says David Howells, 'and the box holders' lounge was open. We watched the other semi-final and had a drink there. Maybe we carried on to Rudolph's next door [a 'legendary' no-frills but plenty of spills nightclub on Tottenham High Road]. I can't be sure. My knee had ballooned up, possibly not helped by the amount of beer we had … That was probably the best footballing day of my life.'

At a sun-drenched Villa Park, Tony Gale – lining up at the heart of the West Ham defence to face Nottingham Forest – was about to experience vastly different emotions.

Brian Clough had confounded expectations with his semi-final selection. Having taken all the shortcuts available to prove his fitness – including pain-killing injections and a reserve team run-out at Stockport – Steve Hodge had particular cause to feel slighted. At the team breakfast, Clough summarily announced that Ian Woan – who'd made just four first-team appearances since signing from the non-league – was in. England international Hodge hadn't even made the bench.

'Later, he gathered us round and said, "If anybody isn't happy, they can fuck off." I knew he was aiming that at me,' says Hodge. 'I was simmering under the surface … I could tell he was nervous. We'd been close to the cup final twice, but this might be his last chance.'

There was little evidence of such anxiety ahead of kick-off as Clough took a calculatedly scenic route past the West Ham fans to the bench. Acknowledging their fulsome applause, he stopped repeatedly to wave and chat. When he finally did dock in the dugout, one cockney voice shouted, 'Oi Cloughie, you're the Guvna. You're the fucking Guvna!' Upon which, Clough coolly turned to Hodge and enquired, 'Darling, what did he say?'

Much had been made in the build-up of the return to the West Ham frontline of top scorer Trevor Morley. He'd been hospitalised as a result of a domestic stabbing incident in March that spawned a spate of salaciously scurrilous rumours to spiral around the team. Manager Billy Bonds had overcome this adversity and a season-ending injury to his captain Julian Dicks to steer the Hammers – sitting top of the Second Division – to the cusp of a potential double of their own.

In the opening 25 minutes, with nothing between the sides, West Ham looked more than ready for top-flight football. That was until referee Keith Hackett thrust himself centre stage. Gary Crosby looped a ball from inside the Forest half beyond the last man in West Ham's unwisely high line. The slowness of Gale's turn encouraged Crosby to give chase. The winger won the race, but the bounce forced him wide of Luděk Mikloško's goal – still at least 25 yards away – when he felt Gale at his back and took a tumble. Perhaps their heels had brushed together. Maybe Crosby felt a faint push. Bobby Charlton, on co-commentary, wasn't convinced. Gale, indignant at the award of the foul, got to his feet incredulously as Hackett reached for his pocket for what the defender assumed would be a yellow card. Instead, with a theatrical flash of scarlet, the referee ordered the inconsolable Gale from the pitch. The embarrassed expression on Stuart Pearce's face as he tried to comfort the West Ham man told its own story.

Hackett's judgement stemmed from an extreme, bordering on fundamentalist, interpretation of the International Football Association Board's (IFAB) newest law: the professional foul. 'If, in the opinion of the referee, a player who is moving towards his opponents' goal with an obvious opportunity to score a goal is intentionally and physically impeded by unlawful means, i.e. an offence punishable by a free kick (or penalty kick), thus denying the attacking player's team the aforesaid goalscoring opportunity, the offending player shall be sent off the field of play for serious foul play in accordance with Law XII (n).'

(This wording is included in full here for reasons that should become obvious later!)

Roger Milford watched on with interest from his living room as John Motson appraised the decision to be a 'sensation'. The 50-year-old Bristolian had already accepted the gig of officiating the final. He could be forgiven if he wondered what he'd let himself in for as Bobby Charlton took Hackett to task. 'It's really quite silly from the referee ... He won't say so, but, nevertheless, he might have ruined the game [with] his decision there.'[18]

Charlton's prediction materialised shortly after half-time. A flurry of goals from Crosby, Keane, Pearce and Charles saw them saunter into the final with a 4-0 victory. 'What a cup final in prospect,' concluded Motson. 'You have to lick your lips at the possibilities thrown up by Nottingham Forest versus Tottenham Hotspur. Two teams who play football the way their managers would say it was meant to be played, on the floor, through the middle of the field to feet. Let's hope they can live up to the occasion when they meet on May the 18th.'

Away from the television cameras, there was a touchingly candid scene in the victorious dressing room. Wet-haired

---

18 While Hackett perhaps got that one wrong, when refereeing the Spurs vs Manchester City cup final in 1981, crucially he'd resisted the temptation to blow for a foul when Ricky Villa was taken out as he supplied the finishing touch to his virtuoso Wembley wonder goal.

smiling Forest players, fresh from the bath and stripped to the waist, surrounded their exhaustedly contented-looking boss – who was quaintly wrapped in a dressing gown. After 34 attempts, spanning his career as a player and peerless manager, Brian Clough would – at long last – contest an FA Cup Final. He allowed a photograph to be taken to commemorate the moment. 'I hope no one tries to take anything away from what we achieved ... Anyone trying to knock our victory by saying we only beat ten men is barmy. We deserved to win, and I don't care if it was against 11 players or six ... or five ... or four. You know me, I don't comment on referee's decisions. It's got nothing to do with me when I'm in the dugout. I'm not bothered we're taking on Spurs. I'm just grateful to be going to Wembley.'

Neil Warnock – wringing everything he could from his time in the media spotlight – rushed to judgement as the BBC's coverage from Villa Park went off the air. 'We don't want the Londoners getting all the glory ... Forest will walk it at Wembley.'

Chapter Thirteen

The Victory Song

GIVEN HOW incensed the Tottenham players had been about the phantom Arsenal cup final song, the staggering revelation that not only had Chas & Dave written but also recorded a Spurs victory number – toasting success 'in the North London Cup' – before a semi-final ball had been kicked is deliciously ironic. Chas's son Nik Hodges tells the sensational story.

'It was the evening of the Norwich game where Gazza proved his fitness. Dad, Dave and all our family – all of us are Spurs – went into the studio to record it. My dad had written it after we'd beaten Notts County and drawn that lot in the semi. The thinking was, let's get ahead of the game because if we win on Sunday, we can hit the ground running on Monday and have it in the shops by the end of the week. People would assume the players were singing on it with Chas & Dave rather than us.'

Chas's wife Joan explains they learned from past experience. 'The other cup final songs Chas & Dave did for Spurs [1981, 1982 and 1987] were all done after they'd got through to the final. Timings were really tight as there was such a small window. In 1981, me and Natasha [wife of Chas & Dave's manager Bob England] had to drive around all the record shops in north London wearing full Spurs kit and skidding across the pavement in football boots to complete the look to make sure the copies of 'Ossie's Dream' were on sale in time.'

Ten years later, Nik remembers watching the Arsenal semi-final through the cracks of his fingers. 'We'd been blown away by how the song sounded when we'd left the studio and were all buzzed up. Dad ordered this big screen – it would probably just be a normal-size telly these days. All of us who'd sang on the record crowded round our house to watch it, crossing everything! The whole song is basically a dig at Arsenal. It would have been absolutely gutting if we'd not been able to use it.'

At this juncture it's worth repeating the song's belting chorus:

'We're off to Wembley 'cos we beat the Arsenal
We're off to Wembley 'cos we beat the Arsenal
In the North London Cup, they was only runners-up
Now they can't get the double up the Arsenal.'

'When Arsenal pulled one back before half-time it was all too much for me as a 17-year-old,' continues Nik. 'I had to leave the room. My mum had to come and tell me we'd got the third goal.

'The next day after the semi-final, we announced that the Tottenham cup final song was called "The Arsenal". Pretty quickly, a fax came through to Chas & Dave's management from Highbury. It was a cease and desist saying "The Arsenal" is a "registered trademark of Arsenal Football Club" and can't be used in the song title. We thought it was hilarious that we'd pissed them off that much. That was literally the whole intention of the song. It was a wind-up, and without it being released or anyone even hearing it, it had done its job. We've still got the fax in our archive, I should frame it really!

'To get around it, the title was changed to the "Victory Song". The only downside was that the club got cold feet about endorsing it as the official Spurs song. So my dad and Dave said, "We'll put it out ourselves independently of Tottenham" and quickly wrote some new lyrics to the tune of one of their old songs, "London Girls", for the players. That became "When the Year Ends In 1". That's why there's the two songs.'[19]

The Spurs commercial manager at the time, Mike Rollo, picks up the story. 'Bob England brought in "The Arsenal" song and played me the demo. I thought it was fantastic but realised I'd better run it by the board before we presented it to the players because it was a bit contentious. It's fine for the supporters and Chas & Dave to sing but to have players on it as an official release? – that was a really difficult one. I think we all felt "The Arsenal" was a better song than "When The Year Ends In 1", but it was discussed at boardroom level. I believe there was a conversation between Irving Scholar and David Dein [the Arsenal vice-chairman] and it was decided the club wouldn't be officially associated with it for PR reasons. There's no doubt it riled the Arsenal fans and players. But Arsenal understood the club hadn't sanctioned it, even though we were quietly smiling about it because it was so good.'

David Howells thinks it was the correct call. 'Quite rightly the club wanted the focus to be on us reaching the final rather than us beating them. You've got to keep your class and as much as they're our rivals, Arsenal were always pretty classy. We needed to maintain our dignity so, although it was a fun song, it was the right decision.'[20]

Remaining dignified proved more of a challenge when it came to the Tottenham squad choosing who would head up the 'players' pool'. This was the tradition among team-mates whereby, on the back of reaching the cup final, all kinds of

---

19 Nik Hodges recalls repeatedly watching a Spurs video released to mark the club's centenary as a child and speculates that the production was the source of many of the facts his dad Chas weaved into the lyrics of 'When the Years Ends In 1'.

20 Nottingham Forest's cup final song wasn't devoid of drama. On the big day, Alex Alexander, the lyricist responsible for 'We Reign Supreme', had stocks of the record – proceeds from which were due to go to international famine relief efforts – confiscated outside Wembley. Trading standards officers warned Alexander, who'd hoped to shift thousands of copies, that he was selling them illegally and could face prosecution.

novel opportunities for additional income were actively sought out and exploited. In addition to recording a single, charging the press for exclusive interviews, public appearances and product endorsements were all considered nice little earners. The money generated was pooled and then divvied up among the players according to how many games they'd each played in the cup run. But who should be the mastermind to tout around for these commercial sweeteners? Several players advocated for Eric Hall. But Hall could be a divisive figure. In fact, with his garish primary-coloured suit jackets, trademark cigar and 'monster' catchphrase, he came to epitomise the enduring caricature of the grasping football agent.[21]

Hall recalled in his autobiography that when Spurs reached the final in 1987, he'd won the vote among the squad to run the pool. However, according to his account, senior players Glenn Hoddle, Ray Clemence and Ossie Ardiles weren't having it. Even after a second vote was taken, which Hall won again, they refused to relent, and the idea of a players' pool was dispensed with.

Things threatened to go the same way in 1991. 'So much energy went into that,' says Gudni Bergsson diplomatically, as he recounts the politics that went hand in hand with reaching a cup final. Erik Thorstvedt shakes his head in amazement. 'You'd think the focus would instantly be "how are we going to win the match", but it was also a money-making exercise … how can we as players squeeze as much money out of this [as possible]. Someone had to run the players' pool, and you had to choose someone to do it. Lots of the boys had different agents, and they were lobbying on their behalf. There was a lot of quarrelling, and even when it came to the vote, there were arguments that some players hadn't been present and some people saying the apprentices shouldn't be allowed a say.'

Eric Hall eventually won the day. 'Gary Lineker didn't like it,' remembers Paul Walsh, 'as he wanted his agent

---

21 Eric Hall died aged 73 in November 2020.

running it.' But unlike in 1987, the democratic process was grudgingly accepted. 'He was a character,' says Walsh of Hall. The striker had been the first Hall had ever acted on behalf of during transfer negotiations. 'Eric was Terry Venables's mate from way back, and sometimes I think there was a conflict of interests there. Eric was supposed to be representing the players in negotiations with him. But deep down, he was a good guy – trying to make a living and be everyone's friend. It was all swagger and showing off with him.'

There was no doubting Hall's connections. He successfully secured a deal with Joe Bloggs, a clothing label synonymous with the 'Madchester' music scene of the late 1980s. For the month leading up to the final, coming in and out of the training ground or speaking to the press, the Tottenham players were human Joe Bloggs billboards. Other endorsements fell into their laps. Nik Hodges explains. 'If you look closely at the cover for the 7-inch single of "When the Year Ends In 1" everyone in the photo is holding one of those little bottles of Lucozade Sport.' Even Chas & Dave – not at their athletic peaks – are in on the act. 'I remember asking my dad about it. He said there was some bloke who just went up to all the players and said, "Hold this, and I'll give you fifty quid." So my dad and Dave had a piece of that too!'

But it wasn't the isotonic beverage that ensured the players' vocal cords were suitably lubricated in the recording studio. 'The players called me Mr Holsten when I was commercial manager,' says Mike Rollo. 'You see from time to time, they all used to get an issue of a crate of 24 beers from our sponsor – of course, some managed to get a few more than that. Anyway, Eric Hall invited me down to the studio and I remember they had various Joe Bloggs tops on. I brought some Holstens down for the recording, and they were all in good spirits. The two things may have been connected!'

'Cup final songs are shit, aren't they?' smiles Walsh. 'But it was lovely to meet Chas & Dave, and they obviously knew what they were doing. It was just a shame we didn't! But when you're singing in a group you just hide if you can't sing. That's what I did.'

'It was mayhem in the studio as there'd been some good drinking going on but so much fun,' recalls Thorstvedt. 'I hadn't heard of Chas & Dave back in Norway, but they're such a big part of the club's history. And I love that we sing to the Manchester City fans now about the Gallagher brothers, "You're just a shit Chas & Dave". That's class.'

'Of course, I knew about Chas & Dave and Spurs,' says Paul Stewart, 'but I don't think it was until we were on the piss recording the song that I found out about the year ends in one stuff. We started thinking our name was on the cup and all those other cliches you'd heard growing up.'

Whereas 'Ossie's Dream' made it into the UK singles chart top five in 1981, 'When the Year Ends In 1' failed to trouble the top 50, peaking at number 52. 'They did get asked to do *Top of the Pops*,' reveals Nik, 'but the producers insisted it had to be with all the players, including Gazza and Lineker, the household names in the team. My dad said that Gary very politely declined. I think he was keen to just be known for his football. It was a shame, but I can understand it.' Perhaps Lineker's reluctance stemmed from his participation in the toe-curling, landfill-destined Stock, Aitken and Waterman effort 'All The Way' for Euro 88. The England squad, including manager Bobby Robson, were made to perform the song 'live' on *Wogan* while stiffly completing a sequence of choreographed dance moves on exercise bikes and weight machines. Embarrassing doesn't cover it.

'The month-long build-up to the final was crazy,' reflects Nayim fondly. 'We were used to training on our own. Suddenly, after Arsenal, there were a lot of journalists coming to the training ground. Most of us were happy with all the attention. We were in the spotlight for that moment. That's what it's all about, to be in the spotlight for positive things.'

True to form, however, even a good news story for the club could swiftly be reversed. *The Mirror* ran an exclusive under the headline 'BANNED, THE UGLY FACE OF FOOTBALL', with a picture of Eric Hall standing guard at the training ground gates. Journalists, invited to Mill Hill for an event promoting the Joe Bloggs summer range, were denied entry unless they paid Hall a fee for the players' pool. 'That was terrible PR,' says Thorstvedt. 'It just pissed off the press, who then reported it. I don't know how the club could allow something like that to happen, but that's how things were.'

Stadium announcer Willie Morgan remembers being phoned up by Hall, who was keen to repair the damage. 'I'd known Eric for donkeys' years. He said, "Can you bring your son down to the training ground as all the press are here, and it will be good publicity for the players to be pictured having a kickabout with him." He must have been about ten, so I went to his school and took him out of class for the morning. His mum knew nothing about it. He got some Joe Bloggs clobber and was on the local news. What memories.'

It was all too easy to characterise Spurs as the callous, mercenary, London big-time Charlies, whereas Forest were Cloughie's endearingly home-spun, humble, small-town sons. It was a depiction the Nottingham *Evening Post* was keen to run with. They produced a graphic showing Forest's team had been assembled for £1.3 million from obscure footballing outposts, including Grantham and Runcorn. Tottenham's acquisitions, by contrast – which didn't leave change from £9 million – came from the game's most illustrious names, the likes of Barcelona and Liverpool. Ramming the point home, the paper ran a series of interviews with the retiring types in the Forest squad, complemented by soft-focus photos of them enjoying simple pursuits with their families in the Nottinghamshire countryside.

One unifying issue among the players at White Hart Lane and the City Ground (and at least one of the managers) was a sharp interest in cup final tickets. Brian Clough went public with his discontent at only being allocated 24, the same number issued to all the other members of Forest's staff as mandated by Football Association rules. 'I've put a bit of time in at this club. I've won a few games down the years and helped make them a bob or two. To turn round and tell me I was getting no more than anybody else – well that's upset me in no uncertain terms. I mean really upset me.'

Indicative of the institutionally breezy nature of Tottenham Hotspur's relationship with rules and regulations, the Spurs players received nearly 100 tickets each. 'That was one of the things that absolutely amazed me with the player power at the club,' says Thorstvedt. 'I know some of the lads gave one or two to their families, and the rest, well … hmmm, hmmm.' Or as one player put it, 'Everyone wanted as many tickets as they could get their hands on, and a lot of that was to sell them to touts. That was the big bunce that came from getting to the FA Cup Final, worth loads more than what came from the players' pool.'

Naturally, the frenzy for tickets was no less intense among fans, as 37,000 tickets of Wembley's 80,000 capacity were to be distributed at the FA's 'discretion', leaving 21,500 allocations for Forest and Spurs fans. Demand immediately outstripped supply. When the first tranche of 11,000 went on sale to City Ground season ticket holders and club shareholders, supporters queued for 16 hours in a snaking line that stretched as far as the Lady Bay bridge. Nottinghamshire constabulary was pleased to report 'no problems of pushing or shoving' in the good-natured crowd.

An editorial in the Nottingham *Evening Post* attempted to explain the fervour. 'They say it takes a lot to get Nottingham folk excited about anything, and there's a deal of truth in that. But even in these days of mass television exposure of soccer there is still nothing to match the magic of the FA Cup … This is the big one. Not even Forest's magnificent exploits in the European Cup in the '70s can match the potential glory of winning the FA Cup. Add to all that natural excitement and anticipation the fairy-tale ingredient of Brian Clough

– making it to an FA Cup Final for the first time in his illustrious career – and it is easy to see why Nottingham is really turning on to this one.'

Those Reds who missed out could legitimately ask how companies like Lincolnshire-based World Wide Sports Tours had somehow come to access 'between 500–1,000 tickets' – offered to Forest fans in a package priced at £299. Pressed on the provenance of these tickets, the firm's sales director could only say, 'I cannot divulge where I get tickets from. This is a commercial secret. There are bona fide sources.'

Remembering the stress of acquiring a cup final ticket brought back a deep teenage trauma for Spurs fan Penny Deller. In 1987, she'd paid a premium to an agency to see Tottenham take on Coventry. Arriving at Wembley that day, she'd chanced her arm hoping to exchange her prized ticket for one closer to where the friends she usually stood with on the Shelf were situated. 'I asked this nice couple if they'd swap, and they said "yes". So we're outside for two hours getting hyped up for the final, singing all the Spurs songs. Then, when it's time to go through the turnstile, the operator shines a light on the ticket they'd given me. Suddenly, he starts banging on the wall. Next thing, this big bloke takes me by the arm and leads me out. It turned out the ticket I'd swapped my genuine one for was a fake. To this day, I think the couple who gave it to me didn't know. I started crying, and right at that moment, a press photographer appeared and began taking pictures of me.

'I remember there was a group of really dodgy-looking guys and one of them came up to me and said, "Don't worry love, we'll get you in." I asked "How?" He replied, "We're going to smash a wall down." I blubbed, "I don't want to." Then a load of police on horses turned up – they must have sensed something – and shepherded everyone away. I ended up watching the game in a pub in King's Cross. Deep down, I have to admit there's part of me that's glad for Gary Mabbutt's own goal and that we didn't win that final.

'So for 1991, I was so relieved to meet all the criteria. I did absolutely everything by the letter. I've still got the programme that had all the application details in. You had to send a stamped addressed envelope to the ticket office with a special form, voucher and an open cheque. The most expensive tickets were £45, the cheapest £12 – different times! That ticket never left my sight once it arrived.'

Chapter Fourteen

Desperate Times, Desperate Measures

AS CUP final fever began to rip through north London's population, the unfortunates in the White Hart Lane boardroom remained unhappily immune. Despite issuing a spectacularly unconvincing defence of Larry Gillick's past insolvency through a club spokesman – 'I don't really know what to say. But people do go bankrupt, and the whole thing is behind him now' – Tottenham – and Terry Venables – were finally forced to accept the flighty Scot could not deliver the club's financial salvation.

It was for the best that the parting of the ways happened when it did. A few years later, press in Scotland would report Gillick missing. They surmised he'd been murdered by north London's notorious Clerkenwell crime syndicate, having double-crossed them in a property deal. Thankfully, news of Gillick's untimely demise proved premature. He resurfaced a decade later, reinvented as a Brazilian steel baron. By then, his reputation as a financial wizard had taken heavy damage. Gillick was the subject of an outstanding financial judgement from the Salvation Army for his part in 'a scam' that, according to the *Sunday Times*, 'defrauded' the philanthropic church 'of more than £6 million ... one of the biggest frauds in British charity history'.

With the Midland Bank now refusing to extend the club's overdraft beyond the end of April, chairman Nat Solomon was compelled to again frantically cast the net in search of a more reputable investor. Five days removed from the Wembley victory over Arsenal, he wrote to Robert Maxwell.

'The purpose of this letter is to let you know formally that my board colleagues have unanimously requested to ask whether you would consider reopening last summer's negotiations with a view to our achieving an underwriting agreement. If, as I hope will be the case, you think that this possibility is worth exploring, I and the company's advisors would be willing to enter into immediate talks with you and your advisors with the aim of reaching an early agreement. You have my assurance that my board recognises fully the need for the importance of absolute confidentiality in connection with any such discussions.'

Unfortunately for Solomon and his board, Maxwell had repeatedly demonstrated during his time as the proprietor of the *Daily Mirror*, *Sunday Mirror* and *The People* that discretion wasn't his forte. His newspapers always needed stories, so much the better, ones that furnished his profile. For now, though, the Tottenham board were kept in suspense. Their letter went unanswered.

Solomon had little choice but to press ahead and flog Paul Gascoigne to the highest bidder at the behest of the Midland Bank. Lazio had burnt off all competition with their world-record bid and astronomical offer that would make Gascoigne a multi-millionaire. On 26 April, after Solomon had spent several days in Rome, the *Daily Mirror* reported Gascoigne moving to Lazio was a done deal. Irving Scholar declared himself to be 'bitterly disappointed and angry' at the news. Self-styled Spurs superfan Morris Keston hysterically told journalists, 'I can't understand the timing with the cup final just a few weeks away. It's like committing suicide,' while season ticket holder Daniel Greenburg summed up the sense of dismay: 'I'm disgusted. It smacks of desperation and will hardly affect the overall debt. No doubt Terry Venables will be the next to leave. Once again, the supporters have been let down.'

Venables, however, wasn't yet ready to call time on his takeover dream. His business adviser Eddie Ashby – a growing influence across the Tottenham manager's soon-to-be sprawlingly arcane financial affairs – was entrusted to source potential dowries. David Gerrard, another property mogul, was briefly substituted into the Venables consortium for the departed Gillick. A new plan was formulated whereby once Venables gained control, White Hart Lane would be sold and leased back to Spurs. The proposed sale of the ground was a worrying development. But as it seemed to permit the club to move forward as a going concern, it received little scrutiny. Venables – to borrow the phrase popularised by football managers – set out his stall. 'It is a constructive offer and consists of a financial package which would permit the retention of Gascoigne and is intended to answer the refinancing requirements of Spurs. I hope the board and Midland Bank accept my offer, which I believe secures the future of Spurs.'

Again, though, the initial £1.1 million down-payment failed to materialise, and Gerrard faded from the scene. Dabbling in some megaphone diplomacy through the press, Venables told Gascoigne to sit tight as he went on yet another financial fishing expedition. 'There are bigger and better clubs for him [than Lazio].'

Lazio president Gianmarco Calleri was suitably riled by these ongoing machinations. 'Please, Mr Venables, leave football and join the lifeguards as you are so good at rescues … It is all very well for Venables to sneer at us and spit venom on Gazza if he goes to Lazio, but it should be clear that he has a share of the responsibility in taking Spurs close to bankruptcy.'

TISA sprang to Venables's defence. Ahead of the season's final league home game against Nottingham Forest – widely characterised as a dress rehearsal for the teams' upcoming Wembley showdown – they issued a punchy statement. 'The proposals put to the board by Edenote PLC on behalf of Terry Venables represent the only prospect of a future for Spurs. The alternative is Paul Gascoigne is sold, and that will be disastrous.'

TISA distributed 11,000 leaflets to fans attending the Forest league match, designed to refocus public attention on the club's ongoing plight. They asked fans, 'What is more important than the FA Cup Final? THE FUTURE OF TOTTENHAM HOTSPUR', and urged them to stage a peaceful sit-in at full time. (There were actually 22,000 leaflets produced. The first batch had to be reprinted after a transcription error down the phone line had led to a typo which called on the board to 'except' Venables's proposals rather than 'accept' them.) Ten TISA members agreed to carry giant placards into the Paxton Road end for a carefully choreographed display. Annelise Jespersen was in their number.

'Bernie Kingsley's mate was a printer, so I presume that's who produced them. I remember they were dished out in front of the Corner Pin pub. Health and safety wasn't such a big deal back then. No one seemed to stop us or ask what we were doing. The turnstile operators were closer to ordinary fans in those days rather than club employees. That said, to be safe, I think we turned the signs horizontally so they were below the turnstile window as we shuffled through. We had to arrange ourselves in the right order – that was our big worry. Thankfully, after one slight mishap, we got it right. I can't remember now what the prompt was, but at a certain point, we held them up in unison before flipping them over.'

On either side, the message – precisely formulated to have the same number of characters – was equally pithy, 'VENABLES IN / SCHOLAR OUT'.

Never easily upstaged, Brian Clough used the match, which had little consequence for either team's league position, to send some sharp messages of his own. Having taken one of his customary in-season breaks to Majorca, he returned ahead of the fixture to discover Forest's reserve team had lost three games in a week and blown the Pontins League title. Coach Archie Gemmill bore the brunt of Clough's displeasure. 'I have suspended him for 44 hours [sic], and he won't be going with us for the Tottenham match.'

Steve Hodge was also in his sights. Clough appeared to take umbrage that Hodge had made a midweek substitute appearance for England in Turkey rather than continuing his rehabilitation from injury by playing for Forest reserves. The midfielder was made to travel down to north London on the team coach, only to be told en route that he wouldn't be involved. The pair exchanged angry words after Hodge – he insists inadvertently – failed to comply with Clough's commandment to sit next to him, like a misbehaving pupil on a school trip, during the game.

The match ended 1-1. Venables conceded afterwards, 'they deserved to win' but he also took comfort in '[picking] up a few helpful hints for the cup final'. While the full time whistle sparked a handful of exercised Spurs fans to try to take their protest against the board on to the pitch, this was swiftly headed off. Thousands, however, did stay behind, peacefully demonstrating from their seats. In the best traditions of protest, estimates of how many vary from 5,000 reported in newspapers to 15,000 in *The Spur* fanzine. Even after TISA co-ordinator Bernie Kingsley was granted access to the PA (hard as it is these days to imagine a club being so accommodating to those calling for its board's removal) to thank participants and kindly ask that they go home, thousands remained. Eventually, Venables strode on to the pitch to express his gratitude. Two hours after full time, the last couple of thousand holdouts finally felt sufficiently content that their point had been made to head for the exits. Irving

Scholar had stayed away in the south of France but was kept up to speed by a stream of television and newspaper coverage.

Steve Davies looks back on TISA's campaign with satisfaction. 'Things had reached a crisis point by the end of the season. We knew Gascoigne was going, and it genuinely felt like the club might go under. We showed the board and Scholar that the situation was untenable. I think it was one of the first campaigns in football that demonstrated fans could effectively organise and did have power. We've seen a lot of fan movements at other clubs since then.'

The week before Wembley, Tottenham all but signed off their league season with a 2-0 defeat at Anfield. They had won just three First Division matches since the end of November. That Gascoigne had appeared in fewer than half of the fixtures during this woeful run of form can't be overstated. Paul Walsh is taken aback when reminded of this sequence of results. 'How many wins? Three? Really? That's pretty shit, isn't it?' He dismisses the idea that the uncertainty surrounding the club lay behind the team's collapse in the league. 'Listen, the reality is footballers are selfish. As long as we're getting paid – which we were – we don't give a monkey's. I can only think once the cup run began, and that was all we had to play for, people started protecting themselves in games. When that happens, you don't get a fully committed performance.'

Looking back at contemporary interviews with the players around the cup final, however, it does seem an impending sense of doom had seeped into the dressing room. Gary Lineker told the press, '[The final] is very much our salvation; something to look forward to with optimism rather than dreading the outcome of all these talks.' Steve Sedgley was quoted as saying, 'Win or lose, it will end in tears,' while when asked about the club's future, Paul Stewart remarked, 'I don't even know if it's got one, has it?'

Given the esteem for Venables in the squad, undoubtedly, the players were taking their lead from his public pronouncements. At a press day previewing the final, he said, 'I fear this could be the end. The thought has crossed my mind. I would like to have announced something to put the players at ease and thank the fans for their wonderful support. But that isn't possible. I have nailed my colours to the mast, and that's where they'll stay.

'In the circumstances to win [the FA Cup] will be my greatest moment. There have been greater achievements, but not under these conditions. I can't remember a season like it. It's my worst ever emotionally. At the start, all the boardroom financial troubles didn't affect the players. But I have noticed in recent weeks it has got to them. When you keep reading about a debt of the magnitude of £20 million, it does increase the pressure on them and the fans. The fact we've not only got through it but reached the cup final speaks volumes of the players.'

Attempting to ease their burden, on the Monday of cup final week, Venables took the entire team to Scribes West, the members' club he'd only just acquired in Kensington, for a boozy lunch. 'I can't think of another manager you'd do that with,' says David Howells. 'Terry was such great company. We loved socialising with him, but he was able to maintain that manager–player relationship.'

'That was fantastic,' says Vinny Samways. 'Not only was Terry a top manager, he also had an amazing voice. I'm sure he sang Frank Sinatra for us.' Venables recounts in his book that Paul Gascoigne arrived late for the festivities. He'd been attending a photoshoot. Eager to catch up, Gascoigne ordered a quadruple Drambuie. Having downed that, he lined up several more and sunk those too. Fortunately, the Scribes barman quietly tipped off Venables, who – despite Gascoigne's voluble protestations – cut him off before things got too messy.

Lineker soon had more legitimate cause to feel aggrieved. On Wednesday morning, *The Sun's* back page was dominated by three words spelt out in block capitals, 'LINEKER FOR SALE'. The exclusive story revealed that Nat Solomon had 'last night told a top European agent: Sell Gary Lineker to

Italy.' *The Guardian* deemed the destructive timing 'days before Lineker spearheads their attack against Nottingham Forest in the FA Cup Final at Wembley extraordinary, even by White Hart Lane standards'. Lineker, reportedly seething at the shambolic way the club was touting him around without even offering him the courtesy of forewarning, showed remarkable restraint. The statement issued by his agent, Jon Holmes, read, 'We have decided to say nothing until after the cup final.' Nat Solomon would by then have apologised to the striker for his part in the shabby affair.

Having been ghosted again by Maxwell following a second furtive letter, Solomon and his board attended a make-or-break meeting with the Midland Bank 48 hours before Wembley. David Buchler presented a recovery plan that confirmed the impending sale of Gascoigne and forecast possible income from a European Cup Winners' Cup campaign. On the back of this roadmap, the bank intimated they would extend overdraft facilities until August. Until that meeting, there had been doubt as to whether it was legitimate for the club to carry on trading due to its possible insolvency. At least 1991/92 season tickets could now go on sale. Gascoigne's agent, Mel Stein, flew to Rome that same day to finalise personal terms on a transfer reported to be worth around £8 million. In addition to a £1 million annual salary, Gascoigne would receive a £2 million lump sum upon passing his Lazio medical the Wednesday after Wembley. Lazio president Calleri was due to fly back to London with Stein to watch his star recruit sign off on English football's biggest stage.

According to Gascoigne, the contract went unsigned before the game because he wanted to take to the field against Forest still feeling like a Spurs player.

Tottenham even managed to spin into drama what kit Gascoigne would wear in his grand farewell. Hummel had been to the High Court seeking an injunction to force Spurs to wear their shirts at Wembley. The Spurs board, however, said that as Hummel had failed to meet its contractual obligations, they were free to wear a new Umbro number ahead of the expiration of Hummel's contract. 'There was a lot of back and forth about it among the players too,' says Erik Thorstvedt. 'Umbro saw big value in us wearing their kit in the final and when it was decided by the club that we would, some of the lads were worried it would jinx it.' This in large part stemmed from the scarred institutional memories of 1987.

* * *

The decision to debut a new strip in the 1987 cup final loss to Coventry had been a fiasco. Roy Reyland picks up the story: 'I was the assistant kit man to Johnny Wallace back then, so I wasn't in the dressing room before the game and was sitting in the stand opposite the tunnel. I remember the players coming out and taking their tracksuit tops off. I could tell something wasn't right, but for the life of me, it didn't click. Then it dawned on me, half the shirts were missing HOLSTEN on the front. I thought, 'I need to get to the dressing room.' But it was too late by then. And, anyway, what could I do? I didn't have any identification on me, so if I'd tried to say "I've got to get in there," the security would have said, "Yeah, course you do mate."'

The realisation was no less excruciating for commercial manager Mike Rollo. 'I was sat in the stand with the Holsten managing director and deputy chairman. I was turning all sorts of colours. I'd noticed. He hadn't. I thought I'd better point it out to him, but I said, "Don't worry, I'll pop down to the dressing room." I had a Spurs Wembley '87 tie on and a blue and white flower on my lapel. A senior policeman was there with stripes on his arm, so I told him the problem. He put his arm around me. "Listen, son, if you've noticed it, then I'm sure your colleagues will have too. They'll put it right at half-time." To my dismay, they came out in the second half in the same shirts.'[22]

---

22 In the event, Holsten weren't too upset about the cock-up as it generated plenty of publicity for the beer.

There remains some debate over the precise cause of the mishap. The most likely theory is two sets of kit had been ordered, one for the final and one for a youth team tournament, where alcohol sponsorship was prohibited. Somehow, a mix-up had occurred when they were sent to the embroiderers to have the final flourish marking the Wembley occasion added below the crest. 'My heart sank for Johnny,' says Reyland. 'I look back now and think, how could it have occurred? But when you're in the throes of things, mistakes happen to all of us.'

* * *

Reyland replaced Wallace as first-team kit manager after the 1987 final. 'From then on, I always did three checks of the kit. I remember getting everyone in with a chance of playing measured with Umbro for the '91 final. When the kit arrived, I hung it on a rail, the type you have in clothes shops, and made sure that everything was on it that should be. My second check was to take the shirts off the rack and fold them in numerical order, low to high, on a table. Then I'd load them from high to low into the big metal skip. Even on the drive to Wembley, I was worrying. 'Did I do the checks right?' I knew I had – but it was still in there at the back of my mind.'

For Reyland, a lifelong Spurs fan who'd grown up in the shadow of White Hart Lane and vividly remembers playing never-ending matches with his schoolmates using the Paxton Road end's vast blue doors as a goal, these were the best moments of his career.

'I headed over to Wembley in my van on the Friday to set up the dressing room. I took my best mate Mark with me. We'd played amateur football together. I didn't tell him where we were going until we caught sight of the Twin Towers. We laid all the kit out in the dressing room – which was pretty basic at Wembley, believe it or not. But all the nostalgia washes over you. I was thinking about all the great players who have been in there ahead of finals, the boys from 1966.

'I looked around the room and thought, "Wow". The butterflies for the final were already going. The groundsmen there were very precious about anyone going on the pitch, but I wanted to check how it would play for the players' boots. We walked up the tunnel and on to the pitch from behind the goal. I could see a groundsman over on the left wing. I said to Mark, "We'd better get a march on here," and got to the 18-yard box at the far end. I had a ball hidden behind my back. So I rolled the ball into the area and hissed to Mark, "Smash it into the fucking net and don't you dare miss 'cos you'll only get one chance before he kills us." No sooner had he hit it, than we hear, "Get off the bloody pitch" ... magic.'

Nayim was experiencing contrasting emotions as he prepared to travel to the Royal Lancaster Hotel, which would again host Spurs on the eve of Wembley. 'Terry had told me I wasn't in the starting line-up, and I was very emotional. My father had come over to London for the first time to see me play. It was hard as he loved watching me play so much. I'd been in the team and scored against Forest at White Hart Lane, but Terry said that was his decision, and I was on the bench. I remember my father said not to be upset. "Take it easy, wait for your moment and see what you can do if you come on."' They would prove wise words.

Venables was nowhere to be seen as the team waited for the coach to take them from the training ground to the hotel. Incredibly, with less than 24 hours until cup final kick-off, he was locked in fresh takeover talks in the Baker Street offices of Philip Green (yes, *that* Philip Green), chairman and chief executive of the Amber Day fashion group. According to Morris Keston's account (Green and Keston were long-standing, Spurs-supporting mates, and Green invited Keston to attend to bear witness to proceedings), Green had agreed to bankroll Venables's takeover. Green called Irving Scholar on the phone, and they went back and forth over a deal that would see Venables pay 80p per share for Scholar's holding (Venables puts the amount at 75p in his book). Scholar offered to drop this to 70p if Venables could persuade Gascoigne to renege on his agreement with Lazio. Venables claims in his autobiography that this 'Gascoigne discount' was a self-serving attempt to generate good publicity for Scholar, who was fully aware that the player's deal with Lazio was by now 'binding'.

Nevertheless, the pair agreed to proceed at the higher price. Both Keston's and Venables's recollections were that it was at that point that Scholar inserted an insurmountable caveat via his lawyer. 'Irving accepts the offer on the understanding that the deal is closed today.' With the working week over, Green tried in vain to reach the decision-makers at the Midland Bank to gain their consent for the transaction. Eventually, with the night beginning to draw in, at 7.45pm, Venables pushed back his chair in exasperation, got up and left to join the team he'd lead to Wembley come the new day.

Venables would bitterly reflect, 'It is my sincere belief that Scholar never had any real wish to sell Tottenham, despite the awful mess he had made of running the company, and that he dragged out negotiations and put obstacles in my way in the Micawberesque hope that something would eventually turn up, allowing him to retain some of his shareholding and his place on the board.'

It was wholly appropriate that Venables's arrival for check-in at the Royal Lancaster coincided with that of the London Fire Brigade – sirens wailing – who'd been summoned by the hotel's fire alarm.

* * *

Given the latest round of north London internecine strife, Nottingham Forest might have hoped a mundane cup final build-up would translate into an on-field advantage. But the immediate days before Wembley proved disquieting ones for them, too. They had completed their league season in a free-scoring flourish, winning five and drawing one – at White Hart Lane – of their last six fixtures. This run of form included a 7-0 schooling of Chelsea and a 5-0 thumping of Norwich and had Ladbrokes pricing them as favourites for the FA Cup Final. Privately though, Brian Clough's celebrated self-assuredness and evangelical conviction was ebbing away. As Wembley beckoned, he began spooking himself.

After Forest's final game of the season, a 4-3 win over Leeds in which he'd admonished and substituted Stuart Pearce for the skipper's attacking brio, he confided to Duncan Hamilton of the *Evening Post* that he was worried the team had peaked too early and as Hamilton puts it, 'that the football that ought to have been saved for cup final Saturday had been spent lavishly the previous month'. Hamilton recalls Clough wagging his finger at him before divulging, 'I want to win the FA Cup very badly – but don't say that unless we do it.'

While the Spurs players had been enjoying their liquid lunch at Scribes, a full-strength Forest turned out in a testimonial for Notts County youth team coach Mick Walker. Although the fixture allowed Roy Keane, who'd damaged his ankle at Spurs, to prove his fitness, even the usually demure Nigel Clough questioned the wisdom of Forest's participation. 'Was this match fixed up by Tottenham? I'm not exactly sure what we are doing here. Let's hope it doesn't turn into a benefit for Terry Venables.'

A day later, three of Forest's back four were selected by Graham Taylor in the England squad to tour Australasia. Des Walker and Pearce were fixtures in the international side, but it marked the first call-up for young right-back Gary Charles. Charles's excitement was immediately overtaken by tragedy.

He was driving his Ford Escort XR3i near the City Ground, seeking a newspaper recording the news of his unexpected international recognition for posterity, when 17-year-old student Stuart Fayle's motorcycle crashed into him. Fayle died in hospital from the injuries he sustained. His father Robert agreed to the inquest into his son's death being delayed – it was potentially due to be held 24 hours before Forest took to the field at Wembley – as he 'wanted to give the lad [Charles] a chance to play in the final'. When the inquest was convened in September, the coroner recorded a verdict of accidental death. It transpired that Fayle had been in a distressed state and riding erratically, having failed his motorcycle proficiency test just minutes before the collision.

Physically unharmed, Charles kept the accident secret from Clough and his team-mates as the squad travelled to London on Thursday ahead of the final. He has since said in a newspaper interview that the untreated psychological trauma he endured contributed to the unravelling of his promising career. Sadly, he suffered repeated injury and descended into alcoholism, leading to two stints in prison before he was able to get sober.

Charles was one of three question marks surrounding the Forest team selection for Wembley. Would Clough opt for him or the more experienced Brian Laws? Would Roy Keane or Hodge get the nod in midfield? Hodge had been excellent in the victory over Leeds. And would Nigel Jemson – who Clough regularly rebuked for being 'the only player with a head bigger than mine' – or Lee Glover provide the focal point of the attack? The discomfort Keane was experiencing in his ankle was trumped by his manager's provocative decision to billet him and Hodge together in the same room of the Bellhouse Hotel in Buckinghamshire. Keane wrote in his autobiography, 'I wasn't sure what Brian Clough's psychological ploy was meant to achieve. I'd never roomed with Steve before, and in the circumstances, both of us felt distinctly uneasy. This arrangement led to a fraught couple of days.' As the players trained at Burnham Beeches on Friday, Jemson believed he'd done enough to make the cut. He'd scored Forest's Wembley winner in the previous season's League Cup Final, and coach Ronnie Fenton had tipped him off that he'd get the chance to repeat the feat.

On the short coach trip back to the hotel, the usual post-training banter and card games were cut abruptly short when the curtain partitioning the players from the coaching staff was suddenly thrown open. Steve Hodge's recollection is that Clough crossed the threshold, marched down the aisle and threw a crumpled piece of paper at Stuart Pearce's feet, announcing, 'Skipper, here is the cup final team,' before turning on his heel and disappearing back behind the curtain. Ian Woan remembers it being either Fenton or Alan Hill who delivered the note to Pearce. Whatever the case may be, it seems an incredible dereliction of duty that Clough left it to his captain to announce the team. As Hodge later wrote, 'I thought Brian Clough bottled it a bit that day – he couldn't face the players he was leaving out.' That charge would be levelled at Clough again before the presentation of the 1991 FA Cup was made.

Charles, Keane and Glover had won their personal selection battles. Laws and Hodge at least had the modest consolation of a place on the bench. Jemson had been omitted altogether. He was inconsolable. When the coach parked up at the hotel, rather than a sympathetic word or explanation, Clough summoned him over to have his picture taken by a press photographer. Jemson's tears flooded the morning's newspapers. The striker would leave the club within six months.

Contemplating his manager's selection a decade later, Pearce wrote, 'I believe Brian Clough picked his favourites instead of the best side that day. I was not alone among the players in that belief.'

Jemson once enlisted the help of those at the table he was hosting at a club dinner and Q&A event to ask Clough anonymously the reasoning for leaving him out. 'Because I could,' came the snarky reply.

In his newspaper preview of the final, Jimmy Hill reprised his plea for Clough to call it a day at Wembley. 'Brian should retire, win or lose. It's time to take it easy before the pressure becomes too much. Management is the most stressful job in football. Managers suffer, you can see it in their faces when the TV camera shows a close-up. Forest's directors should make the decision for him ... he has nothing left to prove.'

The unanimous view among fans and pundits alike was that either Clough or Gascoigne – the two irrepressible personalities of English football – would define the final, perhaps both. They were proved right, of course, but not for the reasons any of them had imagined.

Chapter Fifteen

Countdown to Kick-Off

GIVEN HOW the afternoon would unfold, it's not surprising Paul Gascoigne's behaviour on cup final morning looms large in the memories of his team-mates. Paul Walsh recalls the midfielder being like a 'caged animal'. 'When we stayed in hotels out in the country, he could go and have a game of squash and expend some energy, but there, there wasn't anywhere for him to go.'

Pat Van Den Hauwe wrote similarly in his autobiography, 'As a senior player, I must take some responsibility for not getting a grip of Gazza ... and trying to calm him down. From the minute we had breakfast, he was like a man possessed, and I'm amazed he made it to Wembley for the game as he was that wound up.'

In his first memoir, understandably, Terry Venables is keen to defend himself against suggestions that he'd lost command over his star player. He bristles at the accusation made in Irving Scholar's book that 'Venables had turned the key in the young player to get him psyched up for the occasion'. Venables points out that by contrast to the night before Arsenal, there had been no need to tranquillise Gascoigne. 'All my conversations with him before any game, and the cup final in particular, were designed to calm him down, not wind him up ... The transfer might well have been on his mind ... In any event, he was not as hyped up as normal and certainly nothing like he had been before the semi-final.' Venables doubles down on this in his second autobiography, describing Gascoigne as 'eerily subdued', and 'in his own world', before rhetorically asking: 'Was his apparent pre-match self-control the lull before the storm? I think so.'

Paul Stewart's view is that he saw nothing out of the ordinary from Gascoigne on cup final morning. 'People always ask me if there was anything different about him that day. Of course, he was well up for it, but he was always like that.' David Howells is of the same view. 'I've disagreed with some of the boys on this when we've talked about it in the years since. They felt they sensed something different about him. The move to Lazio was all but done – we all knew he was going, so maybe there was something in that, but honestly, I didn't pick up on anything. He seemed like he always did, mucking about and trying to get a laugh out of everyone.'

The BBC's cameras captured a relaxed-looking Gascoigne sitting at a table with Erik Thorstvedt, Stewart and John Sheridan in the Royal Lancaster's breakfast room. Sheridan soon fell victim to Gascoigne's fondness for practical jokes. Offering to pour the tea for the physio, he sent it cascading out of the pot from a great height, forcing Sheridan to take evasive action. Turning his attention to Thorstvedt, Gascoigne began joshing him about a 'bad week in training' and urging him 'not to drop any today'. The goalkeeper humoured him by immediately dropping his hard-boiled egg. Whatever may have been churning inside, Gascoigne seemed determined to project calm in the press interviews he'd given, too, while acknowledging the burden of others' expectations. 'I've never heard of the word pressure. I don't know what it means. There was supposed to be pressure on me two years ago (sic) when I first came to London, but I've still got the same fat grin on my face. I've got 70 people coming down from Newcastle, and I think they'll stay sober for the match.'

This conscious effort to at least try to contain the mental burden that came with playing in the FA Cup Final rather than lean into it was a ploy of the whole squad. 'We didn't have cup final suits,' says Howells. 'We wore our trackies, which we felt more comfortable in. We'd done that for the semi-final, whereas Arsenal had come suited and booted. You should probably make more effort for the cup final, but it worked for us, so we did it again. I'm a bit sad now not to have an FA Cup Final suit somewhere in the cupboard.'

'I don't think the boys were low-keying it,' reflects Roy Reyland. 'They just wanted to do it their way.'

Howells remembers the bus journey to Wembley being uncharacteristically subdued. 'It was quiet, which was unusual for us. Everyone was focused on the game. Looking out the window, it felt that only Spurs fans were on the pavement. That couldn't have been the case, but that was the impression we got. Maybe they knew the route we'd take. It felt like the support behind us was massive.'

Alighting from the coach, the Tottenham players made the traditional lap of the Wembley pitch, Gascoigne sporting a pair of bedroom slippers. Watching on, Des Lynam was sold. 'He seems to have no nerves at all.' Back in the dressing room, the Spurs players changed into their all-new kit before heading down the tunnel for the warm-up. Gascoigne proceeded to bombard the marching band with driven high balls aimed to knock their instruments from their lips or, better still, topple the ostentatious ceremonial hats from their heads.

Looking on from the BBC's pitch-side studio, Bob Wilson was particularly taken with Spurs' striking knee-length shorts. 'They've borrowed Stan Matthews's shorts, Tottenham, haven't they? 1930s/40s. It's crazy how fashions come back.' According to the *Daily Mirror*'s women's editor – presumably, no one else at the paper was deemed qualified to comment – they looked like 'a cross between a deflated parachute and your granny's bloomers'.

'We were the first [to wear long shorts like that],' asserts Paul Stewart. 'Everyone copied us after the final. That was a typical bit of Spurs. Other teams hated us for it. Thought we were being flash, which we loved.' Paul Walsh was one of the few players in the squad to have reservations. 'I was glad to get rid of the Eighties short shorts. But I wasn't too keen on the big ones. Because when you're only little, like me, it made it look like I had no legs at all. I wanted something that was a shorter version of the long shorts! A kit that bloody fitted, that's all I wanted!'[23]

Brian Clough's sartorial selections also prompted much conjecture. After a pre-match soak in the Wembley dressing room bath, the Forest manager buttoned himself into a light grey club suit, accessorised with a red and white rosette again proclaiming him the 'World's Greatest Grandpa'. Whether this was born of whimsy or a pointed gesture towards the miserliness of the ticket allowance issued to Clough – which, according to the morning's newspapers, had precluded his three-year-old grandson Stephen's attendance – is unclear.

As the Forest players went through their pre-match rituals in the Wembley dressing room, Roy Keane was still scrabbling around and handing over a wad of cash in a desperate attempt to summon up tickets for expectant family members.[24] According to the account in his book, Keane says, 'The ticket crisis had taken its toll. As we began to walk down the Wembley tunnel, led by Brian Clough, I was weary. All the nervous energy dissipated in the previous eight hours had left me drained and virtually legless.'

As the teams emerged into Wembley's pallet of white, red and vibrant green, Clough, without warning, grasped Terry

---

23 There is a sad footnote to Tottenham's famous shorts. Four months after their Wembley debut, Chris Eubank would provocatively wear the same design – complete with Spurs cockerel – in his WBO super-middleweight title fight against Arsenal fan Michael Watson at White Hart Lane. After 11 brutal rounds, the contest was waved off by the referee at the start of the 12th. Watson collapsed in his corner and was carried from ringside on a stretcher having sustained a life-changing injury to his brain stem.

24 Ironically, in 1959, when Forest had last contested the FA Cup Final, then-manager Billy Walker had encountered the opposite problem. He'd come by four spare tickets, which he was trying to sell outside Wembley's entrance – for face value, of course. Eventually, with only 30 minutes to kick-off, he'd had to abandon his sales pitch and gift the tickets to some happy strangers.

Venables's hand. It is one of the FA Cup's most endearing images, made all the more arresting given the supposed antipathy between the pair. Clough had chastised Venables in a post-match interview with Martin Tyler after Forest won a fractious League Cup tie between the clubs the previous season. 'We never crib about fouls, kicks or anything, and I would like occasionally Terry Venables to shake my hand and say "well done".' Venables had been sufficiently antagonised into reportedly responding that 'he couldn't greet a man who had harmed management by striking fans'. (Clough had infamously cuffed two exuberant Forest fans who'd run on the City Ground pitch following a victory.) Now, here they were, in front of a projected global television audience of 500 million across 54 countries, personifying the spirit of the FA Cup Final's great anthem, 'Abide With Me'.

'That was amazing,' says Vinny Samways. 'Brian Clough, what a legend. He could do those types of things off the cuff. What a brilliant moment.'

Not that Venables was altogether comfortable with such a public display of affection. Roy Reyland explains. 'I was at the back of the teams as they walked out and clocked Cloughie grabbing his hand. I couldn't see Terry's face. When you saw it later on TV, you could tell he was embarrassed. But he must have thought, "This is Brian Clough, so I'll just have to go with it." I said to him, "That was a nice gesture, wasn't it gaffer?" and he just looked at me as if to say, "Fuck off Roysie."' In fact Venables wrote later that Clough had said, 'I hope I don't trip over with all the world watching.'

While the Tottenham manager might not have been thrilled about holding Clough's hand, it's absolutely undeniable that the players from both sides were positively giddy at the prospect of greeting Princess Diana – one of four royals they were presented to. Goalkeeper Thorstvedt had been the first player in the Tottenham queue to greet her. 'Prince Charles – or King as he is now – had these long strides, and he'd advanced well ahead of Diana, who was struggling to keep up [the princess had been waylaid by Brian Clough at the end of the Forest line]. She said to me, "My skirt is much too tight," which I wasn't expecting. A couple of days later, you come up with a funny line or two to say in response. But I couldn't think of anything on the spot.'

'To meet Lady Di was one of the best moments of my life,' says Nayim effusively. 'She was so special to the English people.' David Howells describes the experience as 'ridiculous, absolutely ridiculous. That was possibly the most exciting part of the cup final for me. I loved her. I got on well with the press photographers, so I said: "Please make sure you get a picture when Lady Di's shaking hands with me." I've got a couple of photos which are pride of place, and I'm so pleased to have them.' Paul Stewart, flanking Howells, was equally besotted. 'I'd always fancied her. I didn't tell her that, mind. I was just a kid from Wythenshawe. I'd never dreamed I'd be meeting royalty. She said, "You must be really nervous about the game." I replied, "Not as nervous as I am about meeting you," which was true.'

Just as vivid as the treasured memories of their own interactions with the princess are the players' recollections of Paul Gascoigne meeting with her. Stewart recalls the scene. 'Prince Charles had gone off ahead, and as we're waiting for her, I can hear Gazza shouting, "Where's FA Cup-ears gone?" That's Gazza for you.'

'We'd all been told the protocol,' says a smiling Howells, 'not to kiss her hand or anything like that, which Gazza being Gazza he goes and does.' Nayim chuckles, 'Paul could do anything. We were all serious and following the rules, but he was in a different world. He's an alien – we've got an alien here!'

For Jonathan Pearce, who witnessed the presentation from his Capital Gold commentary position, 'She was the beautiful blue-eyed princess from Disney films, and Paul Gascoigne was the ragamuffin, Billy Boots lad in the *Scorcher* comics. They were characters you'd known all your life made real.'

Pearce is right that, as well as humour, there is a poignancy to the scene. Gazza and Princess Di, the two most celebrated figures in the country – pictured together here in the full flush of youth – would soon pay an unbearably dear price for their phenomenal fame.[25]

---

25 The boyish excitement about meeting Princess Diana was no less evident among the Tottenham directors. Befitting the board's conduct throughout the season, two of those in the Tottenham hierarchy contrived to find further grounds for a falling-out over seating arrangements in the Royal Box. While Forest's chairman Maurice Rowoth was to keep Diana company in the first half, tradition dictated that the Spurs chairman should have this honour during the second. Nat Solomon (and his wife) felt his position as PLC chairman entitled him to the princess-side seat. Club chairman, Irving Scholar, however, thought otherwise and wasn't for shifting, provoking a curt exchange before kick-off.

Chapter Sixteen

Things Fall Apart

'ANYONE WHO ever talks to me about 1991 always calls it "the Gazza final" rather than Spurs vs Nottingham Forest,' says Roger Milford breezily. Inside, you suspect he is sighing. 'I was past the retirement age for referees, which was 48, but at the end of the previous season, the powers that be called me up and said, "You're still scoring high up the assessors' list," and asked me to carry on. That happened three times, which I was pretty pleased with!

'I remember getting the call earlier in spring asking if I was free on 18 May. You couldn't have a connection to any of the teams left in the competition, and Bristol City and Rovers – God help us – never took me out of the running!

'Not many things in this country hold the attention of the whole population. The FA Cup Final was one of them. I knocked off early on the Friday to travel up to London. The company I worked for as an area manager were accommodating like that.[26]

'From the moment you wake up on the day, you don't get a minute to yourself. I remember we were picked up in this chauffeur-driven car. First, it was a tour of Lancaster Gate with the FA and then on to Wembley. We got stuck at the lights, and my wife started doing the royal wave out the

---

26 With the professionalisation of elite refereeing in England still a decade away, most refs juggled officiating games with their full-time jobs.

window. You know it's the showpiece game of the season, so it was good to laugh like that. I'd had my hair permed especially – the players always used to ask where I got it done, and I'd jokingly tell them "the same place as Kevin Keegan". My sun tan was from the back garden!

'The referee's room at Wembley was miles away from the dressing rooms. Before the game, all you hear is the clip-clop of boots as the players go back and forth along the tunnel. There was a knock at the door. A guy pops his head in and asks me if I fancy a rub-down. I said no thanks, as I'd already done my stretches. We didn't warm up on the pitch in those days. I didn't tend to get nervous before refereeing. Yes, the cup final is a special occasion, but it's still a game of football, and you can't do things in the final that you don't normally do. I think that's the only way to approach it.

'Everyone was expecting a great match, two good footballing sides. I was really looking forward to it. I loved Brian Clough. He was brilliant. When I used to go in to check the players' studs, he'd tell me, "If you get any trouble from my players today Roger, giving you any mouth, let me know, and I'll pull them off." He used to say, "You're a lucky ref for us."[27]

'Gazza was one of my favourite players to referee. I remember doing a Spurs match before the final. I called him over and said, "Come on, that's three fouls you've done now. Any more, and I'll caution you." He shoots straight back, "You're wrong again, Rodge … I haven't done three fouls, I've done four." You had to laugh.

'I told my linesmen just before we went out, "You've been chosen because you've had a good season, so do your best and try and enjoy it," and that's what we did.'

---

27 Milford had been in charge at Wembley when Forest beat Luton 3-1 in the 1989 League Cup Final. Bizarrely, he'd also taken charge of Spurs' game at Anfield seven days before the 1991 FA Cup Final.

Teamsheet
Wembley Stadium
Saturday, 18 May 1991

Nottingham Forest	Tottenham Hotspur
Colours: red shirts, white shorts, red socks	Colours: white shirts, navy shorts, navy socks
1. Mark Crossley	1. Erik Thorstvedt
2. Gary Charles	2. Justin Edinburgh
3. Stuart Pearce	3. Pat Van Den Hauwe
4. Des Walker	4. Steve Sedgley
5. Steve Chettle	5. David Howells
6. Roy Keane	6. Gary Mabbutt
7. Gary Crosby	7. Paul Stewart
8. Garry Parker	8. Paul Gascoigne
9. Nigel Clough	9. Vinny Samways
10. Lee Glover	10. Gary Lineker
11. Ian Woan	11. Paul Allen
(Subs)	(Subs)
12. Brian Laws	12. Paul Walsh
14. Steve Hodge	14. Nayim

Brian Clough was still settling in on the sideline, having snuck into a recess near the benches for a quick costume change – the grey suit traded for his trademark green sweatshirt (and navy tracksuit bottoms) – when Milford's officiating came under scrutiny. With 48 seconds played of the 110th FA Cup Final, and most players still to have a touch of the ball, Paul Gascoigne set about leaving his indelible stamp on the game and stud marks on Garry Parker's chest. After a tussle for possession on the far touchline between Ian Woan and Paul Allen, the ball broke in between Gascoigne and Parker, 80/20 in the Tottenham man's favour. As he swept his foot through the ball, he allowed his leg to continue rising into Parker's sternum.

'We didn't usually split the commentaries on Capital Gold, but I'm pretty sure I was doing the first part of the game,' says Jonathan Pearce. 'I remember that collective intake of breath around the stadium when he made that challenge. It was a shocker.'

Vinny Samways shudders at the memory. 'It happened so quickly that you didn't take much notice. But as the years pass and you look back, you think "wow". The way football has changed; if that was today, God knows what would have happened.'

Football journalist and Forest supporter Daniel Taylor has his own take. 'I'm probably going to sound bitter now, but I've never seen another tackle like that where both players are stood up, and he's connected with his chest. It's amazing really. Parker must have been about 5ft 10in. I've never seen a higher tackle. It was a red card in any era.' Nayim is of a similar view. 'I thought he was going to be sent off. That was a tackle for a red card. It was a crazy tackle, but the referee was good to him.'

So why didn't Milford take action? His answer is disarmingly straightforward. 'You can only give what you see and I didn't see it. You can't guess. It's one of those where the player went down, and it's obviously a free kick, but when you see it afterwards, you think "Oh blimey." I was in a wide position, I'm pretty sure, and I looked at my linesman on that side, and he hadn't given anything. I asked him later, and he said all he saw was the tackle go in. He couldn't tell if Gazza had kicked him in the ankle or kicked him in the head. I had a word with Gazza. I said, "I don't know what you did – I know you did something because the player went down, and the ball was nowhere near – so you obviously caught him. I'll be watching you." Gazza replied, "You're always watching me Rodge, trying to get tips."'

Perhaps Clough's diktat to his players to never harass the match official worked against Forest, recipients of that season's Football League Fair Play Award. No one in red made any fuss. Parker, after the briefest of treatment, got up and simply got on with it. The past really is a foreign country.

The conventional wisdom in Paul Gascoigne lore is that had Milford reached for his cards, he might have spared Gascoigne from the worse fate he soon destructively inflicted upon himself. Intriguingly, though, in real time, neither John Motson nor Trevor Brooking on BBC television called for any further sanction. Only with the benefit of a replay did Brooking deem Gascoigne 'fortunate not to get more than just a warning'.

Alan Green, providing commentary for BBC radio, observed in the aftermath of the tackle, 'There's no question that Gascoigne, as he was for the semi-final, is very hyped up for this game.'

In the seventh minute, the midfielder gave the briefest glimpse he might just be able to channel this radioactivity to the Tottenham cause. A sweet shimmy away from the close attentions of three Forest players on the left wing granted him the space to flash a menacing cross-cum-shot that forced Steve Chettle into a flying clearing header. The quality of Gascoigne's resulting corner immediately worried Forest into conceding another. This time his back-post delivery landed on Steve Sedgley's head. The defender guided the ball down to Gary Lineker, who, as ever, had somehow found space in the claustrophobic confines of the six-yard box. The forward jabbed the ball past Mark Crossley, but before it could creep onwards to the goal line, Chettle, who had dropped in behind his goalkeeper, booted it clear.

The pattern of the first half had been set. Neither side was seeking a victory of grinding attrition. Instead, this was the type of football – played out on the English game's grandest old stage   to savour. The prevailing sense of abandon was reflected in Gary Mabbutt's decision to sprint forward from his central defensive berth, beyond even Lineker, to participate in a counter-attack. His sense of adventure was almost punished when Forest swiftly reclaimed possession through Gary Crosby on the right wing. His only thought was to run straight at the short-staffed Tottenham defence.

Sedgley went to ground in the box, Crosby declined the invitation to go over his leg in search of a penalty and instead surged onwards. Justin Edinburgh couldn't stop him but at least applied sufficient pressure to force the winger to send his cross in on the stretch, which Erik Thorstvedt gratefully gathered at his near post.

Tottenham's left flank looked vulnerable. Unlike in the semi-final, Venables had deployed Vinny Samways rather than David Howells ahead of Edinburgh. Howells was sitting in front of the back four, tasked with suppressing Nigel Clough's imaginative play. And with Samways's natural inclination tempting him infield, Crosby and the buccaneering Gary Charles were making hay.

In the 13th minute, Crossley collected Pat Van Den Hauwe's misguided pass and bowled the ball out to Charles. The youngster dished it off to Parker and motored forward expectantly. Parker, exemplifying Forest's famed fluid football, slid a pass into Lee Glover, who'd come short to receive it. The Scottish striker turned adroitly with his first touch and dissected Tottenham's centre-backs with his second. Receiving the ball on his left foot, Charles steered it towards the outskirts of the Tottenham area. His next touch was heavy, Gascoigne was tempted, but Charles had the speed to get there first. Gascoigne threw himself into a maniacal lunge, his right leg thrust knee-high into Charles. Both men were sent spiralling across the turf. Amid the wreckage, Gascoigne's outstretched left arm signalled the severity of the harm he'd done himself, even as he writhed in agony under the gaze of his concerned team-mates. To his eternal credit, Charles, just like Parker before him, immediately got to his feet, limping away from the crime scene without so much as a glance in Milford's direction.

Nayim got up from the bench and began pre-emptively readying himself just in case. 'Gazza deserved to be in that final more than anyone. But he couldn't control himself as he did in the Arsenal game. He was mad and you can't play that over-excited in professional football. It's a really thin line to keep inside for a whole game.'

Danny Kelly reaches into the more recent past when searching for a comparison for the mania that had overcome Gascoigne. 'He was massively over-adrenalised, how else can you explain it? Looking back, his performance reminds me of a one-man version of what happened to Brazil when they lost 7-1 in the semi-final of their own World Cup. Under the most intense pressure, they had a collective breakdown. That is what happened to Paul.'

Dave Butler, dovetailed by John Sheridan, rushed on to attend to their stricken star. Butler crouched down and began treating Gascoigne's right knee. Milford approached with a concerned smile and placed a compassionate hand on his head. Forest fan and football writer Nick Miller – a schoolboy at the time and at Wembley with his parents – who'd had a prime view of both tackles from his seat low down opposite the Royal Box, remembers the incomprehension of those around him that no further punishment accompanied the award of the free kick. 'I can remember my dad going mad about this incredible assault. He holds a grudge still to this day against Roger Milford for ruffling Gazza's hair rather than sending him off.' In his commentary, having, by now, seen a replay, John Motson felt compelled to ask Brooking whether Gascoigne was the beneficiary of special treatment from the referee. It was hard to escape that conclusion.

Milford, a chatty, genial character, then as now, tries to explain the competing factors impinging on his decision-making process. 'I stopped the game, I'm hovering around like you do. The Spurs physio looked at me and said, "This is bad. I don't think he's going to carry on." It's funny because I know I said you can't do anything differently just because it's the FA Cup Final, but then there's that creeping thought: somebody once sent someone off in a cup final and got hammered in the press for ruining the game. "Do I ruin the cup final, or don't I?"[28] If it had been a challenge and he's standing straight up – the card's out, bang, bang all over with. But I'm stood there – and it must have been four or five minutes, and I'm thinking, "Blimey, do I do it or don't I?" It goes through your mind. But once the physio said "He's coming off," I thought, "Let it go."

'People say you should have sent him off. But, I'd warned him [after the Parker tackle], "The next time you do something, I'm going to caution you." That's what I said, and that's what I would have had to have done. But once he's carried off on a stretcher, nah, I'm not that type of character. That could be my failure … but, at the time, I thought "no, I can't do that". After the game, one of the Spurs players – I'd rather not say who – came up to me and said, "I wanted to warn you about Gazza because he'd been so wound up in the tunnel before the match."'

It's a thoroughly humane explanation, and probably one Milford – now in his eighties – is weary of rehashing again after all these years. The complication, however, is that Gascoigne wasn't stretchered off directly after the tackle. Once Butler had flexed his injured knee a few times, Gascoigne gingerly got to his feet. In visible discomfort, he limped on to the end of the Tottenham wall constructed to blockade Thorstvedt's goal from the clear and present danger of a forthcoming free kick from Stuart Pearce's mighty left boot.

Pearce had notched up a remarkable 15-goal season from left-back, with no penalties padding the total. Thunderous dead balls were his stock in trade and there was an air of inevitability that his 16th goal of the campaign was imminent as he strode forward. On approach, his cause was helped immeasurably by Glover hauling Mabbutt out of the firing line and creating an avenue down the side of the Spurs wall to Thorstvedt's top-right corner. Forest had disrupted other

---

28 Milford is referring to Peter Willis, who dismissed Manchester United defender Kevin Moran for pulling back Everton's Peter Reid in the 1985 FA Cup Final. Willis was universally lambasted for his decision.

defensive walls like this before. Milford, however, dismisses the notion of foul play which concerned the BBC pundits at half-time. 'Someone said to me afterwards there was a lot of pushing and shoving in the wall and that Pearce shot through the gap. But I couldn't look for things like that. You get the wall back ten yards and take up your position. You can always find something to say about every decision a referee makes or doesn't make.'

The same goal net that had been graced by Gascoigne's free kick a month earlier now rippled from the force of Pearce's strike. In unison, the heads of those in white and navy bowed. The Forest captain turned away, arms outstretched to accept the acclaim of his supporters massed behind the opposite goal. Brian Clough, arms clamped together, sat unmoved on the bench. Forest's lead edged him closer towards a unique feat in the English game. No manager, not Busby, Nicholson, Shankly nor Paisley, had won all three domestic prizes and the European Cup. More significantly, perhaps, it made real the chance of the gilded farewell at least a part of him desired.

From the restart, Stewart passed backwards to Edinburgh. Gascoigne turned to follow the ball's direction. To the delight of the Forest fans and the dismay of all connected to Spurs, his knee buckled under him like a concertina. John Sheridan was already racing on to the pitch before play had been stopped. 'I knew by the way he'd walked and turned when he got up from the tackle what I'd find when I reached him,' recalls Sheridan mournfully. Gascoigne had ruptured his anterior cruciate ligament (ACL), the same injury that had ended Brian Clough's playing career. 'It was devastating. Paul wanted to go out on a high. He wanted to help the club. Wanted to win it for the boys. And for Terry, who he loved. I'm sure he felt extra pressure. He knew Lazio were watching as well. I think he wanted to prove in that final that he was the best player in the world, which he was. So to see him loaded on to that stretcher ...' Sheridan's voice, laced with emotion, trails off.

Covering his face with his hand and then a blanket, Gascoigne, chest heaving, was wheeled between the benches and taken to the Wembley medical room. Sheridan stayed at his side. 'We were in there alone, just the two of us. He looked at me and asked, "How long am I going to be out, John? A month? Two months?" He was crying. I was crying. I said, "I don't know, mate. All I can promise is that I'll get you fit." I wanted to go with him in the ambulance to the hospital. But the doctor told me, "No John, you might be needed here. There's nothing you can do for him." It was traumatic. I felt empty. I don't remember much about the rest of the game. It was my wedding anniversary that day too.'

With Gascoigne went the Tottenham Hotspur PLC recovery plan. David Buchler – mild-mannered and softly spoken – neatly summarises the reaction of those responsible for ensuring the club's financial future. 'What was I thinking when Gazza was stretchered off? "We're fucked" is the honest answer … I felt very sad for Paul on a personal level too. He always had a childlike quality that made it impossible not to like him. There was so much pressure on him with the cup final and the Lazio money being so badly needed.'

For Terry Venables, the profound implications of Gascoigne's calamity posed a problem for tomorrow. His immediate concern was salvaging the cup final. Recognising the magnitude of the moment, he'd taken the unusual step of entering the playing field. Having found a quiet word for the inconsolable Gascoigne, he then turned to the remnants of the team who'd heard again and again since January that the departing midfielder had 'single-handedly' carried them to Wembley. In crisis mode though, the Tottenham manager summoned calm. Here was an opportunity to reshape his midfield and stem Forest's flow. Nayim casts his mind back to those tension-filled seconds, waiting to join the match. 'Just think about me coming on. You're in a final, you're losing 1-0. Your best player is out. It wasn't an easy situation for me.'

Venables instructed the substitute to play from the left. Samways moved centrally with Stewart and Howells. He was now entrusted – in his understated way – with making Tottenham's play as they chased a path back into the match.

Witnessing his great comrade being wheeled away in such evident distress impelled Paul Stewart into making a resolution. 'I remember seeing people's shoulders slump as if "well that's it then". But I told myself, "You've been through a lot to get here, and you might never be back, so just get stuck in."'

* * *

It needs to be said here that Stewart's extraordinary resilience is matched only by his understatement. The interview with him for this book took place not long after he had undergone surgery having fallen seriously ill. During the pandemic, he lost his beloved wife Beverley to cancer, aged just 56. In 2016, with her support, Stewart had gone public with details of the horrific sustained abuse he'd suffered as a child at the hands of the football coach who acted as the gatekeeper to him having a career in professional football. His bravery enabled many other footballers to come forward with their experiences of abuse, forcing the game's authorities to face up to the prevalence of the issue in the sport. So when he says he'd 'been through a lot' to get to Wembley in 1991, it's no platitude. His depiction of his contribution over the next 105 minutes of the final as merely 'getting stuck in' is admirably modest. But it's also absolute nonsense.

From the moment the game restarted, Paul Stewart was utterly magnificent.

* * *

Nimbly plucking a high ball out of the sky in the centre circle before muscularly shrugging off Glover, Stewart started the move that should have brought Spurs level within five minutes. His raking pass set Lineker racing towards goal between Des

Walker and Steve Chettle. The defenders checked his progress but Samways was on hand to resurrect the move. He caressed a pass to Allen's feet inside the Forest box. Pearce, cautious about making a tackle, jockeyed, but Allen had spotted Lineker ghosting in on Chettle's blind side. The winger's low ball across the six-yard box was immaculately timed, Lineker's finish ruthlessly simple. Inexplicably, however, linesman Peter Newton had hoisted his flag. (Perhaps fatefully, the flags used for the final had been proudly made by a Nottinghamshire company.)

Lineker looked across at the official in disbelief. 'If you're level,' explained John Motson in his commentary, 'you're onside. And I thought when Allen actually played the ball, Lineker had a case for saying he was on.' Motson was being courteous to Newton. Lineker wasn't level when Allen released his pass, not even nearly. He was behind two Forest defenders – not a fraction behind, but clear gaping daylight behind. It was fast becoming a less-than-vintage day for the officials. Newton's decision is all the more baffling when you see on the replay angle from his side that he has an excellent, unobstructed view of the 'goal'. It's the type of error that makes you wish there had been recourse to intervention with video technology – well, almost.

With Tottenham's players reeling at this injustice, Forest almost delivered the *coup de grâce*. Woan cut a swathe through the middle of the pitch – supported by five rampaging red shirts – before playing a wall pass with Glover. The winger then weighted an exquisite first-time ball through Edinburgh's legs to set Crosby clear through on goal. Thorstvedt charged from his line to accost him. 'That was the most important save of my career,' assesses the keeper. 'It wasn't a great save, it was a nothing save when you look at it technically. He shot straight at me. But I kept it out. Had we gone 2-0 down, with everything that had gone against us, that would have been tough. Very tough. You have these small moments that matter so much in a final.'

Thirteen minutes from the interval, the sense that the fates were conspiring against Spurs was all but confirmed. Van Den Hauwe, three times a beaten FA Cup finalist, trudged to take a throw deep in his own half. Howells, collecting the ball in midfield, immediately injected some purpose into a rare passage of stodgy play. His vertical pass found Stewart – back to goal and 30 yards out. Walker, unwisely attempting to get tight, had been sucked out of the Forest backline. Fending him off, Stewart rolled clear of the defender's attentions and stroked an inviting pass through to Lineker. Such was the striker's pace – once clear – there was no prospect of him being caught. Panicking, Crossley flung himself to his right – just as Cameroon's Thomas N'Kono had in Naples when faced with the same situation in the World Cup quarter-final a year earlier. As then, Lineker took the ball around the keeper. And, just as then, the keeper brought him down. There was no doubt of the penalty award, but did it clear the threshold to be considered a professional foul? [See IFAB's definition in Chapter Twelve.]

'I could have sent Crossley off,' contemplates Milford, 'but I didn't because he actually went for the ball. He didn't take Lineker out. He went for it, missed it, and then took him out. It wasn't a deliberate foul.' Former World Cup Final referee, Clive Thomas, showed no fraternal inclination in his excoriating assessment of the standard of officiating in the match. 'It was as clear an example of a professional foul as you could see.'

Thirty years later, football writer Alyson Rudd engaged Premier League referee Chris Kavanagh to conduct an experiment. Kavanagh's assignment was to relitigate the final, applying the rules as they were written in 1991. By his exacting standards, the contest was worthy of four red cards and 11 yellows. Crossley, like Gascoigne before him, saw neither. The 21-year-old goalkeeper – who, upon breaking into the first team, was required to turn out for Brian Clough's elder son's Sunday League team in yet another of the manager's unsubtle assertions of power, and who had endured boos from his own supporters during a faltering spell earlier in the season – was about to join a select keepers' club. Lineker, unusually rushed, placed the ball on the spot, turned, and quickly embarked on his run-up. Too quickly. His side-footed shot to the goalkeeper's left is very much one to categorise as 'a good height for a keeper'. Crossley's diving parry made him only the second man, following Dave Beasant in 1988, to save a penalty in an FA Cup Final.

At last Milford's shrill whistle sounded. The first half had barely allowed the crowd to draw breath. But Venables darted along the touchline, keen to make every second in the dressing room count. David Howells vividly relates the scene that greeted him there. 'The first few minutes of half-time, everyone was asking after Gazza. Terry told us it was "a bad one", and we were all devastated for him. Then it all calmed down a bit, and Terry took over.

'He said, "You've got a choice here. Everybody will understand if you lose the game. You've lost your best player, and that's your excuse if you want to hide behind it. But you've had a great first half and should be winning this game. You've been the better side. You can go and show everyone what a team you are without Gazza. It's actually a real opportunity for you. Everyone is expecting you to lose now, but I know you're more than capable of winning. It's up to you."

'That was brilliant management. He put it right back on us, and we looked around at each other and thought, "Of course we can do it."'

Chapter Seventeen

The Rising

'I'M ONE of the most pessimistic Spurs fans, but ahead of the game it never crossed my mind that we might lose the final,' says Terry Deller. 'After doing Arsenal in the semi, I was so confident we'd win – which is a mad thing for any Tottenham fan to say – that Duncan and I, one of the mates I was sitting with behind the goal we attacked in the second half, had shaved SPURS into the side of our heads ... Then, you're barely 20 minutes in, and it seems like everything has fallen apart. You start mentally weighing up: do I cut it all off or wear a hat for the next month?! At half-time, I kept thinking about 1987. We choked that day and blew it. You think that can't happen again. But – oh shit – here it is, happening again.'

The lugubrious looks almost took permanent hold of Spurs fans' faces within a minute of the restart. Ian Woan, shimmying down a left wing plastered with boards advertising Smirnoff, Ouzo, Labatt's and Guinness, was the beneficiary of some tipsy Tottenham defending. His sleek one-two with Nigel Clough enabled him to make inroads into Erik Thorstvedt's box. Steve Sedgley got a foot in. The ball popped out to David Howells on the edge of the area, who tried to chip a delicate back pass into his goalkeeper's gloves.

Pat Van Den Hauwe, however, provided an unwitting barrier to the ball's safe passage. Taking evasive action – the full-back attempted an exotic limbo beneath its flight – he arched backwards, arms flailing. But the ball struck him on the chest and ricocheted as if morphing into a set-up for Roy Keane, who seized on the bounce goal-side of the penalty spot and lobbed it over the helpless Thorstvedt. Just as Keane swerved to poke the ball home, the recovering Howells raced in and smacked it to safety. On such moments cup finals turn.

Journalist Duncan Hamilton recounts how Brian Clough confided in him that 'the strangest sensation swept over [him]' as he sat on the bench at the start of the second half. 'I thought we weren't going to win, and somehow, whatever we did that day wasn't going to be enough.' Stuart Pearce also acknowledges something had shifted in the Forest ranks since the first half but doesn't subscribe to his manager's notion that the outcome was preordained. As he wrote in his book, 'We thought it was too easy … We were one up, Gazza was off, and we felt all we needed to do was play the second half out. I don't know whether it was complacency or whether we thought we had something to hold on to and sat back.' What this explanation doesn't allow for is Tottenham's fierce determination to press the issue.

For all the match's fine football, Spurs' route back into the final was a direct one. In the 55th minute, Thorstvedt leapt to gather a looping header from a Forest corner. Bouncing the ball a few times to encourage his team-mates towards the halfway line, the Norwegian launched a very British up-and-under. Observing its flight with interest was Nayim. Defying orthodoxy, he declined to position himself for a headed flick-on. Instead, the substitute allowed the ball to drop towards him. As it descended to his midriff, he volleyed a sumptuous pass that few players could conceive of, let alone execute. It simultaneously took Keane and Garry Parker out of the game and demanded Paul Allen run at the Forest backline.

Allen, the Stakhanovite of the Spurs side, gladly accepted the invitation and swiftly made for the edge of the box. Sensing his moment, Paul Stewart made a charging run from inside to out. Allen's pass to him was meticulously timed. Stewart took

VENABLES IN — TISA back their man during the final home game of the season. Annelise Jespersen says 'I think I'm holding up the "A" but I can't be sure.' (Mirrorpix)

Recording 'When The Year Ends In 1' with Chas & Dave (Mirrorpix)

Abide with Cloughie – Venables humours the Forest manager

Protocol breach!
Gazza and Lady Di

That tackle on Gary Charles

Gascoigne departs the final on a stretcher as referee Roger Milford looks on

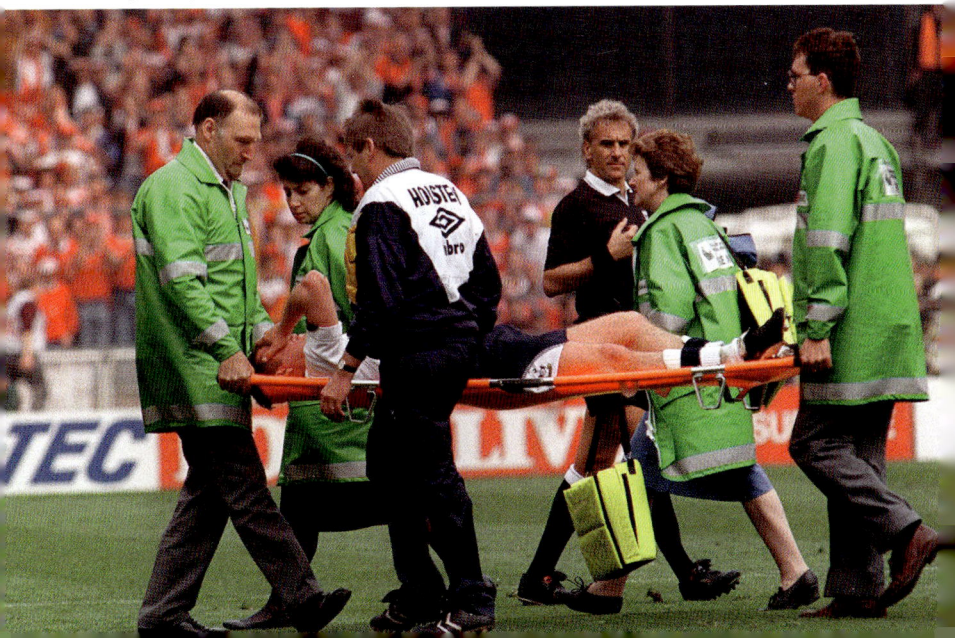

Lineker sees his penalty saved by Crossley

The indomitable Paul Stewart strikes Tottenham's equaliser

Despite appearances, Des Walker is the unfortunate match-winner

Gary Mabbutt holds the FA Cup aloft. Spurs stand alone as eight-time winners.

The boys of 91

Absent friend – this mask was as close as Gascoigne got to the victory parade

The Joe Bloggs' victory bus

1988 launch of Sky TV, Rupert Murdoch and Alan Sugar (centre)

Robert Maxwell pictured in 1991

The short-lived 'dream team'. Venables and Sugar celebrate their takeover in June 1991

one touch to steady himself, then, as four defenders converged upon him, applied a second to pummel a venomously angled low shot between Gary Charles's legs, across Mark Crossley and into the far corner of the net. It was his first goal since Blackpool in the third round. 'To score at the end where the Spurs fans were was just perfect. I sort of felt myself being carried towards them by an invisible tide.'

The sight of Stewart jubilantly jumping over the advertising boards behind the goal before offering a kiss with both his hands to the rhapsodic fans who greeted him will remain forever enshrined in the rich iconography of Tottenham Hotspur Football Club.

But self-effacing as ever, Stewart is keen to heap praise for the goal anywhere but on himself. 'It was Terry who told me to go everywhere with Roy Keane. I think he got sick of me and let me run away from him for the equaliser. You don't think your life has instantly changed scoring in a cup final. You know that if you don't go on to win, it counts for nothing. I couldn't allow myself to switch off. If you do that against a player like Keane – who clearly was going to become one of the best ever – he'll punish you. With that being said, after we scored, I knew we'd win. I could see they were gone. We just got stronger and stronger.'

Tottenham's domination was reflected in Clough's decision to withdraw Ian Woan for Steve Hodge and by the increasing rancour in Keane's tangles with the left side of the Spurs defence. A challenge on halfway grounded Justin Edinburgh. Any pretence that Keane's resulting 'pass' into the prone left-back's head was anything but deliberate was exposed by the Irishman grabbing his nethers while giving Edinburgh a verbal volley.

The pair tangled again with 15 minutes of the 90 remaining. A surging run from the Forest man took him beyond Sedgley. As he crossed the ball, Edinburgh took the opportunity to leave more than a bit on him. Roger Milford had to step in to separate the pair. The referee indicated he had been privy to what the BBC cameraman had missed. The Tottenham full-back had aimed a surreptitious back-heel into Keane's leg as the two men got to their feet. The spat was simmering nicely, but its high (or low point, depending on your sensibilities) was yet to come.

Paul Walsh is brutally honest about his frame of mind on the Tottenham bench as the clock ticked down. He didn't have everything crossed for another Spurs goal. 'Listen, when I hear people say it's all about the team, I think to myself, what absolute bollocks. Things like that are said for other people's benefit. I wanted to get on and score the winner. Alright, you have to play within the framework of the team. And, if you're doing it properly, you have responsibilities and expectations of yourself. But ultimately, you're there for yourself. Football can be pretty selfish.

'So I've always been sceptical of that "as long as the team wins, that's what matters" stuff. My boyhood dream wasn't to sit on the subs' bench in an FA Cup Final. It was to be the match-winner in one. I felt much more a part of it when I was with Liverpool in '86 – even though I was injured for that final – than with Tottenham in '91. I'd deserved to be in that Liverpool side. But I can't say the same about that Spurs cup final team because my behaviour and attitude left me on the outside.[29] That said, I would have probably lost my shit if I'd not made the bench. And I'd been worried in the build-up that Terry might throw in a "fuck you" and leave me off it. Thankfully, he didn't.'

Inside the final ten minutes, Walsh began readying his lustrous hair in anticipation. Venables told him he was coming on for the excellent but exhausted Samways. Once on the pitch, the striker's determination to make his mark further unsettled the weary Forest defence. Walsh willingly chased

---

29 As if to underline his sense of detachment from proceedings while sitting on the bench, Walsh is taken aback when reminded that Spurs had been awarded – and missed – a penalty in the first half of the final. 'Really, did we? Who took it?'

down lost causes. And so, Des Walker and Steve Chettle began thrashing wildly at clearances. One such piece of Walsh ferreting led to a 90th-minute corner. Nayim's outswinger was met firmly by Howells. A scrabbling Crossley and wide-eyed Parker just about combined to prevent it from crossing the line.

The ease with which Spurs players were now making first contact with Nayim's deliveries augured well for the imminent onset of extra time. 'I was pleased that it went to extra time,' says Walsh. 'I knew then that I'd get to play a more significant part in the game.'

* * *

The conclusion of regular time precipitated one of the most bemusing spectacles in FA Cup history. Terry Venables urgently gathered his players around him on the Wembley pitch and attempted to rouse them toward a final 30-minute push to victory. Across the way, the Forest players, clustered in four disparate groups, were left to ponder the whereabouts of their manager.

Brian Clough was nowhere to be seen.

The BBC's cameras eventually located him. He'd secreted himself inside the annexe behind the benches and struck up a conversation with a police constable, who he affectionately touched on both cheeks before returning to his seat. Reflecting on Clough's behaviour before extra time, Bob Wilson struggled to conceal his contempt. 'They needed help from their leader. And at 90 minutes, it was absolutely staggering that Brian Clough stayed on his backside.'

In Clough's defence, it wasn't the first time he'd pulled this particular stroke. During his glorious stint at the helm of Derby County, he'd left the players to their own devices before extra time of an FA Cup tie at White Hart Lane in 1973. On that occasion, following a win for the Rams, the common conception was that it was a typically brilliant piece of Cloughian psychology. Such was his unwavering belief in his players, there was no reason for him to intervene.

He'd repeated the trick in the second leg of the 1984 UEFA Cup quarter-final between Forest and Sturm Graz where his team again triumphed after 120 minutes. The problem in the FA Cup Final, though, was that his Forest players looked shot.

Mark Crossley has since gone on the record to downplay the significance of Clough's extra time aberration. 'I don't think it surprised us that he didn't [come on to the pitch]. What can he say? It looks good for the television that the manager's in amongst things, but what can they say? His philosophy on football was so simple … you had individual jobs: "Goalkeeper, keep the ball out of the net; full-backs, stop crosses, pass it to someone who can play if you can; wingers, get your heels on the line, go one v one, beat them and cross the ball; centre-forward, score me a diving header, preferably get cut while you're doing it, get hold of the ball." So what's he gonna say when he comes on? I know it doesn't look great, but he probably still believed we'd go on and win that game anyway.'

Clough would unsatisfactorily address the matter in his first autobiography. 'I didn't go simply because they didn't want me. I knew the cameras would have been trained on me if I'd stepped forward, so I sent out my coaches. I didn't want my players thinking: "This is the trophy he hasn't won, we mustn't blow it now." I didn't want them freezing after a gruelling 90 minutes, and I'm certain they didn't want me telling them what more they could do. At that stage, I simply had nothing more to offer them. When a team's about to enter extra time in a match as important as a cup final – drained both physically and mentally – the last thing they want is a manager wandering among them, urging "one last mighty effort". They've heard it all, they've had their instructions, they're sick of the sight of the opposition who still stand between them and that wonderful cup-winning feeling, and they know exactly what is needed.'

Given that Clough later told journalist Duncan Hamilton that his extra time non-appearance was a 'mistake', seemingly born of him already being resigned to defeat, it's difficult not to view these words as a hollow justification for his actions after the fact. Hamilton, who – during two decades covering Forest – came to understand Clough's genius and frailties better than perhaps anyone, describes the manager's decision to no-show the extra time team talk as one of the 'crassest he ever made' and considers it to be 'the turning point not just for Forest that afternoon but for Clough's managerial career'.

* * *

The resumption of play saw Spurs kicking towards Wembley's tunnel end. Gary Lineker, fatigued from ploughing a lone furrow in attack for so much of the afternoon, found Walsh a rejuvenating presence alongside him. The striker doggedly pressurised Hodge into surrendering an early corner. Nayim's delivery had found its groove. This one fell right in the middle of the goalmouth. Pearce strained to head it away. His clearance fell centrally on the edge of the box. Paul Allen, an ever-willing retriever, guided the ball back to Van Den Hauwe, who, dispensing with any niceties, lobbed it straight back in the mixer. Walsh – not known for his aerial prowess – had the run on Charles at the back post. The forward's header looped high over the back-pedalling Crossley. As it began to plummet towards the goal, Lineker raised his arms in celebration, only to see the ball ricochet from the crossbar. Pearce was on hand to fire it behind to apparent safety. 'It was almost like someone was teasing me,' says Walsh ruefully, '"You'll nearly score the winner in the cup final, but you won't!"' But Spurs weren't to be denied for long.

After Crossley had been given a few squirts of pain-numbing spray – he'd crashed into the far post in his vain attempt to reach Walsh's header – Nayim received Milford's blessing to take another corner from the Tottenham right. 'We had a signal for me to get the ball into the first post for someone to flick it on. I can't remember what it was now, but we'd scored a couple of goals in the league that season like that, so that's what I went for. I put the ball on to Paul Stewart's head – ah, Stewy, what a fighter. He would compete for every centimetre on the pitch, and he got the touch it needed.' Stewart's intervention diverted the ball to the far post, where Gary Mabbutt appeared ahead of Walker to apply the finishing touch to flash it into the top corner. He'd given Spurs the lead their play undoubtedly merited.

At least that's how Mick Lowes called it in his Capital Gold commentary. Interviewed for this book, Jonathan Pearce lets out a snort of laughter while shaking his head. 'It was chaos. Lowesy had called it Mabbutt's goal, but we'd realised it was actually a Des Walker-headed own goal. So Bobby Moore, Terry Neill, and me, we're all holding up four fingers to Lowesy – Des Walker's shirt number was 4 – to get the message to him. Poor old Lowesy doesn't understand and compounds it by saying, "It's Gary Mabbutt's fourth goal of the season."

'We'd done a deal with Spurs to make a cassette to commemorate the cup run, piecing together our commentary of the goals in each round and interviews with the players. We'd already ordered the tapes, the covers were designed, and the little stickers to go on each of them. It was going to help boost our budget for the next season. But that moment totally fucked it up, and Tottenham ended up pulling the plug on it.'

David Howells remembers being just as confused. 'Even for about an hour after the game, I thought it was Mabbsy's goal. I'd jumped up with Stewy for the flick-on, so by the time I turned around, the ball was in the net, and the skipper was wheeling away. If I'm honest, I was a little bit underwhelmed by his celebration. Especially considering what had happened to him with his own goal in '87. I was like, "C'mon Mabbsy, I thought you'd be running around the stadium." But eventually, someone set me straight.'

There were no big screens inside Wembley, and with the bulk of Spurs fans banked behind the opposite goal, they also assumed Mabbutt had completed his Hollywood script-style redemption arc. Willie Morgan – who'd briefly held the Wembley stadium announcer post – remembers hearing Mabbutt's name being broadcast as the goalscorer over the PA. 'We all started singing the "Super Gary Mabbutt" song,' remembers Steve Davies. 'It was the loudest I've ever heard singing at football. It wasn't until later, when we were out for a drink, that we discovered it was Des Walker. That was astonishing in itself because he was such a reliable player – "You'll never beat Des Walker" and all that.'

Having buried the ball in his own net, Walker disconsolately buried his head in the Wembley turf. Aside from the pleasing circularity of Mabbutt erring in '87 and now likely lifting the trophy thanks to another own goal, there were further narrative strands to Walker's *tempus horribilis*. The England international had never managed a goal at the right end in his City Ground career. Furthermore, the Forest stalwart was Enfield-born and had been on Spurs' books as a youngster, until – legend has it – Bill Nicholson took exception to his unkempt hair and tardiness.[30] It was a decision they'd long regretted as he'd since established himself among the outstanding centre-backs in the First Division – long regretted until the fourth minute of extra time in the cup final, that is.

There was little to suggest a Forest footballing fightback. With no Nigel Jemson to call forth and Lee Glover a spent force, Clough's only option was to send on Brian Laws and push Keane forward. The disgruntled Hodge channelled his multifaceted frustrations into a series of murderous tackles, the worst of which – a flying effort that landed halfway up Nayim's calf – finally prompted Milford to issue the game's first card, in the second period of extra time. Hodge was fortunate it was only yellow. Tottenham continued to string

---

30 The less sensational but more likely rationale for the defender's White Hart Lane release is that Spurs had considered Walker insufficiently at ease with the ball at his feet.

passes together, sapping Forest's dwindling energy reserves. Spurs were liberal in their use of the back pass, too. Stewart played one particular beauty to his keeper from almost the halfway line. Thorstvedt gladly picked them up, rolled them out and waited to receive the next.

It was all proving too much for Keane, who, before viewers' very eyes, was transforming from the lithe colt into the snapping, snarling force of nature who would dominate English football's midfield for the next decade. When Justin Edinburgh indulged in some taunting verbals after Keane was flagged offside in a shooting position in the final minute, he couldn't resist thrusting his head toward Edinburgh and firing back. This prompted Steve Sedgley to deliver a wanker sign at Keane straight down the barrel of a BBC camera, which John Motson didn't dare ignore. 'There are one or two gestures there not worthy of the cup final.'

The commentator followed this magnificent line with another pearler as Lineker ran down the clock by hemming the ball into the corner. 'We're now in stoppage time at the end of extra time, and Spurs are in touching distance now of the FA Cup. The Forest fire seems to have faded. They're virtually burned out.' Tottenham almost ended the match with a flourish of keep-ball: 20 'Olé' serenaded passes were completed before a shattered Stewart – soon to be named Man of the Match – momentarily let it run beneath his foot.

And with that, the navy blue and white ribbons were tied to the FA Cup – a tradition believed to have been started at a celebratory dinner by the wife of a Spurs director in 1901 when Tottenham, playing outside the ranks of the Football League, had lifted the cup for the first time. Now, having scaled the 39 steps, a glowing Gary Mabbutt received the trophy from the Duchess of Kent. This eighth victory elevated Spurs into rarefied air above Aston Villa and Manchester United as the club that had won the FA Cup more than any other.

Chapter Eighteen

Congratulations and Tribulations

BRIAN CLOUGH, momentarily emerging from the catatonia that had enveloped him for so much of the afternoon, acknowledged the Forest fans as they hailed him as he walked back to the dressing room. He would rage that the FA had not struck medals for either manager and later borrowed his son Nigel's to have one cast for himself in gold. Roger Milford's performance also came under Clough's fire. In his first autobiography, he described the official's benevolence to Paul Gascoigne as 'the worst refereeing decision in my 40-odd years in football ... Wembley stank to its rafters ... here was a referee copping out of his responsibilities.' There's an irony in Clough levelling that specific allegation at Milford, given the flak he took over his team selection and his inertia before and during extra time.

The post-final traffic on the M1 was so bad that some Forest fans vacated their vehicles and cheerily commenced an impromptu roadside kickabout. The mood on the team bus was far more sombre. According to the account in Steve Hodge's book, Clough insisted on a diversion to East Midlands Airport so that he could fly off to Majorca. It's a false memory, reflecting Hodge's aversion towards his manager by the end of their strained relationship. Clough attended the civic reception held for the team the next day. Hodge – soon to sign for Leeds – did not. Thousands of fans gathered to fill the streets between County Hall and the Old

Market Square. Faced with a sentimental outpouring from his adoring public, Clough – against his better judgement – couldn't resist uttering the words the crowd craved to hear. 'There's no way I'm going to retire ... I'll be back trying to get there [to Wembley] next year.'

It would prove a fateful decision.

**

Inside the Tottenham dressing room, the victors complied with all the sacred traditions of FA Cup liturgy. Roy Reyland recalls, 'I was the one who got thrown in the bath. They all just picked me up and chucked me in.' But, amid the jubilation, an absent friend was never far from the squad's thoughts. Rather than heading straight to the Hilton Hotel, which was to play host to an all-night celebratory function, Terry Venables and the players made a detour to the Princess Grace Hospital. Gascoigne had been admitted in time to watch the culmination of the final from his bed. He described his misery in the 2015 documentary film *Gascoigne*. 'All I ever wanted to do was walk up them steps being a winner ... Once I'd seen Gary Mabbutt ... lifting up the trophy, that destroyed us 'cos that was all I wanted to do. If I could have done that, I wouldn't be bothered if I played another match.'

Gascoigne asked for a sleeping tablet to temporarily escape his new gut-wrenching reality. But he was soon confronted by the bitter-sweet arrival of his tracksuited team-mates, who presented him with the silverware and his winners' medal. Gascoigne, in his book, says he could barely meet their eyes. 'I felt I didn't deserve it. I'd acted like a mad bastard ... I felt I'd let them down when it mattered most ... I had finally buggered everything up for good, all through my own stupidity.'

'That's what I remember the most, going to the hospital to take the cup to Gazza,' recalls Nayim. 'More than anyone, he deserved it as he took us to the final. We wanted to share it with him. I was crying around his bed. I think we all were. It was an unbelievably emotional moment.'

'I'm not sure we knew the full extent of the injury,' says Erik Thorstvedt, 'but it was just important to tell him how much we appreciated him as a person and what he'd done to win us that trophy. He was someone you were used to as always laughing and joking, so to see him like that was very sad.'

'It was tragic. I kept thinking what must be going through the kid's mind,' reflects Reyland, 'and he was just a kid. He's blown his chance of playing in a cup final. He's jeopardised his move to Lazio. And, he must have been thinking: "Will I be the same player again?"'

Paul Walsh remembers the challenge of striking the right tone. 'We didn't want to be too euphoric as he's laying there with his leg all wrapped up. You're gutted for him until you leave the room, where the celebrations carry on without him.' Gascoigne asked to be temporarily discharged to join the night's revelry but was given a stark choice by the doctor: 'It's either the party or your career.'

Inevitably, the hospital room reunion with Gascoigne had a subduing effect on the players' official celebrations. The Hilton gala reception eventually burst into life when Steve Sedgley insisted on joining Chas & Dave on stage to belt out a spirited version of 'Ain't No Pleasing You'. 'Once it got going, the party was amazing, it carried on straight through until we got on the bus for the parade in Tottenham the next morning,' says a smiling Paul Stewart while involuntarily massaging his head as he recalls the joyously foggy memory.

Interviewed in a plush wood-panelled suite for that evening's episode of *Match of the Day*, Venables, with the FA Cup in tow, tried to savour the moment while deflecting questions from David Davies about Gascoigne and the club's future. 'I'm not going to think about that tonight. We're going to relax … and then business as usual on Monday morning, I would say … [winning] was a bit like a fairy story, the fact that we've had these problems. The fact I've got involved, sometimes I've thought: "Is this worthwhile?" Then you look at people – and the supporters – and you think "yes, we've got to keep going to the death" ... Seeing those supporters today when I was walking around was special. And I was really thrilled for them.'

When asked, 'Could there be a better day?' Venables smiled before replying, 'I haven't seen one yet. Let's hope there is a better day, but it was a special day for me, and I think for lots of people. Staff, the players and the supporters: everyone's been unsure about what's been going on, and there's nothing you can say to appease them at the moment. We've all hung on in there, and it's been a fairy-tale ending.'

The following morning, Venables – accompanied by his dad Fred – and the bleary-eyed players climbed the steps of a blue and white open-topped Routemaster bus. It was plastered, of course, with Joe Bloggs branding, while cans of Lucozade Sport were strategically snuck into the shot as television interviews were conducted on the upper deck. An estimated 250,000 people lined the streets as the parade crawled past White Hart Lane towards the Tottenham Town Hall. Several in the crowd were wearing rubber 'Gaz masks' moulded in their now fallen hero's image which had been sold by *The Spur* fanzine as the cup run had unfolded. The enduring soundtrack emanating from the crowd was a chant of 'Don't go Terry. Don't go'. Venables joked that he had spied the club's bank manager amid the crowd before declaring the welcome to be 'as good as I have ever seen it in this country. It's just unbelievable.'

'Those scenes will stay with me forever,' says Stewart. For David Howells, 'It felt like an out-of-body experience. You're suddenly involved in something that wasn't meant to happen to you, something you see on telly, not something you actually get to do. It was brilliant, just a blur of faces.'

'All my family were Spurs,' reminisces Vinny Samways, 'so I'd watched those open-top bus parades as a kid. To be part of one was mind-blowing. Thousands upon thousands of people and one of the most memorable experiences of my career. It doesn't change you as a person, but it's something you're incredibly proud of. To win it with the club where you've come through the ranks and supported is very special. My medal is securely in the safe!'

'That was the first time in my life I'd seen that number of people chanting and screaming,' says Nayim. 'Without the fans, there is no football. To be able to enjoy that ecstasy with them is what football is about. You are in the spotlight, and you know, all around the world, people have watched you play a final. So a little bit, your life has changed. But inside, you've not changed too much. You're a professional, and you try to get to more finals.

'But you know it has changed a lot of fans' lives, and that's what happens in this marvellous game. You can change people's lives. They still remember that final after all these years. They keep those memories with a smile, and when you have problems, you can put on that final and have two hours to be happy.'

Watching a video of the parade, it's noticeable that Erik Thorstvedt holds a monopoly over carrying the trophy. The goalkeeper explains, 'Because I was holding it for so long, someone asked me on the bus, "Have you glued the FA Cup to your hands?" I tried to pass it around, but everyone was saying no – I got a bit of stick for that, but I don't mind. The main thing was I didn't drop it!

'It was a life-changing moment, although I didn't know it then. Growing up, I wasn't one of these guys who just knew I'd be successful. I had to fight for it mentally. Having that success in football gave me the confidence that I could perform in other areas. I now work in television. I would never have thought I could do that, as speaking to big audiences or on-screen felt very hard. But the experiences you have through football, having some triumphs – along with failing miserably on many, many occasions – helped me grow.

'And now that I've allowed myself to look back and feel pride in winning that FA Cup, I've come to peace with all my demons which try to bring me down somehow – more often than not, you remember the bad stuff instead of the good, don't you? But having that winners' medal – it's not that my life has taken a totally different direction, but it has been extremely meaningful and important to me and made a difference in my life.

'Not long ago, someone approached me about restaging that open-top bus parade and getting all the players who'd been on board back together for a charity thing,' says the smiling Norwegian while rolling his eyes. 'You can imagine the reaction if we did that – Spurs can't win a trophy, so they're restaging the 1991 bus parade … a recipe for disaster.'

When, after several hours, the bus reached its Town Hall terminus, the players were ushered inside to receive the acclaim of the civic dignitaries. 'I remember I went out on to the Town Hall balcony with Gary Mabbutt and the cup,' laughs Gudni Bergsson. 'Everyone cheered very loudly for me and a little for Gary – or maybe it was vice versa. I think Mabbsy dragged me out there saying, "Come on Gudni, let's lift this cup together." He knew how much I had wanted to play in the final and how disappointed I'd been to be left out. That was really nice of Mabbsy – typical of him – to think of a team-mate at that moment. It's a very fond memory.'

For TISA founders Annelise Jespersen and Steve Davies, who'd invested so much energy into securing a future for the club, the parade is a cherished memory. 'What a mad thing to do really,' says Jespersen, 'to stand around for hours waiting to catch a glimpse of them as they come past for a few seconds – particularly as Tottenham Green where we were standing was covered in dog shit – but it was well worth it. We were a cup team. *The* cup team. To think there are fans in their 30s now who haven't seen us win the FA Cup. The things you take for granted.'

'It's such a shame we've not had another one,' echoes Davies. 'People hanging off every building – a chance for those who can't come to games to be involved, which is so important. It's just a great community feeling. I'd love to have that again.'

Danny Kelly is one of the few who didn't attend the parade. 'That morning, I woke up in a massive celebratory mood and somehow ended up at a garden centre – I suspect it wasn't my idea. There before me was this navy blue and white striped deckchair, which I had no choice but to buy to commemorate Spurs' victory. That chair has followed me through moves across London. Eventually, when I emigrated to Ireland, we were packing up the pantechnicons. The current Mrs Kelly gave me the side eye as I started folding it up. "Don't ask," I said.

'Now the sunshine has faded it to more Brighton and Hove Albion colours, and I must confess the other summer, my sister-in-law – who is a West Ham fan – put her arse through it. But I always get it out if Spurs are in a really big game, hoping it will somehow help. The plan now is to find some new navy and white striped fabric and resuscitate it to its former glory of 34 years ago.

'Whenever I hear the term "Spursy" bandied about to mock us, I think back to 1991 and that final. Even now, all these years later, what little hair I have left is standing up on the back of my neck. We overcame tremendous adversity. That's just as much what "Spursy" means to me.'

For physio John Sheridan, however, memories of the day after the cup final are far from rosy. 'That Sunday was awful. Everyone was on the parade except for Gazza and me. I was with him at the hospital for his operation. I always wanted to be there in the operating theatre when players had surgery, as it put them and their families at ease. That could be very tough as once the surgeon got in there, the extent of the injury became apparent. You know it's going to be a long road back. That was definitely the case with Paul. There was no guarantee that he'd play again. I'd been through the same with Danny Thomas at Spurs three years earlier. I remember Danny asking me, "Will I play again?" That's what Gazza kept asking.' Thomas's knee ligaments had been severed in a tackle, and despite a series of operations, he'd been forced to retire in 1988 aged only 26.

'Whenever you took a player to hospital with Spurs, the press would turn up, but the level of interest with Gazza was frenzied, newspapers and television crews around the clock. The hospital management came up to me and said, "We've got a lot of other patients in our care beyond Paul Gascoigne who we need to consider, so you'll need to issue a statement to the media so they go away." I rang White Hart Lane to explain the situation, but no one answered due to the parade, so the hospital said I'd have to do it. I jotted down a few hand-written notes and then walked out to face them. All those cameras and reporters, it was like *whoosh* – unbelievably intense.

'Once I'd finished, I wondered whether I'd said the right thing. I'd basically asked them to respect Paul's privacy and leave him alone. And then, as I headed up the road, I realised they were following me. It was terrible, a real insight into Paul's life. When I got home, I put on the evening news, and there I was on the screen. Terry did phone me and ask how it had gone. He told me that he'd seen me on television and "well done" for how I'd handled it.'

The Sun's front page on the Monday morning showed little regard for the wellbeing of the man they'd hyped to the stratosphere. 'GAZZA: IS IT THE END?' Below the headline, a surgeon said to have carried out many similar procedures to that undergone by Gascoigne told readers that the player's chances of 'returning to the game at the top level were very slim'.[31]

---

31 Unhappily, the other story vying for attention on the front page of that edition of *The Sun* told of 'Charles and Di's rift over Camilla'.

Further newspaper reports did little to soothe Gascoigne's multiplying fears. '£8.5m deal collapses', stated *The Times*, quoting Lazio president Calleri as saying, 'If the long recovery period is confirmed, then the deal for the purchase of Gascoigne will be definitely off.' Elsewhere, Calleri spoke even more candidly. 'It looks like being a disaster as far as we are concerned.' Taking his lead from the despondent club president, Lazio fan Marcello Acciai told the press, 'I feel like laying some flowers at the gates of the Olympic Stadium after what's happened because he was going to be our superman … He would have taken over Italy because he was the type of personality to make it happen. But now it's all over. Like every other Lazio fan, I feel like committing suicide.'

Reading journalist Martin Barrow's assessment in *The Times* of where this left their club, it was a sentiment with which Spurs fans could empathise. 'The inevitable collapse of the agreement with Lazio as a result of Gascoigne's untimely injury has thrown Tottenham's tentative rescue plans into chaos and appears to have left the club with little option but to submit to being put into the hands of administrative receivers appointed by its creditors.'

Chapter Nineteen

The Dream Team

ALAN SUGAR courteously declined to be interviewed for this book, but according to the account given in his autobiographical tome, *What You See is What You Get*, he decided to invest in Tottenham Hotspur on little more than a whim.

'On Saturday, 18 May 1991, I was at home watching the FA Cup Final. Spurs were playing Nottingham Forest ... To this day, I don't know what possessed me, but on the following Monday, I put out a call to Spurs' manager, Terry Venables ... I'll say it again – I have no idea what prompted me to get involved.'[32]

Venables would have been preparing to travel to Old Trafford to complete the season's final league fixture when Sugar's call came through. With United revelling in their European Cup Winners' Cup triumph over Barcelona and the Spurs players running on boozy fumes after Wembley, the 1-1 result was of no consequence. The abiding image from a game that resembled a love-in more than a First Division match was that of respective captains Bryan Robson and Gary Mabbutt displaying the two trophies to the crowd before kick-off. The Tottenham Hotspur PLC farce had not discouraged those

---

32 While support for Spurs ran in Alan Sugar's family, very little of that interest seemed to have rubbed off on him. In a newspaper interview ahead of the 1991 Charity Shield, he failed to successfully identify the decade, let alone year, in which the club had won the double.

determining Manchester United's future. Within a month of the match between the two clubs, United embarked on their own flotation. Timing is everything. The upshot was that the Old Trafford outfit were primed to dominate English football for the next two decades.

Back at Spurs, Venables's contract as manager expired at the end of May. He took a dim view of Irving Scholar's offer – typically communicated to *The Mirror*'s Harry Harris – of a new deal to remain in post. Only the acceptance of his terms and a seat at the boardroom table would keep him at Tottenham.

'I have indulged sentiment enough already by doing what I'm doing and trying to buy and help save the club. But you can't make really silly decisions. I'm prepared to get involved in things, but not to the extent of getting myself into a position where I can't win. I'm not prepared to buy Tottenham at any price. Why should I pay double – or treble – what it is worth? It's nonsense. I'm not scared to leave Spurs, and if anything, winning the FA Cup Final has made it easier.'

As if to underline that Venables was serious about calling time on his Spurs stay, press reports began linking him to Marseille and Juventus. Even if the veracity of these stories was in doubt, they served to pile even more pressure on Spurs' major shareholders to sell up and ship out.

After a series of meetings between the Sugar and Venables camps – 'financial guru' Eddie Ashby was in charge of running the numbers on Venables's side of the ledger – the two men settled on a 50/50 partnership. Bidding to end the stalemate between Paul Bobroff and Irving Scholar by buying the warring pair out, Sugar and Venables would put up £3 million each.

Under their proposal, Gascoigne would have to be sold as a down payment on the debt. Not that Venables ever said so publicly, but perhaps he too had had his fill of Gazzamania/Gazza's mania. A statement from John Browett, the surgeon who had operated on Gascoigne's knee, had by then assuaged fears that the injury might prove terminal for the player's career. Accordingly, Lazio officials began indicating their deal for the player could be revived.

News of this 'dream partnership' to salvage Spurs hit the press as the team participated in a post-season tournament in Japan. Gary Lineker's appearance in the final match in Tokyo – which necessitated him flying in from Australia, where he'd just captained England, to ensure the organisers didn't renege on the tour fee promised to Tottenham – helped facilitate his 1992 transfer to Nagoya Grampus Eight for just under £1 million.

Harry Harris had been on the other side of the world covering the England team for *The Mirror* when, without warning, Robert Maxwell summoned him home. The publisher's interest in buying the club had suddenly been rekindled. Harris began pumping out columns championing his boss's cause, which was presented as a piece of altruism in service of the interests of the British public. *The Mirror*'s back page on 12 June read, 'SAVE OUR GAZZA'. Harris followed it up a day later by telling readers, 'Robert Maxwell – who is making a dramatic move into Tottenham – is aware that keeping Gazza in English football would be like protecting the national inheritance. And Maxwell is the only man who can save him.'

But what was behind Maxwell's latest gambit? Why now – when he'd ignored Nat Solomon's correspondence which all but begged him to come to Tottenham's aid? The obvious answer was publicity. Here was another opportunity to thrust his name into the headlines, and by linking himself to Gascoigne, he was guaranteed reams of them. He certainly had plenty of form for such stunts. But there is little doubt Maxwell's interest must have been piqued by Alan Sugar entering the Tottenham fray. Perhaps he suspected Sugar was acting as a proxy for his bitter rival Rupert Murdoch. He would not have been alone in that prognostication.

The week before Tottenham and Arsenal had contested the semi-final in April, the uneasy status quo in English football was torn asunder with the leak of the Football Association's 'Blueprint for the Future of Football'. It gave the governing body's blessing for the 22 First Division clubs – led by the long-standing 'Big Five' plotters (Arsenal, Everton, Liverpool, Manchester United and Tottenham Hotspur) – to break away from the Football League and its unwelcome commitment to sharing out television money across all four of its divisions. On the very same day in June that the FA officially presented these plans to the sports minister – confirming it was willing to seek a High Court ruling to legitimise its right to create the all-new Premier League – Maxwell signalled his renewed interest in Spurs.

While Alan Sugar may be unclear on what motivated his bid for Tottenham, Murdoch – like Sugar, a man with no previous passion for football – was keen that Sugar win the day. Their relationship had been consummated in 1988 when Murdoch launched Sky TV. In his book, Sugar recalls taking the call from Murdoch that started it. During that decade, Amstrad (Alan Michael Sugar Trading) had scrapped its way to the front rank as the UK's largest manufacturer of home computers. However, as the 1990s dawned, following the release of a faulty new model and increased competition, things had gone awry. The inexorable rise of Amstrad's share price was over and the company badly needed something new to sell. As Murdoch laid out his satellite television plans, Sugar's excitement grew by the second.

'I knew ... the punters would go bananas for an extra 16 channels if it could be done cheaply ... I told Rupert I was so confident about this that he didn't need to underwrite any orders.' Amstrad would use its know-how to knock out the dishes and set-top boxes required to view Sky, enabling them to be sold on the high street for an affordable £199. But while both men had stood smiling shoulder to shoulder on stage at Sky's glitzy launch, it was not long before Sugar's hectoring voice down the line became familiar to those at Sky HQ.

The fundamental problem was that there was precious little on any of Sky's 'extra 16 channels' that viewers wanted to see, and definitely nothing they were going 'bananas' for. As a consequence, unsold satellite dishes were piling up in Amstrad's warehouse. What's more, with viewing figures so low, advertisers were hard to come by. And the only subscription channel from which Sky could draw meagre revenue – movies – offered low returns as rights fees were costly. Adding to Sky's woes, in the spring of 1990, rival British Satellite Broadcasting (BSB) had launched – also offering film subscriptions. An already emaciated market was saturated. With both companies haemorrhaging money, a merger quickly became inevitable. In November, Murdoch's deep pockets enabled Sky to gobble up BSB. (Initially, the 'merged' company was badged BSkyB, but that didn't last long.) The favour he curried with the Conservative government – Margaret Thatcher had hailed Sky for providing 'the only unbiased [TV] news in the UK' – worked in his favour. Not for the first time, questions as to whether Murdoch had flouted UK monopolies and mergers regulations went unanswered.

Nevertheless, the situation needed a lot more than the hurrahs of free marketeers. With BSB's losses added to its own, Sky was £2 billion in the red. At one point, it was said to be losing £14 million per week. Whispers even began circulating that the entire Murdoch empire might be taken down by this foray into satellite television in the UK.

Tasked with turning things around, Sam Chisholm jetted in from Australia. Such was the urgency of Sky's need, he got cracking before the necessary work permits had been issued. His rescue plan was simple. Sport was Sky's route to salvation. He'd used this playbook at Channel 9 in Australia, where he'd deployed media mogul Kerry Packer's millions to entice some of the best cricketers on the planet to the breakaway competition World Series Cricket. Packer's Channel 9 became

Australia's most popular station. Chisholm understood that only top-flight English football could bring in the subscribers required to save Sky. The FA's announcement that the Premier League was on its way meant the secessionist clubs would soon have to decide on the new league's broadcast partner. The vote, whenever it came, was a fixture Murdoch, Chisholm and Sky dare not lose.

It certainly wouldn't hurt their cause if Tottenham Hotspur – who'd long pushed for the Premier League and would have a pivotal role to play in canvassing the other clubs ahead of the vote – was owned by someone who shared a burning desire for Sky to succeed. As Sugar recalls in his book, 'I was really hyped up to ensure that Maxwell would not scupper the deal [for Spurs]. Andrew Neil [Sky's executive chairman], now back as editor of the [Murdoch-owned] *Sunday Times*, called me, trying to be helpful by bringing me up to date on what the market was telling him about Maxwell's intervention.'

In a 1992 interview for the Channel 4 documentary series *High Interest*, Sugar confirmed Murdoch had contacted him directly about Tottenham too. 'Rupert rang me up one day and said, "What's going on with this football club you're thinking of buying? I'm seeing this clown Maxwell is trying to buy it also." I think I might have said to him at the time, "Well he's got the power of his newspaper to hype up the thing. I haven't got a newspaper so perhaps one of your journalists could put in a good word for me in *The Sun*." … The conclusion was him saying, "Well, it sounds a good deal, wish you the best of luck, get on with it."'

Maxwell wasn't going to vacate the field without a fight. Attempting to head off the multi-ownership issue that had frustrated his attempt to buy Watford, *The Mirror's* back page on 14 June proclaimed, 'DERBY SOLD NEXT STOP SPURS'. David Buchler recalls meeting Maxwell at the upmarket Harry's Bar to discuss his 'offer' for Spurs. 'He seemed sincere. I don't know what was in his heart, but I must confess I found him to be personable and charming. At the end of our conversation, he told me he was going away on business. But he insisted on giving me phone numbers where I could contact him on his yacht, helicopter, or anywhere else he might be.'

Three days after the Derby sale scoop, another Mirror article claimed that the Football League had given Maxwell's Tottenham takeover 'the green light'. As so often with Maxwell, neither claim was accurate. Derby hadn't been sold, and the Football League – wisely – insisted they'd require written confirmation of any such divestment before its management committee would consider ratifying any Maxwell takeover at Tottenham.

Even forced on to the back foot, Maxwell continued to stir the Spurs pot. On 18 June, *The Mirror*'s back page declared to Tottenham fans, 'BOB'S YOUR UNCLE', warning them not to give any credence to mischievous stories circulating in rival outlets about a player mutiny at White Hart Lane should Maxwell's bid triumph. Amid newspaper reports that Sugar and Venables's proposals had won the unanimous support of the Tottenham board, it looked as though Maxwell had finally accepted defeat. On 21 June, Harry Harris was given *The Mirror*'s front page and three more inside the paper to explain that 'Robert Maxwell last night dramatically withdrew a near £9 million offer for Tottenham Hotspur which would have kept Paul Gascoigne at the club.'

After nine months of wrangling, Tottenham's future appeared secure as that afternoon Sugar and Venables arrived at the offices of Ansbacher Bank expecting to complete the purchase of Scholar and Bobroff's shareholdings. But even as Sugar prepared to hand over his share of the money, Maxwell reinserted himself into proceedings. Scholar, in Monte Carlo, and Bobroff, in attendance at Ansbacher, were taking calls from Maxwell, who again dishonestly claimed to have sold Derby and promised to pay more than Sugar and Venables were offering. Despite having been repeatedly let down by Maxwell, Scholar was inexplicably up for it. This time, at least, he issued Maxwell with an ultimatum. No more obfuscation. A deal had to be completed by the end of the day.

With Scholar onside, Maxwell gatecrashed Ansbacher by sending a battery of lawyers and financial advisors to talk Bobroff round to him too. Bobroff sheepishly told Scholar, 'It's alright for you, sitting in Monte Carlo. They're all shouting at me here.'

When Maxwell came on the phone and tried to discourage him from partnering with Venables, Sugar brought matters to a head in his pugnacious style. '"I've been told you don't have any money. Does this mob you've sent down here have a bankers' draft with them?" Maxwell went nuts, spouting off a load of rubbish ... I cut him short. "You don't have the money, right? So in that case, you'd best tell your team of lackeys to piss off and let me get on with this deal." He hung up.'

Robert Maxwell was definitively out of the Spurs picture.

Before the year was out, Sugar's instincts were proven to be spot on. Maxwell's inability to do a deal for Tottenham was symptomatic of more serious problems. The money men who had loaned Maxwell the funds to build his billion-pound business empire were becoming increasingly twitchy about his ability to service his debts. He was due in London on 5 November 1991 for a crunch meeting with the banks where his complete financial meltdown would finally be exposed.

In the early hours of that morning, Maxwell disappeared from his yacht, the *Lady Ghislaine*. Shortly before 6pm, his naked body was found floating in the Atlantic Ocean.

Harry Harris led the eulogies in the *Daily Mirror*, 'A MAN FOR ALL SEASONS'. Harris told readers that 'Maxwell loved the game [of football]', which 'was his passion'. Maxwell, Harris continued, was 'a soccer saviour they all went running to in their hour of need ... He was the man who saved two clubs from extinction, Derby and Oxford. He even put up £35,000 to rescue the Christmas club money of Southend fans. Yes, Robert Maxwell was that sort of man.'

Less than a month later, the tone at *The Mirror* had changed dramatically. On Wednesday, 4 December, the paper's front page read 'MILLIONS MISSING FROM THE MIRROR'. This was followed up a day later with 'MAXWELL: £526m IS MISSING FROM HIS FIRMS'. Maxwell had stolen it. Tottenham Hotspur had dodged a cannonball. Had it struck, the club may well have been sunk.

* * *

Having seen off Maxwell at Ansbacher, Sugar and Venables completed their takeover. There was a slight hitch in that Terry Venables's money hadn't arrived in time, which required Sugar to stake him. Meanwhile, Eddie Ashby rummaged down the back of the proverbial sofa and gave the magic money tree a vigorous shake on Venables's behalf. As Venables later wrote, 'The purchase of Spurs took practically every penny I owned.' Having enabled Venables's dream, Ashby was rewarded with a handsome general manager's salary at White Hart Lane – and he kept that position even when in June he was declared bankrupt with a string of 43 failed companies behind him, which by law should have disqualified him from the role. Venables's relationship with Ashby and the loans secured to complete the deal would return to haunt him, but that was for the future.

The morning after the Ansbacher summit, Tottenham's new smiling owners held a press conference at White Hart Lane. TISA's Annelise Jespersen and Steve Davies – understandably elated with the club's continued existence finally secure – were among the fans invited to line the pitch to greet them. It's striking, watching the archive news footage from that day, how the crowd's admiration is almost exclusively directed toward Venables, who is front and centre with the FA Cup. The overshadowed Sugar, who no doubt noticed this too, cuts an awkward figure bringing up the rear.

In his remarks to the press, Sugar set out how he saw the state of their union. 'Terry Venables will look after the 11 players on the field; I'll take care of the £11 million [debt] at the bank.' It was a good line but within it lay the seeds of the disharmony ahead. Venables – who became managing director of the PLC – had no intention of sticking strictly to on-pitch matters. One of Venables's first acts in his new post was to appoint Peter Shreeves as his successor in the Tottenham dugout. Gary Mabbutt expressed his regret at this development in a 1999 press interview. 'I was disappointed with [Terry] after the 1991 FA Cup Final. It was the highlight of my career to lift the trophy and we could have gone on after that Wembley triumph. But his mind was never again on the coaching side. Had he carried on, it could have been so good. But he wanted control of the club. From that victory over Nottingham Forest, we hardly saw him again at training.'

'The sale of Paul Gascoigne' was circled in red and twice underlined on the agenda of Tottenham's new managing director. Lazio's officials found themselves in an invidious position. They had placed so much reputational stock on signing Gascoigne – and aroused such excitement among the club's fans – that they were almost obliged to pursue the deal against their better judgement.

Gascoigne's recovery was going well. Spurs physio John Sheridan recalls the diligence with which his patient tackled his rehab even under the most trying conditions. 'I'd often take him out of London during that time. I remember being at my house in Bedfordshire and getting a call from a friendly journalist who said "you might want to have a look out your front door". There were photographers there who'd followed him. You couldn't escape it – they wanted to get something on him.' The pair – plus Gascoigne's entourage – escaped to Portugal to continue their work in the sunshine. It was a trip Sheridan remembers fondly, not least because actress Brigitte Nielsen was staying at the same hotel and was a willing table-tennis partner.

With Gascoigne making progress, a new offer came in from Rome. Lazio would no longer pay a world record fee but were offering £5.5 million, the money to be held in escrow while Gascoigne rehabilitated his knee. Only if Gascoigne passed a stringent medical, eventually set for a year to the day from his cup final catastrophe, could Spurs lay their hands on the money.

Programmes made in 1993 by BBC *Panorama* and Channel 4 *Dispatches* looking into Venables's tangled financial affairs raised concerns about the involvement of Kensington-based Italian restaurateur Gino Santin in the transfer. Venables claimed not only had Santin helped clinch the deal, but that he had even gotten Lazio to bump up their amended offer from £4.8 million and was therefore good value for the £200,000 commission he subsequently received. *Panorama* and *Dispatches* cried foul, demonstrating that Spurs and Lazio had agreed on £5.5 million before Santin's involvement, citing a fax from Lazio's solicitors and securing an interview with Lazio's finance director to back up their allegation. Venables insisted no such fax had been shown to him.

There must have been a bout of buyer's remorse at the Olympic Stadium when Gascoigne was arrested in Newcastle in mid-July. He'd been out in the town with his sister when she was knocked over. Gascoigne – not thinking clearly – saw red and indiscriminately threw punches at both the man who had bumped into her and another who had come to help. In court, he later admitted to assault and received a conditional discharge. Trouble seemed to keep seeking him out.

Two months later another trip home to the North East ended in personal disaster. Gascoigne was in a nightclub when he was the victim of an unprovoked attack. His surgically repaired knee crumpled beneath him and bystanders reportedly heard him screaming, 'It's my career. It's my career. Get me an ambulance!' John Sheridan remembers receiving a call from the Royal Victoria Infirmary where an inconsolable Gascoigne was being treated. X-rays revealed his kneecap had snapped into two pieces and that he'd damaged his ligaments. 'That was a career-threatening injury on its own,' says Sheridan. One small mercy as Gascoigne braced himself for further surgery was that his reconstructed ACL had remained intact.

'That was a horrible time,' says Sheridan with a puff of the cheeks. 'There was huge pressure on me to get him fit. We had such a small window to do it and after that second injury, that window became even smaller. That money from Lazio was desperately needed to give Spurs breathing space and I've heard people say without it the club could have gone down the drain. There were rumours – I don't know if there was any truth to them, but I still heard them – that there were problems with the insurance policy for him too, and that all contributed to the huge burden of responsibility I felt to get him back playing. Other than Terry, who was always supportive, I felt isolated from the club working day after day with Paul, racing against the clock. It reached unbearable levels.'

* * *

On 18 May 1992 at Mill Hill, Paul Gascoigne lined up for the kick-off in a specially arranged game. It was his first appearance for Spurs since his injury, and his last time in Tottenham colours. Sheridan, flanked by three Lazio officials, watched on nervously from the sideline.

'It was pouring down with rain and he scored in the mud. That shows you what a man Gazza was and his passion for the game. A lesser player might not have made it back.' After the match, Gascoigne withdrew as much money as the local cashpoint permitted and gratefully handed it over to the apprentices who'd comprised the opposition. His move to Lazio was confirmed soon after when he passed further tests in Rome. 'Gazza got to resurrect his career, Spurs got their money, and I flew home,' says Sheridan. 'When I got back from Italy, I was ready to jack it in.'

Emotionally and physically spent, he wasted little time in tendering his resignation.

Chapter Twenty

A Whole New Ball Game

THE SIGNIFICANCE of 18 May 1992 in English football goes far beyond Paul Gascoigne's return to fitness. That Monday morning, Alan Sugar and Terry Venables arrived at the Royal Lancaster Hotel – the venue from which Venables had set out with his team for Wembley precisely one year earlier – for a vote that would shift the paradigms of English football forever.

The top brass of England's 22 First Division clubs were assembling to determine which broadcaster would receive the television rights to the all-new Premier League. The kick-off to its inaugural season was only three months away.

By the time of the ballot, the equilibrium of Venables and Sugar's alliance had fundamentally altered. As 1991 had drawn to a close, Alan Sugar had ploughed nearly £5 million more into Tottenham, underwriting a rights issue to refinance the club that took his total investment to £8 million. It was a fascinating move from somebody who barely six months before had felt at a loss to explain what had compelled him to buy into Spurs, and who had spent the time since feeling as though he was 'being taken for an idiot'.

Venables, already stretched to fiscal breaking point, could not match the financial pace set by Sugar. Venables later alleged that before he'd consented to the rights issue proceeding, Sugar had promised not to use the votes that would come with his enlarged shareholding – a claim that

Sugar vehemently denied. Much to his chagrin, after the rights issue went ahead, Venables was very much demoted to junior partner.

Both men entered the Royal Lancaster's Westbourne Suite, aware that the deadline for bids for the Premier League contract had elapsed at midnight. Sky and ITV's best offers should have already been lodged with Premier League chief executive Rick Parry. ITV, however, decided to up the ante. Their executive director of football, Trevor East, attempted to outfox Sky by placing a new and improved offer worth £262 million before the assembled clubs. Sugar bolted out of the meeting room. A desperate search for a phone led him to the hotel lobby. Decorum be damned, there was too much at stake. 'Do you understand what I'm telling you? ... These are the figures, take them down ... Get your fucking arse round here and blow them out of the water.' The recipient of Sugar's call was Sky's Sam Chisholm. Chisholm got straight on the case. He dialled New York, where it was 4am, to wake Rupert Murdoch. He needed Murdoch's blessing to bid whatever it took. Murdoch was all in: £304 million ought to get the job done.

Under the Premier League's constitution, the winning bid required the support of at least two-thirds of its clubs. Sky's strategy had been to lobby those outside the Big Five. That very term needled the other clubs. ITV, on the other hand, promised the Big Five that they would show more of their matches throughout the five-year contract and assumed that where they went, enough of the other clubs' votes would follow.

When war-gaming how the vote would play out, ITV had not counted on Alan Sugar. Nor had they reckoned on Terry Venables suddenly being called away before the vote could take place to attend to some apparently 'not encouraging' news at the Spurs training ground related to Gascoigne's Lazio medical.

Sugar was left alone to cast Tottenham's ballot. Before he could do so, Arsenal vice-chairman David Dein and

Manchester United's Martin Edwards argued that Amstrad's partnership with Sky represented a potential conflict of interests and queried whether Tottenham should be allowed to participate in the vote. In his memoir, Sugar says he initially offered to abstain. But then, in an apparent volte-face, this offer was withdrawn. Entreaties from those clubs outside the Big Five swayed him. They felt Spurs' vote could prove decisive, doubtless in the knowledge that Sugar would go for Sky – the more lucrative offer for them.

Sugar says he was disappointed with the sniping going on about whether Spurs should be allowed to vote, and his back was up because he thought he could see agendas forming.

'The big clubs were trying to bully the rest – it was undemocratic. It seemed clear that they wanted to line their own pockets by favouring ITV. I was annoyed, so I went into bat big time for BSkyB.'

Lofty sentiments indeed! Although a sceptical reader might be forgiven for noting that things seemed to work out just as Sugar might have wished had this been the plan all along. Two clubs, Chelsea and Crystal Palace, did abstain. Of the remaining 20, 14, including Tottenham, plumped for Sky and six for ITV. Sky had gotten over the line without a single vote to spare, securing the majority required under Premier League rules. It was Alan Sugar's vote 'wot won it'. Amstrad's quoted market value immediately shot up by £7 million. Greg Dyke, then chairman of ITV Sport, pulled no punches when summing up how he felt about what had transpired: 'We were stitched up.' Dyke called for the result of the vote to be voided and for the whole bidding process to start again. Rick Parry maintained the outcome was 'irrevocable'.

A total of 91 Members of Parliament put their names to a motion, 'That this House deplores the new contract signed by the Football Premier League which restricts live television coverage of matches to homes with satellite dishes, thus depriving the vast majority of the football-watching public of their chance to see live matches on their sets; notes that this continues a trend set by the World Cup Cricket competition which was also largely kept off main British television channels; and condemns the swamping of the concept of public service broadcasting by narrow commercial interests.'

Ninety of the signatories came from the opposition Labour benches. Dyke reflected it was a matter of realpolitik. 'In other countries, politicians intervened when it looked like their major football leagues were likely to end up on pay television, in Britain they didn't. Winning elections is too important to British politicians, and the Murdoch press can influence who wins and who loses. As a result, most of them don't have the nerve to take on Murdoch.'

And so what Sam Chisholm called the 'greatest corporate romance of all time' between Sky and the Premier League was waved through.[33] Those football fans who could afford a subscription scrambled for an Amstrad dish to watch Sky's much-heralded 'whole new ball game'. Sky's fortunes quickly turned. By 1994 the satellite broadcaster announced profits of £93 million; later that year the company was floated with a valuation of £4.4 billion.

With the onset of the edacious Premier League era, the erosion of reverence for the FA Cup began at pace. In the view of Jonathan Pearce, 'It's almost as if that Tottenham–Arsenal semi-final and the final against Forest in the old Wembley were two of the last great occasions in the UK phenomenon that was the FA Cup.'

---

33 The relationship between Chisholm and Alan Sugar flourished too. When Chisholm eventually left Sky in 1997, he was appointed to the Tottenham board.

Chapter Twenty-One

What Happened Next

'I THINK Terry would have seen the Premier League stretching out before him, the riches that were on offer and wanted a part of it. He could see a Spurs with more Gascoignes and Linekers. I honestly believe Tottenham would have won the league if he'd stayed,' laments Jonathan Pearce, before quickly checking this thought. 'But Sugar/Venables was never going to work. They were two diametrically opposed human beings, oil and water.'

Looking back on the Terry Venables and Alan Sugar 'dream team', it seems remarkable that their marriage of inconvenience endured for two years. Both men wanted ultimate power. Neither was ever really minded to share it. Everything – be it the signing of Gordon Durie (which Venables committed the club to without Sugar's say-so), the transfer fee received for Gary Lineker, the specifications of the kit being supplied by Umbro, the hosting of official Tottenham Hotspur functions at Venables's club Scribes, television rights for friendly matches, the computerisation of the club using Amstrad tech or even the use of Venables's office by Sugar for meetings – proved contentious and fuelled the pair's corrosively mutual suspicion.

After Arsenal had narrowly seen off Spurs in the 1993 FA Cup semi-final, Sugar moved to orchestrate Venables's involuntary extraction. (Both that year's last-four ties were played at Wembley despite assurances that 1991 had been a one-off.) On 6 May, he presided over an outrageously ill-tempered board meeting at White Hart Lane. When the suitability of Amstrad equipping the club came under renewed scrutiny from Jonathan Crystal, Venables's ally on the board, Sugar flew into a rage. According to the account in respected journalist Mihir Bose's biography of Venables, *False Messiah*, Sugar 'leapt out of his chair and ran towards Crystal, screaming, "You fucking arse-licking cunt",' but then regained sufficient composure to return to the chairman's seat. At this point, he tipped on to the table a letter which had clearly been burning a hole in his briefcase, tossed it in Venables's direction, and swept out of the room.

The careful wording of the letter reflected the no-doubt costly input of the formidable law firm Herbert Smith, involved in its drafting.

> 'I am unable to continue with matters as they are. I feel that the past two years have been enough for me to form an opinion on the way things should be run and I feel now that I have to take total executive control of the company. I therefore ask you to stand down as chief executive and leave the employment of the company as soon as possible.'

Sugar offered to buy Venables out to hasten his departure.

Venables gave this offer short shrift at a board meeting convened without notice and held at Highbury, of all places, where Spurs were playing their final match of the first Premier League season. (A rare away win in the fixture ensured an unremarkable eighth-place finish. It would prove one of the decade's better league outcomes. Thereafter Tottenham became perennial also-rans in the table's bottom half.)

But Sugar had the numbers. Three days later, on the eve of the FA Cup Final between Arsenal and Sheffield Wednesday, Terry Venables was sacked as managing director of Tottenham Hotspur PLC and shoved off the football club's board. Venables gained a reprieve via an injunction from the High Court that night. The judge ruled he must be restored to all his positions at Tottenham as no resolutions from the day's board meeting could be implemented before a full court hearing occurred. The deferral of his ousting didn't hold for long.

'It was a tragedy really,' reflects TISA's Steve Davies. 'Both Sugar and Venables talked to me a lot about what was going on. Sugar's perspective was that Venables had essentially done things that were dishonest and that he couldn't work with him. I always got chapter and verse on what they were – ordering tablecloths for Scribes, things like that – but they seemed to me to be an excuse. I felt it was really about power. Sugar didn't like the fact that Venables got all the credit and thought that they equally deserved it. I kind of get that. He thought Venables was dispensable. Sugar called and invited us one Sunday night to see the legal documents his team had prepared. His solicitors said, "If you look at these, you'll understand why we must get rid of him." I read them, but I couldn't see why Venables had to go. It was all stuff I felt was a pretext for Sugar's ultimate goals.

'During that time, I remember being at home and taking a call. The voice said, "Can I speak to Steve, please? It's Bill Nicholson here." I was like, "Bloody hell, it's Bill Nicholson." It was like being called by God! I can barely think about it now without crying. He said, "This is a really terrible idea getting shot of Terry. What can I do to help?" We organised a big meeting in a sports hall with about 800 people there. When Bill Nic came in, there was a ten-minute standing ovation. The whole football community was behind Terry, which again probably made Sugar feel unappreciated. I'm sure he thought, "I put my money in, why don't they care about me like this?"

'We tried to support Venables through his legal action in court and put a lot of pressure on Sugar. It generated a lot of publicity, but ultimately it failed because the legal basis of

Venables's case was weak. He hadn't paid enough attention to corporate documents and things like that. So he was edged out. He may have shown poor judgement towards some people he got involved with but essentially he was a guy who wanted the club to do well.'

Annelise Jespersen recalls her thinking while she stood outside the High Court's steps on the Strand in solidarity with Venables. 'Honestly, I felt we didn't know what was going on. But we were going to support the football person in this because why wouldn't you? Sugar didn't have football or the football club at heart. I think it was during that trial I became disillusioned. Maybe I realised then that we didn't have as much power as we thought we had. In the other campaigns like Left on the Shelf and TISA in 1991, we'd been able to radicalise other fans, get things in the press and maybe even have a say in the boardroom. But when Venables was sacked, we were powerless. I didn't renew my season ticket after that.'

After three days of evidence, Venables's dismissal was upheld. He vowed to fight on, but his cause was lost.[34] The trial also wounded his old managerial adversary Brian Clough, who was caught in the relentless crossfire. An affidavit by Sugar claimed that during Tottenham's ultimately successful attempt to sign Teddy Sheringham from Nottingham Forest, as a replacement for Gary Lineker, Venables informed him that to lubricate transfer deals, Clough 'likes a bung'. 'Mr Venables told me that what actually happened was that people would meet Mr Clough in a motorway cafe and hand him a bag of money.' The timing of this allegation was particularly sore for Clough. Forest had just been relegated, having finished the season bottom of the Premier League. Clough had resigned immediately, a diminished figure, visibly struggling with alcoholism. Venables denied making the remark to Sugar, or that the £50,000 handed over in cash from Spurs to agent

---

34 At the start of September 1993, 'with very deep regret and sadness', Venables sold his Tottenham Hotspur PLC shares and resigned as a director.

Frank McLintock (the former Arsenal captain) – which in turn made its way to Forest's assistant manager Ronnie Fenton – was an illicit payment to secure Sheringham's signature. Clough threatened to sue Sugar if he repeated the claim outside the sanctuary of the courtroom.

Off-the-books payments had been an open secret within the game for years. But now the whole sorry business – not to mention the word 'bung' – had entered the national conversation. Football's early Nineties renaissance among the wider population meant the authorities couldn't afford to be seen turning a blind eye. As a result, the Sheringham affair led to a near-four-year Premier League inquiry into bungs. The image of Clough and Venables walking together like good sportsmen from the Wembley tunnel at the 1991 FA Cup Final lost some of its shine as both men fell under suspicion of corruption.

Clough always maintained his innocence. He wrote caustically in his first autobiography, 'Asking me what it's like to make money out of a transfer is like asking what it's like to have VD? I don't know. I've never had it.' However, Clough couldn't have failed to understand that his reputation had been blemished. He tacitly acknowledged, 'I know, now, that I should have retired after the 1991 FA Cup Final ... I could have gone [out] with my head held high after watching my team play its last match for me on the grandest occasion of them all ... [I] knew in my heart that in deciding to carry on after the FA Cup Final I had made a mistake.'

Rick Parry, chief executive of the Premier League at the time of the inquiry, would later say, 'On the balance of evidence, we felt [Brian Clough] was guilty of taking bungs. The evidence was pretty strong. I was very surprised when the FA took no action against him or Nottingham Forest.' The FA seemingly chose not to act on the evidence gathered by the Premier League because by then Clough was no longer working in football and was in seriously ailing health. Venables also received no punishment because, although according to the inquiry's report, his 'conduct cannot be justified', he hadn't personally profited from the £50,000 handed over.

Nevertheless, the cloud surrounding Venables's finances dogged him throughout the 1990s. When he was appointed England coach to widespread acclaim at the start of 1994, the FA were very keen to signpost that he had not been bestowed with the title of 'England manager'. They were clearly attempting to keep their distance from his chaotic financial affairs which were the focus of a second BBC *Panorama*. This examined how some of the money used to buy his stake in Tottenham was raised against assets that Venables either didn't own or which didn't exist. That the now disgraced journalist Martin Bashir was the principal reporter on the two *Panorama* take-downs of Venables – and that Venables expressed reservations about the methods employed to acquire, and the veracity of, some of the documentary evidence used to discredit him – only further muddies already murky waters.

The prospect of a string of court cases meant Venables announced he would step down from the national team after just one tournament in charge, Euro 96. A few months later, Sugar won a libel action against his erstwhile partner over claims Venables had made in his first autobiography. Most observers agree that had he gone on to lead England into the 1998 World Cup, the tactical acumen Venables blended with skilled man-management – which set him apart from other contemporary English managers – could have taken the team close in France.

Rather than World Cup glory, however, 1998 proved a different kind of landmark in the Venables story. Following an investigation by the Department of Trade and Industry into his mismanagement of Scribes, Edenote and Tottenham Hotspur, he was banned for seven years from being a company director. The particulars of the £1 million loan Venables had raised in 1991 to buy his Spurs shares was central to the case against him. By the time of the DTI's verdict, Eddie Ashby had already served a four-month jail sentence for a 'flagrant' breach of bankruptcy laws while working for Venables at Spurs and Scribes.

If Alan Sugar felt vindicated by Venables's plight it didn't stop him describing his tenure as Tottenham chairman as his life's 'wasted' decade. Spurs fans might echo the sentiment given the club's lack of success on the pitch during his custodianship. It's worth noting, however, that thanks to the Premier League's phenomenal success, Sugar was able to cash out his shares in the club for a reported £47 million. Not a bad return on his initial investment.

By 2007, Sugar felt ready to sell Amstrad too. Sky was by then accounting for three-quarters of the company's revenue. Sugar asked James Murdoch – by then in charge of Sky – whether he might be interested. 'Then I pulled out what I considered my final trump card … he [James] just might want to run the idea past his dad.' A deal of £125 million was agreed. As Sugar explains: 'It was Rupert's final gesture, as payback for the effort I'd contributed to BSkyB's fantastic success story.'

* * *

After their 1991 Wembley victory, Tottenham Hotspur stood peerless as eight-time winners of the FA Cup. They have not played in the final since. They have, however, reached the semi-finals eight times – losing all of them.

The 2001 defeat at that stage to Arsenal gave notice that 'It's lucky for Spurs when the year ends in one' doesn't seem to apply in the 21st century.

Agonisingly Nik Hodges confirms, 'To my knowledge, there are three very good cup final songs that Chas & Dave wrote that we've never been able to use.' Spurs fans will be hoping that before too much longer, there will be cause to release at least one of them …

Postscript

The Class of 1991

Erik Thorstvedt – The goalkeeper's Tottenham career ended in 1996 when he was forced to retire due to injury. He has since established himself as the 'Gary Lineker' of Norwegian television, where he is known for his irreverent analysis. Thorstvedt briefly lost his FA Cup medal while it was on loan to a football museum which unexpectedly closed down. Happily, it was found and returned to him.

Thorstvedt was invited to play in the 'Legends' game against Inter Milan to open the new Tottenham Hotspur stadium. 'My body is gone, and I hadn't played for ten or 15 years. But I couldn't resist. And yes, I threw one in, but it was still worth it. Being part of that Tottenham family is something precious in my life. I've managed to raise my two sons to support Spurs, and for the three of us to have that in common is extremely special.'

Justin Edinburgh – The left-back remained a mainstay of the Tottenham team during the 1990s and was the only man to win two trophies with Spurs in that decade. Despite being sent off in the 1999 Worthington Cup Final, Edinburgh collected a League Cup winners' medal to complement his 1991 FA Cup honour. In 2019, Edinburgh successfully led Leyton Orient to promotion to the Football League as manager. He was widely tipped to have an outstanding coaching career ahead of him.

Just days after returning from Spain having watched Spurs play Liverpool in the Champions League Final, Edinburgh suffered sudden cardiac arrest and died in hospital soon after. The Justin Edinburgh 3 Foundation, created in his memory, campaigns for legislation to mandate the installation of automated external defibrillators at health and sports facilities while raising awareness of cardiac arrest and delivering CPR training. Leyton Orient versus Tottenham Hotspur for the JE3 Trophy is now a regular pre-season fixture.

Pat Van Den Hauwe – Van Den Hauwe joined Millwall in 1993 and then relocated to South Africa. In his autobiography, he revealed how his life had spiralled downwards as he'd been overtaken by paranoia induced by his consumption of cocaine. Reaching rock-bottom, he pulled a gun on an associate who owed him £100. Thankfully, both men walked away unscathed. The incident forced Van Den Hauwe to take stock. Returning to the UK, he found a role with his former club, Everton, working in their community centre and hosting fans on matchdays.

Steve Sedgley – The story of Paul Gascoigne bringing an ostrich to the Tottenham training ground in Sedgley's 'honour' has passed into English football lore. Sedgley left Spurs in 1994 and played more than 100 times for Ipswich and Wolves before retiring. He now owns a construction company which celebrates his allegiances in its name: COYS Construction Limited.

David Howells – Howells made 335 first-team appearances for Tottenham between 1986 and 1998, when he left White Hart Lane for Southampton. Given his consistency, he was unfortunate never to be capped by England. He also participated in the 'Legends' match against Inter and still looked more than capable of doing a job. Howells has built a career in player development, working in both education and the professional game. He remains as passionate about Spurs as ever and is great value in telling Tottenham tales on the after-dinner speaking circuit.

Gary Mabbutt – If there were a Tottenham Hotspur Mount Rushmore, Mabbutt would surely be in the mix. Despite having to fight his way back from a catalogue of awful injuries, he made 611 appearances over 16 years. This means that in the club's entire history, only Steve Perryman ran out wearing Tottenham colours more times.

Mabbutt's unwavering service to the club since his retirement in 1998 has only enhanced his reputation. He never has a bad word to say about Tottenham and is often found fighting Spurs' corner on national television and radio, even when the club's actions aren't worthy of such loyalty. The steadfast friendship and support he's offered to Paul Gascoigne throughout his troubled life helps explain why so many of the 1991 team still deferentially refer to Mabbutt as 'Captain' or 'Skipper'.

Paul Stewart – Stewart has the distinction of being one of the players used in the Sky Sports television commercial to launch the Premier League in the summer of 1992, in which he drives a red Porsche convertible into White Hart Lane, where he is mobbed by adoring fans. By the time the new league kicked off, however, Stewart had signed for Liverpool.

He has since recalled how, at his Anfield medical, he'd had to stall for time when asked to provide a urine sample because an alcohol and drug addiction had taken hold of him. He quickly fell out of favour with Liverpool boss Graeme Souness, leading to a series of unremarkable spells at Crystal Palace, Wolves, Burnley, Sunderland and Stoke as his career ebbed away. In truth, few beyond White Hart Lane had given Stewart much thought since his retirement from the game.

Then, in 2016, he went public with the story of the abuse he suffered as a young player making his way. His bravery has had a transformational effect on football, and his legacy will forever go beyond his man-of-the-match display in the 1991 FA Cup Final. Stewart is now at the forefront of safeguarding in the game, working with the English Football League to deliver education to clubs. His work resulted in him being awarded an honorary doctorate from the University of Salford. And in 2024, he received the EFL's Contribution to League Football Award – the most prestigious honour the English Football League can bestow. 'When I do my work speaking to the young players in academies, I tell them I played for England and show them my goal in the cup final. But none of them have a clue who I am now. It's a long time ago!'

Paul Gascoigne – While Gascoigne's time with Lazio was punctuated by flashes of brilliance, injury lay-offs and ill-judged (not to mention poorly received) 'banter' characterised his time in Rome. He may be entitled to dispute the many assertions made from both inside and outside the game that he was physically never the same player after his knee injury in the 1991 cup final, but it is undeniable that he failed to hit the heights of his thrilling Spurs form again. Ahead of Wembley and that tackle on Gary Charles, he was rightly considered among the best players in the world. After the final, he was never again held in such regard.

Gascoigne never played at another World Cup. The high point of his career post-Spurs was his participation in Euro 96. In the tournament, he scored a goal against Scotland to rival his Wembley free kick masterpiece and was a stud's length away from scoring a 'golden goal' against Germany to send England through to the final. That this brief renaissance came during Terry Venables's time as England manager is no coincidence.

While there can be no excuse for the violence Gascoigne perpetrated against his wife Sheryl during their turbulent marriage, the pernicious influence of the tabloid press in his life's unravelling is staggering. The BBC's 2022 documentary

Gazza set out how Rebekah Brooks ingratiated herself with the couple and was then able to harvest exclusive stories about them while scaling her way to the top of Rupert Murdoch's affections. Brooks rose to edit both the *News of the World* and *The Sun* before becoming CEO of News International. She was forced to resign, receiving a £10 million pay-off, over the shocking revelations about the practice by News International reporters of illegally gathering confidential information on celebrities. Rebekah Brooks was subsequently arrested and stood trial charged with conspiracy to hack voicemails, conspiracy to pay public officials and conspiracy to pervert the course of justice. She was cleared on all counts. Astonishingly, given what had occurred on her watch, she was rehired by Murdoch to head up his UK newspaper division. Suffering from paranoia and alcoholism, Paul Gascoigne came forward as one of the most high-profile victims of what became known as the phone hacking scandal. He eventually received 'substantial damages' from News International Newspapers.

In February 2008, Gascoigne was sectioned under the Mental Health Act. Later that year, he was rushed to hospital following a suspected overdose. He has reportedly been to rehab seven times. In 2015, Gascoigne received damages from The Mirror Group, which had also been found to have intercepted messages on his phone for 10 years. Speaking at the time, he said 'I'd like to trade my mobile phone in for a coffin because these guys have ruined my life.'

Vinny Samways – The midfielder proved something of a novelty in the 1990s as a rare English player who ventured abroad. Having left Spurs for Everton in 1994, Samways was part of the Toffees squad that won the 1995 FA Cup Final. He didn't play in the match but did score the winning goal in that year's Charity Shield. A year later, he swapped Merseyside for Gran Canaria, where he joined islanders Las Palmas. His debut lasted only 13 minutes as he was sent off, and his robust play saw him dismissed a further nine times in his first

88 games in Spanish football. Given Samways was under-appreciated for being a 'technical' player in the rugged climate of English football, this tally – combined with 47 bookings – was more indicative of Spain's less liberal refereeing than malice on Samways's part.

His commitment to the Las Palmas cause saw him hailed as one of the club's best players in the modern era and led to a brief spell with La Liga giants Sevilla. Since retiring from football, Samways has relocated permanently to Spain, where he has worked as a coach and agent.

Gary Lineker – The striker enjoyed one more goal-laden season at White Hart Lane after the FA Cup win before embarking on his Japanese adventure. Injury limited him to 18 appearances across two seasons in the J-League, and he was forced to retire in 1994. His skilled cultivation of the media during his playing career paid dividends. He was as much in demand as a pundit as he was a goalscorer, and the BBC quickly signed him up. Despite never kicking a ball in the Premier League, as the witty and knowledgeable host of *Match of the Day*, he has become one of the country's most well-regarded and influential public figures. He is set to finish his term on the flagship show in 2025, but will continue to work for the BBC and his Goalhanger stable is the leading independent podcast production company in the UK.

Paul Allen – Allen was one of the players caught up in the fall-out of the fast and loose practices at White Hart Lane during the 1980s. A 1993 *World In Action* documentary for ITV, *The Club Who Liked To Say Yes*, revealed that Allen was among several Spurs players signed during the previous decade to receive 'loans' that they were never expected to repay, and ex-gratia payments in breach of Football League rules. The Tottenham file was passed to the FA, who completed their investigation in 1994. Allen's testimony to the Commission of Enquiry was damning. Spurs were hammered with a 12-point deduction, banned from the 1994/95 FA Cup and fined a record £600,000. The sporting sanctions were later overturned on appeal.

Upon leaving White Hart Lane, Allen joined Southampton before winding down his long career at Swindon, Bristol City and Millwall. He now works for the Professional Footballers' Association to ensure members are aware of the support and services the PFA provides.

Paul Walsh – The fiery striker stuck it out for a further season at Spurs before his frustrations at his limited first-team prospects boiled over. Walsh recalls Peter Shreeves telling him he'd be given every chance to stake a claim but felt Shreeves wasn't true to his word. Having been substituted in a reserve match played at White Hart Lane, Walsh punched reserve team coach Ray Clemence in full view of the crowd. The red-top press seized on the story. After serving a suspension, Walsh was rehabilitated into the fold but remembers seeing little first-team action thereafter. 'The last game of the season was Manchester United away, and I wasn't even in the squad. When I found out, Peter Shreeves was doing some filming, so I went and smashed balls at him while he was on camera as a "fuck off" to him. Then I went into London and got bladdered. My contract was up.'

Walsh then enjoyed two spells at Portsmouth, becoming a cult figure with Pompey fans. Post-retirement, he transitioned into broadcasting and was a regular contributor on Sky Sports' *Soccer Saturday*, where his candid analysis proved popular with viewers.

Nayim – There can be no other player who has won a trophy for Spurs who is more celebrated by the club's fans for a goal they scored while wearing another team's colours. And there can be few goals that have conferred legendary status on a player at two clubs simultaneously. But Nayim's effort from the halfway line (at least that's the distance according to the terrace chant) for Real Zaragoza in the final seconds of extra time to defeat Arsenal in the 1995 Cup Winners' Cup Final was extraordinary. There is a street in Aragon, the province to which Zaragoza belongs, called *Gol de Nayim*. Many Spurs fans would have been thrilled for Haringey Council to have copied the initiative.

There is an intriguing footnote to Nayim's wonder goal. A young Cafu had signed for Zaragoza midway through the season and watched the match from the stands. Seven years later, when he was captain of Brazil at the 2002 World Cup, Cafu told Ronaldinho of Nayim's goal against David Seaman and encouraged him to try to lob the keeper when Brazil met England in the quarter-finals. The advice proved telling as Ronaldinho's winning goal sailed over Seaman's head from almost the same spot on the pitch as Nayim's strike. Today, Nayim writes a regular column about Zaragoza for the Spanish daily sports newspaper *Marca*.

Irving Scholar – The pain caused by his Tottenham demise seeps into every page of Scholar's eminently readable 1992 autobiography. He left Spurs a disappointed man and used the book to try to settle scores and apportion blame for the crisis that engulfed his chairmanship, accepting little of it himself. There can be no doubting Scholar's passion for the club. And it would only be human if, watching on from the sidelines as the Premier League he'd helped bring into existence became a juggernaut, he felt envious of his other Big Five co-conspirators who reaped such rich rewards.

Perhaps it explains why – despite his saying in 1992, 'I've no desire to return to English football, although in recent months several clubs have been offered to me for sale … There is no question of my going to any club other than Spurs, and I do not hanker or even wish for a return' – Scholar decided to make a comeback. In March 1997, he headed up a consortium that bought Nottingham Forest for £16 million.

What happened next may sound more than a little familiar. A holding company was formed, and Nottingham Forest Football Club became a subsidiary of Nottingham Forest PLC. In the esteemed investigative journalist David Conn's view, it was 'probably the shabbiest' of all English football's stock market flotations. It raised a derisory £2 million. In short order, the consortium split into warring factions which soon began threatening each other with legal action. A member of the Scholar camp even took to making secret recordings of board meetings as Forest's losses stacked up. Despite taking on the grandiose title 'director of football', Scholar lost control of the football club when a local fan stepped in to invest in it directly rather than bailing out the ailing PLC. Scholar resigned from the board in protest but continued to hold on to his sizeable tranche of shares, ensuring an impasse at the City Ground that endangered the club with bankruptcy. Finally, in 2001, a High Court ruling went against Scholar. Forest fans were delighted to see the back of him. Having almost crashed at the wheel of two of England's storied clubs, he was to have no footballing third coming.

Alan Sugar – Being associated with Tottenham Hotspur did wonders for Sugar's public profile. In 2005, he was cast as the boss in the BBC's *Apprentice* series. It has been on UK television ever since, making Sugar a household name. In 2009, he was elevated to the House of Lords. He can regularly be found on social media proffering views on Spurs' fortunes.

Terry Venables – On 25 November 2023, it was announced that Venables had passed away following a long illness. Tributes poured in from across the footballing fraternity. A fulsome minute's applause was held before the kick-off of Tottenham's fixture against Aston Villa the next day. He remains the only man to have led Spurs to the FA Cup separately as player and manager.

Tottenham Hotspur 1990/91
Season Record

First Division Results (final league position: 10th)

Date	Venue	Opposition	Result	Score	Goalscorers
25/08/90	H	Manchester City	W	3-1	Lineker 2, Gascoigne
28/08/90	A	Sunderland	D	0-0	
01/09/90	A	Arsenal	D	0-0	
08/09/90	H	Derby County	W	3-0	Gascoigne 3
15/09/90	A	Leeds United	W	2-0	Howells, Lineker
22/09/90	H	Crystal Palace	D	1-1	Gascoigne
29/09/90	H	Aston Villa	W	2-1	Lineker, Allen
06/10/90	A	QPR	D	0-0	
20/10/90	H	Sheffield United	W	4-0	Walsh 3, Nayim
27/10/90	A	Nottingham Forest	W	2-1	Howells 2
04/11/90	H	Liverpool	L	1-3	Lineker
10/11/90	H	Wimbledon	W	4-2	Stewart, Mabbutt, Walsh, Lineker (pen)
18/11/90	A	Everton	D	1-1	Howells
24/11/90	H	Norwich City	W	2-1	Lineker 2
01/12/90	A	Chelsea	L	2-3	Gascoigne, Lineker
08/12/90	H	Sunderland	D	3-3	Walsh 2, Lineker
15/12/90	A	Manchester City	L	1-2	Gascoigne
22/12/90	H	Luton Town	W	2-1	Stewart 2
26/12/90	A	Coventry City	L	0-2	
29/12/90	A	Southampton	L	0-3	
01/01/91	H	Manchester United	L	1-2	Lineker (pen)
12/01/91	H	Arsenal	D	0-0	
20/01/91	A	Derby County	W	1-0	Lineker
02/02/91	H	Leeds United	D	0-0	
23/02/91	A	Wimbledon	L	1-5	Bergsson

02/03/91	H	Chelsea	D	1-1	Lineker (pen)
16/03/91	A	Aston Villa	L	2-3	Samways, Allen
23/03/91	H	QPR	D	0-0	
30/03/91	H	Coventry City	D	2-2	Nayim 2
01/04/91	A	Luton Town	D	0-0	
06/04/91	H	Southampton	W	2-0	Lineker 2
10/04/91	A	Norwich City	L	1-2	Hendry
17/04/91	A	Crystal Palace	L	0-1	
20/04/91	A	Sheffield United	D	2-2	Edinburgh, Walsh
24/04/91	H	Everton	D	3-3	Allen, Mabbutt, Nayim
04/05/91	H	Nottingham Forest	D	1-1	Nayim
11/05/91	A	Liverpool	L	0-2	
20/05/91	A	Manchester United	D	1-1	Hendry

League Cup (lost in the fifth round)

Round	Venue	Opposition	Result	Score	Goalscorers
Second round (leg 1)	H	Hartlepool United	W	5-0	Lineker, Gascoigne 4 (1 pen)
Second round (leg 2)	A	Hartlepool United	W	2-1	Stewart 2
Third round	H	Bradford City	W	2-1	Gascoigne, Stewart
Fourth round	A	Sheffield United	W	2-0	Stewart, Gascoigne
Fifth round	A	Chelsea	D	0-0	
Fifth round (replay)	H	Chelsea	L	0-3	

FA Cup (winners)

Round	Venue	Opposition	Result	Score	Goalscorers
Third round	A	Blackpool	W	1-0	Stewart
Fourth round	H	Oxford United	W	4-2	Mabbutt, Lineker, Gascoigne 2
Fifth round	A	Portsmouth	W	2-1	Gascoigne 2
Sixth round	H	Notts County	W	2-1	Short (o.g.), Gascoigne
Semi-final	N	Arsenal	W	3-1	Gascoigne, Lineker 2
Final	N	Nottingham Forest	W	2-1	Stewart, Walker (o.g.)

First Team Total Appearances & Goals

Player Name	First Division	League Cup	FA Cup	Goals
Allen, P	36	6	6	3
Bergsson, G	12			1
Dearden, K		1		
Edinburgh, J	16	5	5	1
Fenwick, T	4	2	2	
Garland, P	1			
Gascoigne, P	26	5	6	19
Gray, P	6		1	
Hendon, I	2			
Hendry, J	4			2
Howells, D	29	6	4	4
Lineker, G	32	5	6	19
Mabbutt, G	35	6	6	3
Moncur, J	9	2		
Moran, P	1		1	
Nayim	33	5	5	5
Samways, V	23	4	5	1
Sedgley, S	34	6	5	
Stewart, P	35	6	5	9
Thomas, M	31	5	2	
Thorstvedt, E	37	5	6	
Tuttle, D	6	1		
Van Den Hauwe, P	32	2	5	
Walker, I	1			
Walsh, P	29	6	4	7

Acknowledgements

THERE IS so much to agonise over when writing a book. Will I finish it? Is it any good? Will anyone ever read it? But perhaps most anxiety-inducing of all is the worry of unintentionally leaving someone out of the thank-yous. Here's very much hoping I haven't.

Firstly, thanks to all those who generously agreed to be interviewed. I would be lying if I didn't confess to being a bit starry-eyed when meeting the 'boys of '91'. I was nine when Tottenham won the FA Cup Final against Nottingham Forest, and they say you should never meet your heroes. But the experience of talking to David Howells, Erik Thorstvedt (who even humoured me by allowing me to show him the fan 'art' I'd drawn of him at junior school), Gudni Bergsson, Paul Moran, Paul Stewart, Paul Walsh, Nayim and Vinny Samways could not have been more edifying. John Sheridan, Mike Rollo, Roy Reyland and Willie Morgan all provided tremendous testimony and insights about life at Tottenham during the Terry Venables years and have hugely enriched this book. Thanks also to Donna Cullen and Tony Stevens at the club for their help contacting THFC alumni.

I'm sure barely a day goes by in referee Roger Milford's life when someone doesn't mention the 1991 FA Cup Final to him. But he shared his memories with all the enthusiasm and vigour of someone recounting them for the first time.

Annelise Jespersen and Steve Davies were both incredibly helpful in recalling TISA's campaign and giving the perspective of Spurs fans in the early Nineties. As were Penny and Terry

245

Deller. It was a pure delight speaking to Joan and Nik Hodges about Chas & Dave and the duo's cup final songs. I came away with a sore jaw from laughing so much at their stories.

David Buchler replied to a message I sent to his work email address on spec and kindly invited me to his central London office for a thoroughly illuminating chat, which provided invaluable context to the club's financial struggles.

Danny Kelly and Jonathan Pearce are two broadcasters I've long admired. They are also two of the greatest storytellers I've ever had the pleasure of meeting. Their memories and magnificent turns of phrase have enhanced this book immeasurably. Football writers Peter Gillatt (Blackpool), Martin Brodetsky (Oxford United), Colin Farmery (Portsmouth), Jon Spurling (Arsenal), Daniel Taylor and Nick Miller (Nottingham Forest) all gave enlightening perspectives on their clubs in 1991. As did Forest fan Pat Riddell.

Roy Ackerman's documentary *Sick as a Parrot*, which Steve Tollervey tracked down for me at the British Film Institute, was a real find. Thanks to Roy for his time on the phone to discuss his memories of making it.

A massive note of gratitude to my big Spurs pal and journalist Mike Collett for his wisdom, his lovingly kept cuttings from the 1991 cup run and for his encyclopaedic football knowledge which saved me from scoring a few own goals in the draft of this manuscript. Thanks to football writer Brendan Madden for his help and friendship. Thanks also to Lars Sivertsen, Martin Cloake, Sam Blair, Sampson Collins, Sian Allpress, Jonathan Wilson and Toby Leigh.

Thank you to the team at Pitch Publishing – Graham Hales, Dean Rockett, Katie Field, Duncan Olner and Paul and Jane for being so easy to work with and for the beautiful way they have produced this book. Thanks also to Jack Pitt-Brooke and Max Rushden for their fantastic testimonials for the book's cover.

Lastly, thanks to my partner Esther for her unwavering support and encouragement.

Bibliography

Books

Adams, T, *Addicted* (Collins Willow, 1998)

Bose, M, *False Messiah: The Life And Times Of Terry Venables* (André Deutsch, 1996)

Bower, T, *Broken Dreams: Vanity, Greed and the Souring of British Football* (Simon & Schuster, 2003)

Bower, T, *Maxwell: The Outsider* (Mandarin, 1991)

Clough, B, *Brian Clough: The Autobiography* (Corgi, 2005)

Clough, B, *Cloughie: Walking on Water* (Headline, 2003)

Collett, M, *The Complete Record of The FA Cup* (SportsBooks Ltd, 2003)

Dalglish, K, *Dalglish: My Autobiography* (Hodder & Stoughton Ltd, 1996)

Dein, D, *Calling The Shots* (Constable, 2023)

Dyke, G, *Inside Story* (Harper Collins, 2005)

Fenwick, T, *Earning My Spurs* (Mainstream, 1989)

Fynn, A & Guest, L, *Heroes And Villains* (Penguin, 1991)

Gascoigne, P, *Gazza: My Story* (Headline, 2005)

Hall, E, *Monster* (Boxtree, 1998)

Hamilton, D, *Provided You Don't Kiss Me: 20 Years With Brian Clough* (Fourth Estate, 2007)

Harris, H, *Down Memory Lane* (G2 Entertainment Ltd, 2011)

Harris, H, *Hold The Back Page* (Know The Score Books, 2006)

Hodge, S, *The Man With Maradona's Shirt* (Orion, 2011)

Hodges, C, *Chas & Dave: All About Us* (John Blake Publishing, 2010)

Horrie, C, *Sick As A Parrot* (Virgin, 1992)

Horsman, M, *Sky High* (Orion, 1998)

Inglis, S, *Football Grounds Of Britain* (Collins Willow, 1996)

Keane, R, *Keane: The Autobiography* (Michael Joseph, 2002)

Kelly, G, *Sweet F.A.* (Collins Willow, 1999)

Keston, M, *Superfan: The Amazing Life Of Morris Keston* (Vision Sports Publishing, 2010)

Mabbutt, G, *Against All Odds* (Century Hutchinson, 1989)

Merson, P, *How Not to Be A Professional Footballer* (Harper Collins, 2012)

Pearce, S, *Psycho: The Autobiography* (Headline, 2014)

Preston, J, *Fall: The Mystery Of Robert Maxwell* (Viking, 2021)

Reyland, R, *Shirts, Shorts And Spurs* (John Blake Publishing, 2011)

Robinson, J & Clegg, J, *The Club: How the Premier League Became The Richest, Most Disruptive Business In Sport* (John Murray, 2018)

Scholar, I, *Behind Closed Doors* (André Deutsch, 1992)

Seaman, D, *Safe Hands: My Autobiography* (Gollancz, 2001)

Sheridan, J, *The Limping Physio* (Pitch Publishing, 2021)

Smith, A, *Heads Up: My Life Story* (Constable, 2018)

Stein, M, *Chris Waddle* (Simon & Schuster, 1998)

Stewart, P, *Damaged: My Story* (Trinity Mirror Sports Media, 2017)

Sugar, A, *What You See Is What You Get* (Macmillan, 2010)

Sugar, A, *The Way I See It* (Macmillan, 2011)

Van Den Hauwe, P, *Pat Van Den Hauwe: My Autobiography* (John Blake Publishing, 2015)

Venables, T, *Born To Manage* (Simon & Schuster, 2014)

Venables, T, *Venables: The Autobiography* (Penguin, 1995)

Walsh, P, *Walshy: My Autobiography* (Trinity Mirror Sports Media, 2015)

Webb, S, *Clough, Maxwell & Me* (North Bridge Publishing, 2016)

Wilson, J, *Brian Clough: Nobody Ever Says Thank You* (Orion, 2012)

PhD Thesis

King, A, *The Premier League and the new Consumption of Football* (University of Salford, 1995)

Newspapers, Fanzines & Podcasts

Daily Express
Daily Mail & Mail On Sunday
Daily Mirror & Sunday Mirror
Evening Gazette (Blackpool)
Evening Post (Nottingham)
Evening Standard
Financial Times
Reservoir Red Dogs
The Guardian & The Observer
The Independent & Independent On Sunday
The News (Portsmouth)
The People
The Spur
The Sun & News of the World
The Times & Sunday Times

Documentaries

Dispatches, *Sugar & Venables: The Inside Story* (Channel 4, 19 September 1993)

Gazza (BBC, 13 April 2022)

High Interest, *Sick As A Parrot* (Channel 4, 29 November 1992)

On The Line, *Tottering Hotspur, Where Did All The Money Go?* (BBC, 16 May 1991)

Panorama, *The Manager* (BBC, 16 September 1993)

Panorama, *The Manager And His Money* (BBC, 31 October 1994)

World In Action, *The Club Who Liked To Say Yes* (ITV, 13 December 1993)

Index

INDEX

About the Author

EWAN FLYNN is a freelance football writer focusing on the game's rich history. His work has been featured in *The Independent*, *The Blizzard*, *When Saturday Comes*, *Four Four Two* and on BBC Radio. His first book, *We Are Sunday League*, is a bitter-sweet real-life story from football's grassroots.

Born in Edmonton, north London, he is a lifelong Spurs fan and attended his first game at White Hart Lane in the 1988/89 season – a 1-1 draw with Charlton Athletic. He was an itinerant season ticket holder in the Paxton Road and East Stand from 1993 to 2017 and attended most of the eight FA Cup semi-finals the club has lost since 1991. He also owned 20 shares in Tottenham Hotspur PLC until the company was taken into private ownership.